W9-BQK-681

Presented to Purchase College
by
Gary Waller, PhD Cambridge

State University of New York
Distinguished Professor

Professor
of Literature & Cultural
Studies, and Theatre &
Performance, 1995-2019
Provost 1995-2004

The Ash Wednesday Supper

La Cena de le ceneri

La Cena de le ceneri

The
Ash Wednesday
Supper

by Giordano Bruno

Edited and translated by
EDWARD A. GOSSELIN
and
LAWRENCE S. LERNER

ARCHON BOOKS   1977

Library of Congress Cataloging in Publication Data

Bruno, Giordano, 1548-1600.
    The Ash Wednesday supper—La cena de le ceneri.

    Bibliography: p.
    1. Copernicus, Nicolaus, 1473-1543. 2. Occult sciences—
Early works to 1800. I. Title. II. Title: La cena de le ceneri.
QB36.C8B8713—1977   523.2   76-46562

Edited, translated, and with an introduction by Gosselin,
Edward A.   and Lerner, Lawrence S.
ISBN 0-208-01610-4

©Edward A. Gosselin and Lawrence S. Lerner 1977

First published 1977 as an Archon Book, an imprint of
THE SHOE STRING PRESS, INC., Hamden, Connecticut 06514

All rights reserved

Printed in the United States of America

Acknowledgement

To Claudia Hoffer Gosselin and
Graziella Pozzebon for
their assistance in the translation and
editorial preparation of this work

CONTENTS

PREFACE

This translation is the result of several years' labor. It began in 1971, when we were preparing to offer an interdisciplinary seminar in the General Honors Program at California State University, Long Beach. The seminar was entitled, "Case Studies in the Interaction between Science and Society: The Galileo and Oppenheimer Affairs." It occurred to us that in order to put Galileo in his proper historical setting we might ask our students to read an earlier "defense" of the Copernican system. We thought immediately of Giordano Bruno's *La Cena de le ceneri* (London, 1584).

After searching for a translation of the *Cena* and finding none, we sought someone who could competently (and quickly) translate the work. Funds for this translation project were made available through the good offices of Professor William M. Resch, then Director of the General Honors Program. We had the good fortune to employ Ms. Graziella Pozzebon, a graduate student in the Department of Comparative Literature at the University of California, Irvine, to make a rough translation of the *Cena*. In the final weeks of the summer vacation, we began to refine the translation and to add footnotes. The translation was in a usable form for the seminar by the opening day of the semester.

The task of correcting, revising, and polishing our translation has continued over the intervening years. So has the process of gaining a more accurate and deeper understanding of this difficult work.

We wish to acknowledge our debt to those who have aided us

9

in this endeavor, and to express our gratitude to them. First of all, there is the influence of Dr. Frances A. Yates of the Warburg Institute, London. Through her deeply perceptive works on Bruno and his times, she has done much to give shape to our approach to the *Cena*. Dr. Yates has also kindly responded to our queries about Bruno, and has enlightened us on several abstruse points.

Closer to home, we are deeply grateful to Ms. Pozzebon for her unstinting efforts at the outset of our project, and for the lasting impetus which they provided. Equally deep is our gratitude to Ms. Claudia Hoffer Gosselin, a graduate student in the Department of French and Italian at the University of California, Irvine, and the wife of one of us. She has contributed many hours of fruitful work to the refining and editing of the translation. Our thanks are also due to Professor Gene L. Dinielli, Dr. Resch's successor as director of the General Honors Program, for his continuing encouragement.

Finally, we are grateful to our students in the seminar, whose enthusiasm for the subject encouraged us to extend our interest in Bruno beyond the course itself, and to all the others who have served as resonant sounding boards.

Needless to say, the blame for all errors of translation and interpretation is solely ours.

California State University,   EDWARD A. GOSSELIN
Long Beach   LAWRENCE S. LERNER

INTRODUCTION

Giordano Bruno is one of those semi-legendary figures of whom nearly every educated person has heard the name and very little more. For all too many people, that little more is mainly mythical. Much of the content of the Bruno myth arises from his own messianic self-assessment and from the intricacies of his literary style. But much more stems from the moral imperatives implicit in the intellectual climate of an era long after Bruno's death.

Like all myths, the Bruno myth has a foundation in fact. But it has come, for the sake of the intended moral, to have a life of its own quite independent of the life and work of the man who is its protagonist.

The Bruno myth can be summarized as follows: An itinerant renegade friar, Bruno defied contemporary ecclesiastical authorities and doctrines. In addition, he vehemently rejected the commonly held Ptolemaic belief that the earth lay at the center of the universe, and engaged in mystical speculation which centered about his pioneering support of the Copernican view. In connection with his Copernican beliefs, he held also that the universe contains an infinite number of worlds populated with intelligent beings. On account of these teachings, Bruno was tried for heresy by the Inquisition and burned at the stake in 1600. He thus became the first martyr of modern science at the hands of the Church, and thereby a precursor of Galileo. The moral of this

---

See page 53 for Notes to the Introduction.

11

nineteenth-century story is that Science, the bearer of knowledge, struggles to an inevitable victory over the Church, the champion of ignorance and superstition.[1]

The facts in this myth are true, though sketchy to the point of poverty and generally misleading in their emphasis. The interpretation—or rather the moral—likewise has some truth to it, though that truth has been bent to serve a preconceived purpose. This is a pity, because the complex and turbulent facts of Bruno's life and career support a far richer interpretation. Such an interpretation cannot be so clear-cut as a simple homiletic moral, but it contributes greatly to an understanding of the way in which the modern world-view emerged from the late Renaissance. And Bruno himself is far more than a mere Galileo *manqué*.

Good myths are neat self-contained packages. It is easy for the unsuspecting to fall prey to the notion that the myth contains all that is worth knowing about its protagonist. If one is thereby led to overlook the real three-dimensional Bruno, it were indeed a pity. For Bruno was an extremely complex man, extraordinarily brilliant, self-centered, contentious, obstreperous, vain, opinionated, and wrong-headed. To paraphrase his own words he was, like his own work,

> great and small, professorial and studentlike, sacrilegious and religious, joyous and choleric, cruel and pleasant, Florentine in his leanness and Bolognese in his fatness, cynical and Sardanapalian, trifling and serious, grave and waggish, tragic and comic.

He was often ignorant of his opponents' views, and he was not at all above misrepresenting them to his own advantage when he did understand them. He was a magnificent literary stylist and innovator. His writings reach soaring heights of majesty and swoop precipitously to nadirs of burlesque. He had an uncanny aptitude for starting with false premises and proceeding through faulty reasoning to correct conclusions.

This infuriating intellectual brawler lived in a time suitable to his mentality, if not to his personal well-being. The last quarter of the sixteenth century was a period of extreme violence, at once political and religious. Divided by conflicting religious ideologies and torn by international as well as domestic conflicts, many still hoped to restore harmony and unity between and within states. And Frances Yates has shown, in her seminal studies of previously neglected and ill-understood intellectual movements, that Bruno's holistic mode of thinking fitted in well with them. For these movements called upon the whole encyclopedia of human knowledge in their efforts to restore the lost *harmonia mundi*. It is perhaps fitting that the precise significance of Bruno's role in these efforts is still subject to some controversy (as is his role in the emergence of modern science). We do not presume, of course, to settle that controversy, nor even to set forth a comprehensive study of Bruno's life and works.

Rather, it is our purpose to use the Bruno myth as a key, and this translation of *La Cena de le ceneri* as a gateway, to a broader understanding of Bruno and his times. *The Ash Wednesday Supper,* published in London in 1584, is Bruno's major exposition of the Copernican picture of the universe. Or, better, as we shall see, it is Bruno's major use of that picture as a foundation of and a metaphor for his own vast philosophical-theological-political-social program.

With such a purpose in mind for this translation, we have aimed at a happy medium in the editorial apparatus. On the one hand we have endeavored, through this Introduction and through the notes to the text, to furnish enough background and interpretive discussion to enable the general reader to follow the argument without immediate recourse to other works. On the other hand, we have taken care not to drown him in footnotes. We have assumed, for example, that the reader who may not remember the story of Lycaon is nevertheless familiar with Jove. We have not indulged in long expositions of unimportant points. In order to preserve the bilingual flavor of the original, however, we have left Bruno's Latin quotations in the text and have furnished English translations in footnotes. We have not "explained" every untranslatable Italian pun—indeed, we cannot possibly have caught them all—but some of them are too good to miss. Where we could, we have given an idiomatic English equivalent for puns, aphorisms, idioms, and so forth, with a note to the effect that the translation is not literal. In the case of a relatively small number of serious ambiguities of meaning, we have furnished the original word or phrase in a footnote. In general, however, we have refrained from commenting on every technical difficulty of translation, since we do not think it right to burden the general reader with the pains of our task.

In short, this is not intended to be a definitive translation of *The Ash Wednesday Supper*. We believe such a thing to be a contradiction in terms; the serious Bruno scholar must always have ultimate recourse to the original Italian. Of the original there is a fine diplomatic edition,[2] replete with scholarly apparatus which has been as valuable to us as to many others. We have also relied on two other excellent modern editions; these include passages at the end of Dialogue II and in Dialogue III which are lacking in the above-mentioned edition and which, we believe, must be included in the translation.[3]

We hope that this translation, with its accompanying explanatory material, conveys the flavor and ferment of the original faithfully enough to strike the modern English-speaking reader as the original must have struck Bruno's contemporaries. We have tried to do as little damage as possible to Bruno's style in rendering it into modern English. We realize that the endless sentences of Renaissance writing, with the involuted logical order of their parts, require sometimes drastic restructuring if they are not to be both bewildering and tedious to the modern reader. We have chopped, disjointed and disentangled wherever we thought it necessary for comprehensibility and smooth flow. But in doing so, we have preferred to err on the conservative side. After all, Bruno's style is nothing if it is not discursive, and its obscurities are sometimes deliberate; we have not tried to hide this from the reader.

In conveying Bruno's style, we have been particularly careful not to meddle with the satirical and derisive passages, where the humor often depends in an essential way on a deliberately extreme ponderousness of phrase or on a cataloguing *ad nauseam*. This not uncommon form of Renaissance humor is now more or less extinct, but it still has its appeal; it would be presumptuous of a modern translator to try to "improve" or modernize the original. In our treatment of the satirical passages

in particular, we have been guided by the style of Samuel Putnam's translation of *Gargantua and Pantagruel*,[4] to which the
Supper has strong stylistic resemblances.

In the technical task of translation, we have depended heavily upon the Italian-English dictionary of Bruno's friend, John
Florio.[5] The existence of this dictionary is the greatest stroke of
luck for the translator of Bruno; not only were Florio and Bruno
friends, but Florio drew extensively from Bruno's Italian works
for examples in compiling his dictionary. Many passages which
seemed obscure, and which have given endless trouble to us and
to others who have translated various passages of the *Cena*,
become perfectly clear when Florio's dictionary is used as the
final authority on the meaning of words.

While our main purpose has been to present Bruno in a dress
agreeable to the general reader, we believe that English-speaking
Bruno scholars will find it sufficiently faithful to the original to
make it useful as an interim or working text, for purposes of
general quotation, or for classroom use. It goes without saying
that no scholar will want to found a crucial argument on a
passage he has not checked with the original.

Bruno's Life

Giordano Bruno was born in 1548 in the small city of Nola,
which is somewhat less than twenty miles to the east of Naples.
The Emperor Augustus died in Nola in A.D. 14, and legend has it
that one of its early bishops, St. Paulinus of Bordeaux (354-431),
invented the church bell; clearly, the town has had an unremarkable history.

Bruno's father was a professional military officer; nothing is
known of his mother. After a presumably uneventful childhood
of which we know nothing, he joined the Dominican Order at the
age of fifteen. In the Order he received a thoroughly scholastic
education, and seems to have been regarded as showing great
promise. In time Bruno was ordained a priest, and began to
pursue the career of a scholar in Naples. He appears to have been
in demand as a teacher of the then-fashionable art of mnemonics,
on which he wrote several books during his lifetime. It must be

pointed out that mnemonics was not then conceived as a mere set of mechanical rules for aiding memory, but was freighted with a very large content of mysticism and magic. Bruno's study of the substantial literature on mnemonics, and his own youthful contribution to the art, must have been among the most important influences in shaping his later thought on larger matters.[6]

Bruno's studies were not, however, confined to mnemonics narrowly construed. It was at this time that his unorthodox streak came to the surface, or at least first manifested itself in a manner serious enough to warrant official notice. In 1576 he found himself surrounded by a cloud of accusations of heterodoxy. Among these charges the most serious was that of suspicion of Arianism. The one which evokes the most amusing image was that he had read the suspect works of Erasmus, and had hidden them in his privy.

Though no formal prosecution or other disciplinary proceedings arose immediately from these charges, so that we cannot know how grave they actually were at that time, the twenty-eight year old Bruno found it advisable to cast aside his monk's habit and flee to Rome. We can speculate that part of the reason for this action was a youthful taste for adventure in a wider world. But it seems reasonably clear that had Bruno elected to remain in Naples he could not have continued to express himself with the same freedom which was the presumptive first cause of his troubles.

Indeed, throughout his life it was not only Bruno's views but his unbridled outspoken manner and his penchant for making enemies, sometimes quite gratuitously, which got him into trouble again and again. He used his sharply-barbed pen not only against abstract ideas and generalized types of persons, but too often against individuals thinly veiled in caricatures. In this he was no respecter of persons; some of the butts of his assaults were potentially sympathetic to his views or even inclined to help him. His gift for withering satire needs no comment here, since it is amply displayed in *The Ash Wednesday Supper*.[7]

We will discuss aspects of Bruno's philosophical ideas in more detail later. It would appear, however, that by the time he left Naples his basic religious and philosophical views had already solidified. He had embraced the system of belief called Hermetic Neoplatonism or Hermetism, and on it his entire career was based. For the moment we need only remark that Bruno saw Hermetism as a basis for reconciling Catholics and Protestants in an era of violent religious warfare.

Bruno's flight from Naples took him to Rome, but he did not remain there long. He wandered through northern Italy, Switzerland and southern France, attaching himself more or less peripherally to various universities, both Catholic and Protestant. On some occasions he appears to have represented himself as a monk and on others as a layman. He eked out a precarious living by lecturing, tutoring in the art of memory and on other subjects, and proofreading Latin for various printers. He was eventually excommunicated, and seems to have taken the excommunication seriously. While he frequently participated in church services, he seems to have been punctilious in not taking communion, and on at least one occasion he entered into negotiations to have the ban lifted. On the other hand, he was received as a communicant in several Protestant churches, some of which later excommunicated him themselves.

Bruno's personal life must have been totally unremarkable by the standards of the time, for in neither the writings of his friends nor of his enemies do we find any comment on it. His public life was quite a different matter; wherever he went his unorthodox views, together with his tactlessness and belligerency in dispute, left hard feelings behind. Though Bruno attempted repeatedly to gain some sort of official post at a university, his attitudes (and later his reputation) precluded any real possibility of such good fortune.

In 1581 Bruno's wanderings brought him to Paris. There he attached himself to the Palace Academy, a group of literary men and intellectuals in the court of Henri III.

Henri is often represented as a weak and indecisive king, wavering continually and dishonorably between the ultra-orthodox Catholic faction led by the politically ambitious and powerful Guise family and the equally ambitious and powerful

17

Protestant faction led by the Bourbon-Navarre family. Henri's personal life, his favors to his *mignons*, his excessive religious devotions and his anti-Spanish foreign policy caused him to be misunderstood and despised by his contemporaries. This negative view has survived until recent times. Only really in the past thirty years or so has it been realized that Henri labored—not entirely without success—to avert the utter disintegration of a France polarized and torn by civil war.[8] His purpose in founding the Palace Academy was to nurture a nondoctrinal philosophical basis for the political reconciliation of the Catholic and Protestant factions, through which alone he could hope for a consolidation of his precarious and limited power. It was in this atmosphere that Bruno's message of religious reconciliation fell upon receptive ears.[9] In turn, Bruno absorbed the political consciousness of the French court and its intellectuals, which prepared him for his attempts in England to apply his philosophy to the political and religious reconciliation of France and England.[10]

In 1583 Bruno received royal letters of recommendation to Michel de Castelnau, Marquis de Mauvissière, who was Henri's ambassador at Queen Elizabeth's court. Upon arrival in England, Bruno seems first to have gone to Oxford, where he arrived fortuitously in time to participate in the academic ceremonies which the Queen had ordered to honor the visit of the intellectually-inclined Polish Prince Albert Laski. Perhaps because of Laski's origin, one of the disputations arranged for him was on the subject of the theory of his countryman Copernicus. In this debate Bruno took the pro-Copernican position against one or more Oxonian Ptolemaists. The debate caused considerable furor, and neither side emerged with much credit. The level of scholarship at Oxford at the time was not what it had previously been;[11] indeed, Queen Elizabeth reproved the Chancellor in the wake of Laski's visit. Bruno's adversaries distinguished themselves mainly by their pigheaded pedantry. But Bruno was laughed off the stage when his opponents showed that he did not have the details of the Copernican system correct.[12] This incident is transformed into a triumph for Bruno in *The Ash Wednesday*

Supper (see the Fourth Dialogue and especially notes 56-58), but it seems that in the intervening year or so Bruno still had not got his Copernicus straight.

Any hopes Bruno may have entertained of a lectureship at Oxford were dashed. It was then that he repaired to London, where, on the strength of his letter from the King of France, he joined the household of Mauvissière.[13]

The two years or so that followed were probably the most stable and relatively serene, and certainly the most productive, of Bruno's adult life. In the amiability and security of the Mauvissière household he wrote the six Italian Dialogues, the first of which was *The Ash Wednesday Supper*.[14]

As we have already noted, *The Ash Wednesday Supper* contains most of what Bruno had to say concerning the Copernican theory, and it is thus on this work that there rests the view of Bruno as a scientific precursor of Galileo.

In the early fall of 1585, Mauvissière was recalled to Paris as a result of political realignments at home.[15] He was replaced by the Guisard Guillaume de l'Aubespine, Baron de Châteauneuf, from whom Bruno could not hope to obtain support. It would seem, moreover, that Bruno had not succeeded in cultivating any influential Englishmen to the point of obtaining patronage. In part this may have been due to his penchant for gratuitously offending his friends, as he managed to do at one time or another with both Sir Fulke Greville and Sir Philip Sidney. But the major barrier in this direction was almost certainly the political situation. The French embassy now had close connections with Mary Queen of Scots, Elizabeth's kinswoman, prisoner, and *bête noire*. For this and other reasons, the French had suddenly become very unpopular in England, and this exacerbated the general English xenophobia. Bruno's connection with the French embassy—and particularly the identification with at least some French goals which could be read into his writings—made his future in England a dim one.[16]

Bruno's attachment to Mauvissière was also to be ruptured. Mauvissière, as was true of almost all ambassadors in the sixteenth century, had experienced serious financial reverses during his stay in England, and had enjoyed scant monetary support from his royal master. To exacerbate matters, the ship carrying his possessions home was captured by pirates, and a great part of them were lost for good. Mauvissière was ruined, and there was no possibility of Bruno remaining for long in his private household.

In any event, it should be clear from Bruno's remarks (see especially the Second Dialogue) that he was not fond of English society. He may have been more than ready to try his fortunes elsewhere by the time Mauvissière's embassy ended.

But perhaps the most important consideration leading to Bruno's departure from England was what he may have considered to be the end, in at least partial failure, of his mission there. For Bruno stated on several occasions later in his life that his mission to England had been an official one, as a sort of intellectual ambassador, and that his letter from King Henri was tantamount to an official appointment. Although there is no incontrovertible evidence to support the claim, there is no doubt that Bruno's philosophical aims were entirely in line with the political goals of the French monarchy. We will explore these matters in detail when we come to consider the text of *The Ash Wednesday Supper*. But it would appear, and this is supported by other evidence which we shall cite below, that the change in ambassadors signaled a shift in French policy. By that time, too, Bruno may well have become disillusioned, and disabused of his vision of Queen Elizabeth as the universal, utopian monarch he sought to implement his grand program. Two years should have been long enough to convince even Bruno that neither the very pragmatic Queen herself nor her courtiers aspired to any such role for her.[17]

After 1585 Bruno resumed his wanderings through Europe, lecturing and writing and almost always managing to remain a center of violent controversy wherever he went. He continued to develop his "true philosophy," which he hoped would be a basis for a reconciliation not only of Catholic and Protestant but also of Man and God. In 1591, he cast Henri IV in the same role in which he had previously envisioned Henri III and Queen Elizabeth. Believing that the recent accession of the *politique* Henri de Navarre to the French throne and his victories over the Guisard *Ligue* forces presaged the culmination of his own mission, Bruno rashly returned to Italy. He accepted the invitation of the wealthy Venetian nobleman Zuan Mocenigo, who wished to have Bruno teach him the art of memory. Bruno's goal, however, lay beyond Venice: he aspired to return to Rome, there to convert the Pope to his Hermetic philosophy and thus, under the joint captainship of Henri IV and the Pope, to usher in the return of the Hermetic Golden Age.

Venice would certainly have been the safest place in Italy for Bruno, had he been able to remain *persona grata* with his influential patron. Venice was pro-French and would likely have been sympathetic to Bruno's associations with the French court. Besides, Venice prided itself on its very real independence of the Papacy, as the later example of Paolo Sarpi was to show, and the Serenissima had never handed heretics over to Rome merely because Rome willed it.

It turned out, however, that Mocenigo's real interest lay in what we would today call black magic, of which he believed Bruno to be a master. He soon began to importune Bruno to teach him magic spells. When Bruno repeatedly refused, claiming ignorance as well as distaste, Mocenigo fabricated a grab-bag of accusations and betrayed him to the Venetian Inquisition. Once this step had been taken, he had by law to be turned over to the Roman Inquisition, whose interest in his heresies was substantially deeper. More importantly, as we will see, Bruno was a potentially useful pawn in Rome's involved relationship with Spain.

Bruno remained in the prisons of the Inquisition for eight years. Part of the time he seems to have been neglected—kept in cold storage as it were. During these long stretches, his main communications with his jailers were requests for clothing, a blanket, or more food. At other times, he and the Inquisitors carried on a sort of macabre colloquium, both orally and in writing, in which each side tried to convince the other of the correctness of its views, as though it were a university debate and not a life that was at hazard.[18]

Bruno was not a real political danger to the Papacy. He had no following and few sympathizers. In the normal course of events, he might have remained in prison for decades, as many other accused heretics had done. But the Spanish, who had just put down the Calabrian Revolt in southern Italy (which had been led by another Hermetist, Tommaso Campanella), had far more against Bruno than did the Papacy. Bruno was the most infamous Hermetist of his day, and his execution would thus be ripe with symbolic meaning; it would teach the lesson that such utopian Hermetic movements were ended forever. Thus, apparently as a part of a minor political *quid pro quo* with Spain, involving the apprehension of an adulterous couple who had eloped to Spanish territory from the Papal court, Bruno was condemned to death. Early in the morning of February 17, 1600, he was led from his dungeon by the friars of the Company of St. John The Beheaded, an order dedicated to the comfort and conversion of condemned prisoners. He was conveyed the short distance to the Campo dei Fiori. There, after he had scoffed at his executioners and averted his eyes from the proffered crucifix, his tongue was spiked and the now-silenced heretic was burned at the stake. It is not known if his executioners intended to heighten the symbolism of his execution by offering this *auto da fè* on the day after Ash Wednesday; it is clear, however, that his execution early in 1600 served the purpose of showing all present and future Hermetists that their dreams of ushering in the Golden Age in that symbolic year, 1600, were illusory.[19]

Here again, the Bruno legend is worth mentioning. It is not clear just how or when it came into existence, but it attracted wide attention in the late nineteenth century in connection with the Risorgimento and the extraordinarily bad light in which the latter cast the ultrareactionary Catholic Church. It was obvious that Bruno was a martyr. But in terms of the spirit of the times, it was much less clear just what was the cause for which he was martyred. Since the Church of the late nineteenth century was obscurantist, antiscientific, and anti-intellectual, and since the late nineteenth century saw science as the standard-bearer of progress and enlightenment, it was easy to reflect the current situation back three hundred years and to cast Bruno as a martyr for science, a proto-Galileo. Bruno's support of Copernicanism, the seventeenth-century persecution of Galileo, and the retention of both Copernicus' and Galileo's books on the Index of Prohibited Books: all these together made a plausible case for a neat lesson with a fitting moral.

Any reading of Bruno, no matter how superficial, makes it evident that there are great differences between his works and those of Galileo. These differences were conventionally accommodated to the overall picture by proper insertions of the very appropriate adjective, "mystic," in comparisons of the two figures.

It is clear that the Bruno of legend was something of a hero to liberals and intellectuals in the years following 1870. A collection was raised internationally for a memorial statue, which was executed by H. Ferrari and dedicated with great pomp on the Campo dei Fiori in 1889. An ode commemorating this event was written by Swinburne in 1899.[20] The Pope, in his "prison" of the Vatican, played his part, too. He solemnly condemned the proceedings and declared a day of prayer and fasting.

This view of Bruno is perhaps best summarized by A. D. White in his monumental work, *A History of the Warfare of Science with Theology in Christendom:*[21]

> In the latter half of the sixteenth century these evolutionary theories of the universe seemed to take more definite form in the mind of Giordano Bruno, who evidently divined the fundamental idea of what is now known as the "nebular hypothesis"; but with his murder by the Inquisition at Rome this idea seemed utterly to disappear—dissipated by the flames which in 1600 consumed his body on the Campo dei Fiori.

This intriguing though largely artificial controversy has long since simmered down, since it is not much suited to the realities of our day. Certainly thousands of Romans pass Bruno's statue every day without a glimmer of interest, while in the Mezzogiorno, in the sun-drenched Piazza Giordano Bruno, a monument stands in memory of Nola's most distinguished son, and casts not a shadow of controversy.

There are no known portraits of Bruno drawn from life, and it seems unlikely that any will be found.[22] We know from his contemporaries that he was short and dark, but that would hardly serve to distinguish him from the greater part of his Neapolitan countrymen. It is perhaps most fitting that nothing remains of Bruno himself except his ideas.

The Background of The Ash Wednesday Supper

As we have already remarked, Bruno came to England in the belief that he had a mission from the King of France.[23] Henri III was beset by a tangled mass of perils internal and external, which we have summarized above. There was a Europe-wide struggle for power between the Catholics, led by Hapsburg Spain, and the Protestants, whose less powerful and certainly less enthusiastic champion was Elizabeth's England. This struggle was reflected in a lengthy and destructive series of French civil wars. Henri's aims were of course mainly political, but they had inevitable corollaries in the areas of religion and philosophy.

Bruno's mission in England, as he himself saw it, was in line with Henri's aims.[24] Spain had gained the upper hand in the long struggle, and it was natural for France to seek closer ties with England as a counterbalance. The French crown, however, was committed at least nominally to the Catholic side, which made any English alliance a very touchy matter indeed. Internal reaction to such a move could lead to a victory for the Guisards, while any increase in Catholic power in England strengthened the claims to the throne of Mary Queen of Scots, the Guises' kinswoman.

Bruno saw as his immediate task the search for bonds which could be forged between the liberal Catholic intellectuals in France and their influential, liberal Protestant counterparts in England. Such intellectual links could become a powerful counterbalance to the doctrinal objection to a French-English alliance. The very moderate and ambiguous Protestant position of

24

Queen Elizabeth seemed an attractive beginning point, while the more extreme and uncompromising Puritan view appeared to be well under control at court.

Bruno thus needed to establish a favorable relationship with the circle of English court intellectuals. This circle included such many-sided Renaissance men as Sir Philip Sidney, the poet-philosopher; Thomas Digges, the savant who had written the first account in English of the Copernican system; William Gilbert, the physician, natural philosopher and sometime mystic who was later to become royal physician; and Sir Fulke Greville (later Lord Brooke), the courtier-intellectual-poet. *The Ash Wednesday Supper* and the later Italian dialogues were addressed to the members of this circle. Indeed, the *Supper* is supposed to take place in Greville's house, while the later *Spaccio* and *Eroici furori* are dedicated to Sidney.

It is in terms of this special audience, for which Bruno intended his London writings, that we can explain the otherwise curious use of the Italian language. Bruno certainly did not know English well enough to write in that language, but Latin was of course understood by everyone who made any claim to education. Indeed, most of Bruno's other works were written in Latin. But the court intellectuals were not typical of educated Englishmen in general. Much more common among the latter were the rigid pedants whom Bruno pillories at length in the *Supper,* and the Puritans and Presbyterians who could be expected to oppose Bruno's aims with all their might. Most such persons did not know Italian.

In fact, knowledge of Italian was rather closely confined in England to a group of relatively broad-minded intellectuals living mostly in and around London. There, an interest in "advanced" Italian culture, which stemmed from the "finishing school" visits to Italy of educated young men, had been cultivated by a group of Italian Protestant émigrés, among them Bruno's friend John Florio and his late father Michael Angelo.[25] As a consequence, knowledge of Italian was widespread among Bruno's intended audience. Queen Elizabeth herself was fluent in Italian, and took pleasure in showing off her abilities before foreign visitors.

Among other segments of educated English society, Italian culture was seen as dangerously corrupt, and knowledge of the language thus conducive to a life of immorality. Consequently, by writing in Italian, Bruno could be assured that his writings would be read by precisely those persons who constituted his intended audience, and by almost no others.

This fortuitous state of affairs was a stroke of good luck in another way. Bruno is a master stylist in Italian, and perhaps only by writing in his native tongue could Bruno have brought forth the rich and intense poetic, religious, and philosophical language we find in the *Supper*.

Given this audience, the use of the Copernican theory was a serviceable polemic device, quite aside from its adaptability to Bruno's overall philosophy. There had been considerable interest in Copernicanism in English intellectual circles; Digges' exposition, *A Perfit Description of the Celestiall Orbes*, had appeared in 1576, and had its third and fourth printings during Bruno's stay in England. William Gilbert's *De magnete*, with its strong (though to the modern reader unconvincing) defense of the Copernican theory, was not published until 1600; however, it was entirely or essentially complete in manuscript by the time Bruno came to England.[26] If Gilbert's work was not known in manuscript form to at least some of the court circle, his views must have been.

While not all members of the audience to which Bruno directed the *Supper* were convinced Copernicans, most of them had at least a passing interest in the theory.[27] Hence Bruno could at a minimum expect a sympathetic initial interest in a work which introduced him to his reading public as a Copernican. And, as we shall discuss below, Copernicanism was one of several themes in the *Supper* which linked the English courtiers to the intellectuals of the French court.

We will soon see that *The Ash Wednesday Supper* is concerned with the Copernican theory only in a subsidiary and metaphoric way. Indeed, the title itself suggests this. Having secured the interest of his reading public, Bruno hardly mentions the Copernican theory at all in his later Italian dialogues, which deal with matters metaphysical and theological for the most part. Nevertheless, Bruno uses the theory skilfully and in an intriguing manner.

We have discussed Bruno's immediate aims, and have shown their close relationship to the aims of French policy. Bruno's ultimate aims, however, were far wider. Ultimately, he hoped to establish a universal Christian commonwealth on the basis of his Hermetic "true philosophy." At various points in his career, he envisioned different personages in the office of universal monarch: Henri III, Elizabeth I, and Henri IV. This dream of a universal empire, which would heal the wounds of sixteenth-century society, reform it, and attune it to the harmony of all natural terrestrial and celestial phenomena, was a commonplace conceit in the last half of the sixteenth century. It was adopted as the rhetoric in the Holy Roman Imperial, English and French courts.[28] It also formed the basis for other mystical, utopian philosophers of the age, notably Guillaume Postel[29] and Tommaso Campanella. It would seem, however, that the rhetoric of the imperial and royal courts was exceeded by the sincerity of Postel, Campanella and Bruno. Postel, who advocated the *restitutio omnis* through the agency of the French king, was considered an eccentric by the King of France, and he ended his days under Jesuit house arrest. Campanella was welcomed by Urban VIII for a brief moment, then thrown off only to be welcomed next at the court of Louis XIII. The universal monarchy which Campanella hoped the French king would initiate was, for all practical purposes, scorned in Paris; all that was adopted was the Hermetic rhetoric of the Sun King. There is little doubt that Henri III also would have been ill-pleased with Bruno's practical aims had he been aware of their full scope.

*The Relationship
between Bruno's Cosmology and His Physics*

Bruno's enthusiasm for the Copernican system arose, as we shall see, from its felicitous applicability to his philosophical and religious views. This applicability goes considerably further

27

than a mere conformity or consistency; Bruno uses the Copernican system as a grand metaphor or hieroglyph for his insights into the fundamental nature of the universe, into the relationship between Man the microcosm and the external macrocosm, and (by extension, since the matter is not consistently treated in this particular work, but in later ones) into the relationship between Man and God.

Since Bruno sees his own views as revolutionary both in their progress beyond those of his immediate predecessors and in their powerful applicability to the solution of practical social and political problems, the Copernican system has the additional attraction of possessing, in the view of Bruno and some of his contemporaries, a revolutionary flavor. For all that Copernicus himself did not see his work as extending beyond the sphere of astronomy, his contemporaries and successors—especially those who were not astronomers—saw his system as holding much potential for universal change. By implication, at least, the Copernican system swept away the confining and impenetrable celestial spheres which ever had hemmed in the human body if not the human soul. Bruno makes much of this.[30] He was surely not the only man of his time to read broad implications into the Copernican cosmology, but certainly no one else developed these implications to the extent that Bruno did.

In contrast to Bruno's cosmology, his physics is essentially traditional and Aristotelian. Indeed, Bruno sees Copernicus and Aristotle in basically the same light, as inspired geniuses who saw part of the truth and vaguely glimpsed some or all of the rest, but who failed through their own limitations to see the ultimate truth as he himself did.[31]

Bruno's essential adherence to Aristotelian physics places him, however, in a delicate position. The physics of Aristotle and his cosmology are very tightly knit together. Indeed, the great appeal of the total system lies in its unified account of both the commonplace and the celestial.

Faced with the same problem, Galileo vigorously and boldly rejected Aristotelian physics, and in doing so laid the groundwork for the modern science of mechanics. Bruno, who was no physicist, took the more conservative pathway of effecting a reconciliation between Aristotelian physics and Copernican cosmology. In spite of his limitations as a physicist, he did this with great skill and subtlety; in making his modifications appear as natural if subtle outgrowths of Aristotelian physics, he was able to adduce Aristotle as a supporter of his own unorthodox and revolutionary metaphysics.

In order to see this clearly, let us begin with a brief review of the standard Aristotelian physics of the Middle Ages and the Renaissance, with emphasis on the way it fitted the generally accepted cosmological picture.

The earth lies at the center of the universe. The fixed stars are embedded in the surface of a hollow crystalline sphere which revolves daily on an axis passing through the earth—what we today would call the earth's axis. (In the Aristotelian-Ptolemaic view it is improper and somewhat confusing to call it this, since it is the celestial sphere and not the earth which turns on it.) The planets, the sun and the moon are located on other similar spheres nested within the celestial sphere; the axis of each sphere is embedded at two diametric points in the next outer one. By introducing a sufficient number of "dummy" spheres which contain no visible heavenly bodies, it is possible in principle to account for any motions of the stars and planets whatsoever which may be observed.

Unfortunately, if one tries seriously to account for the celestial motions as they are actually observed, the system of spheres becomes very complicated and thus loses its principal attractiveness. From a practical point of view, calculation based on the model is very awkward. Finally, certain observations (e.g., the periodic variations in the apparent diameters of the sun and the moon, and the variation in the brightness of Venus) cannot be explained in a simple way using the model.

The Ptolemaic system, with its deferents, epicycles, eccentrics, and equant points, is more suitable for calculation. It retains the central features of a geocentric universe, and of observed motions all of which are compounded of fundamental uniform circular motions. It does not, however, possess a strong esthetic appeal,[32] and the astronomers who used it as a practical tool for centuries held widely differing attitudes as to the seriousness with which the model should be taken. A by no means uncommon view, which concorded with the late medieval and Renaissance views of the relationship between God and the material universe, was that the Ptolemaic system was a mathematical tool useful for more or less accurate predictions of the positions of heavenly bodies, but should not be regarded as a representation of the "real" structure of the universe. The universe, being the extraordinarily subtle creation of the mind of the omnipotent and omnicompetent God, could have been created by him in an infinite number of ways, some or all of which are entirely beyond our comprehension, actual or potential. Thus, while one might make observations and calculations, it was at least suggestive of heresy to argue that one had discovered the "actual" structure of the universe.[33]

It is this view which is set forth in Osiander's spurious preface to Copernicus' *De revolutionibus*, and which is so vehemently rejected by Bruno.[34]

Uniform circular motion—or at least a motion compounded of elementary uniform circular motions—is essential to a reconciliation of Aristotelian physics with the geocentric cosmology. With a few exceptions needing special explanation (notably the irregularity of the surface features of the moon) celestial observations over many centuries strongly suggested that the heavens were a place where no essential changes ever took place. The matter of the heavens, unlike that of the earth, was eternal and unchangeable. It was requisite, in the Aristotelian view, that such matter engage in the motion (in the modern sense of change of place) appropriate to it. Such motion is circular, since no point on a circle is essentially distinguishable from any other, and since circular motion has neither beginning nor end. The importance of this correspondence between unchangeability (or incorruptibility, to use the Aristotelian term) and uniform circular motion appeared far deeper to the Aristotelian than it does to us. In part, this is a matter of terminology. When we speak of motion, we mean what was then called *local motion;* i.e., the change of position as a function of time. But as Drake has pointed out,[35] *kinesis* (the Greek word universally translated as "motion") meant to Aristotle not only local motion, but any kind of continuous change. It was meant to be the opposite not of stasis, but of mutation, or discontinuous change. Thus the only kind of local motion in which matter, immobile in the broader sense, can engage is that kind which is perfect and eternal.

Terrestrial matter, on the other hand, is constantly changing—that is, it is in constant motion in the broader sense. The natural motion proper to it is that which leads to a terminus where it can come to rest and cease to change; i.e., linear motion inward toward the center of the universe for heavy bodies and outward motion toward the periphery of the universe for light ones. It is this point to which Bruno refers when he says,[36] "Two are the kinds of motions: straight, by which bodies tend to conservation, and circular, by which they conserve themselves."[37]

In removing the earth from the center of the universe, Bruno is obliged to remove from it its unique status as the only body in the universe whose matter is corruptible. He does this by a felicitous compromise. On the one hand, the earth, though it is in constant change in its parts, as is necessary for a living, ensouled being, does not as a whole pass from youth through middle age to decline and death, as would an ordinary living creature. This is because the separate parts of the earth undergo the cycle of birth, growth, decline, death and rebirth individually and separately, so that the whole maintains an eternal state. This eternal state, however, is distinct from the corresponding Aristotelian state in that it is dynamic.

On the other side of the coin, the other stars, while maintaining an eternal quality, likewise possess it in a dynamic sense. Indeed, they are not fundamentally different from the earth. All the stars, including the earth, must move in circles in order to maintain the motion proper to eternal beings, but Bruno paradoxically maintains[38] that the motions cannot either be precisely circular or composed precisely of circles, even though the motion of the earth (after Copernicus) must be composed of exactly four circular motions. While the reason for this paradoxical statement

31

(which Bruno attempts not very successfully to clarify with the example of a spinning ball thrown into the air) cannot be accounted for with certainty, it seems likely that it represents Bruno's compromise between the circular motion necessary for "conservation" and the noncircular motion necessary for change. For Bruno, however, it is perfectly possible for opposites to concord:[39]

> Do consider that, even if we say that the motions are four, they nevertheless contribute to a compound motion. Secondly, consider that, even though we call them circular, none of them is really circular. . . . There are thus four motions, and there must not be more nor less . . . of which one irregular one.necessarily renders the others irregular. . . .

In a similar spirit, Bruno retains Aristotle's view of the natural upward or downward motion of ordinary objects by asserting that the infinite universe contains an infinite number of centers, rather than the single center of the geocentric universe. Each star is the natural center for its own matter. Since (again after Aristotle) matter is weightless in its proper place, the substitution of many centers for one satisfactorily accounts for terrestrial as well as celestial observations.

To all this, Bruno adds a justification, or cause, which we would call metaphysical. All objects revolve around all others. This motion is requisite to the vital interchange necessary for living beings. In this way, Bruno dispenses with the necessity of a prime mover. Such a prime mover—an engine that turns the whole celestial works—is not absolutely necessary to an Aristotelian cosmology; as we have seen, eternal circular motion is natural to celestial bodies without any external impulse being required. But such a prime mover was easily added to the system, and served the double purpose of giving employment to the angels and establishing the necessity of continual intervention by God. Thus was the universe of Aristotle Christianized.

Bruno must in any case dispense with this prime mover, which in the Aristotelian system moves the outer sphere which then communicates the motion to the inner spheres. But this dispensation is entirely in line with Bruno's Hermetic view that all living beings—and certainly the stars, which he considers to be living beings *par excellence*—possess natural motion as a direct expression of their immanent divinity. That is, the divinity within them provides the natural impulse to motion (which is mutual since they all participate in this divinity), and there is no need for a continual push provided by an external God. Bruno is careful to point out that such an external push smacks of the violent motion[40] which is inconsistent with celestial beings. Moreover, as Bruno points out, stars are so large that it would take an implausibly large and esthetically awkward force to move them if they did not move naturally.[41]

Perhaps Bruno's most important contribution to the physics (as distinguished from the cosmology) of his day was his implicit stress on the dynamical steady state. The idea that such a state could properly be part and parcel of an eternal universe may or may not be original with Bruno, but his stress on it is unique in his time. Needless to say, a willingness to deal with a dynamic universe is absolutely necessary to the development of modern physics. Galileo went much further, and dismissed completely from his discussions a consideration of the teleological final state. It is an intriguing speculation that Bruno's thought helped to launch Galileo's own.[42]

In his consideration of the parts of the earth, Bruno is thoroughly Aristotelian. He stresses the constant change of the earth, going to the extreme point of claiming that sooner or later everything is interchanged with everything else, with respect to form, matter and interaction. All this, however, is quite consistent with standard Aristotelian views. In his citation of instances of climatic and geological change, Bruno seems to be quoting from standard sources. In view of this, one should probably be cautious in evaluating Bruno's originality in contributing to the theory of geological uniformitarianism. Nevertheless, the possibility remains that the *Supper* had direct or indirect effect on later geological thought.

We must also note that, whereas Bruno draws upon many standard sources and ideas concerning physics, one should be extremely cautious in arguing for Bruno's conscious interest in and contributions to physics and astronomy *per se*. His interests in the *Supper* were not essentially physical, and his statements on physical matters are mainly either derivative or intuitive, based on his own religious and philosophical imperatives. As we will see, his astronomical and physical arguments carry deeper meanings and are offered both to convey these deeper meanings and to display already existing intellectual links between France and England.

The Ash Wednesday Supper

The *Ash Wednesday Supper* is not an easy work to approach for the first time. While it is tightly organized, the organization is closely entangled with Bruno's main purposes. These do not coincide with the normal expectations of the modern reader who has, because of the Bruno myth, come to expect to find a defense of the Copernican system. Moreover, the organization of the work is not linear but recursive. The arguments that Bruno makes in one place are often related in a complex way to arguments and comments made elsewhere. This plan of organization, irritating to the modern mind, is entirely in harmony with Bruno's universe, in which everything interacts with everything else as a vital precondition of its existence. The purpose of this section is to forearm the reader so that he can make substantial sense of the *Supper* on the first reading.

It must be made clear, first and foremost, that the central subject of the dialogue is not the Copernican System, but the Ash Wednesday Supper.[43] The title tells us as much. Having said this, however, we must examine closely the relationship of the heliocentric theory (and Bruno's natural science in general) to the Ash Wednesday Supper. As we will see, this reciprocal relationship is the key to Bruno's philosophy.

As we have said above, Bruno hoped to effect a political and religious union between France and England. In terms of political practices both in his day and in ours, the means by which Bruno strove to accomplish this alliance was most unusual.

Bruno saw the religious differences separating England and France as paramount, and he espied their reconciliation in and through his philosophy, a philosophy which was deeply influenced by Nicolaus of Cusa's concept of the reconciliation of opposites.

The political danger posed to France and England by Hapsburg Spain did not, in Bruno's view, constitute the starting point for political and religious reconciliation. Such crass considerations of self-interest and political expediency were not part of Bruno's method, however important they may have been to the politically-minded rulers of the day. Rather, the belief that *liberal* Protestants and Catholics could be reconciled is the nodal point of *The Ash Wednesday Supper.* In Bruno's view, the doctrinal difficulties that separated these two groups could be overcome. That this is Bruno's goal is made perfectly clear by an analysis of the dialogue.

La Cena de le ceneri is translated "the Supper of Ash Wednesday." Which supper? In Italian, *la cena* means the Eucharist or, as the Protestants called it, the Lord's Supper.[44] It was entirely reasonable for Bruno to choose the Eucharist as the subject of his dialogue, as the debate over the nature of the Eucharist among various Protestant confessions and between Protestants and Catholics was one of the thorniest of the Reformation era.[45] Was Christ physically present in the bread and wine? Was the Real Physical Presence to be explained by the doctrine of transubstantiation or by that of consubstantiation? Was Christ only spiritually present? Was the Lord's Supper simply a memorial service, Christ not being present either physically or spiritually?[46] As we shall see, Bruno hoped to transcend these doctrinal enigmas, and to teach a Hermetic theory of the Eucharist acceptable to all men of liberality and good will.

Bruno hoped that liberal English Protestants and French Catholics would accept his transcendent notion of the Eucharist. The necessary consequences of such acceptance would be *unification* of religion, and political alliance between France and England. This goal of unification is also evident further on in the title of the dialogue: "five subjects . . . four interlocuters . . . three reflections . . . two subjects . . . sole refuge." Herein we see the main current which characterizes the *Supper*: the progression from multiplicity to Unity, from superficial differences to essential similarities, from apparent chaos to universal participation in oneness.

This majestic theme of Unity is expressed again and again in the *Supper*. We find it, for example, in Bruno's discussion of geological transformations in the Fifth Dialogue and in his discussions of the earth and other "stars." Drawing upon Plato's *Timaeus* and Aristotle's *Meteorologica*, Bruno asserts (see pp. 213ff.) the constant interchange of the parts of stars and their mutual relationships. Every internal part of a star becomes an external part, and vice versa. What has been dry becomes moist, land sea and sea land. Every part, in other words, becomes every other part, however antinomial they may seem to be. Moreover, the earth and the other innumerable stars are generally similar in terms of both their physical characteristics and their inhabitants. If such a reconciliation can be effected for the infinite universe, with all its bewildering variety, the unification of Protestants and Catholics is surely within reach.

The reconciliation of opposites is seen in another guise in the opening pages of the Prefatory Epistle. *The Ash Wednesday Supper* is itself no thing, all things, and one thing. Bruno leads us through an excursus on Cusan negative theology: "this book is not a banquet of nectar, . . . not a protoplastic one, . . . not that of Bonifacio Candelaio for a comedy." The book, and the Supper itself, can thus be defined negatively by what they are not; this is the Cusan *Minimum*. The Cusan *Maximum* [47] follows immediately in the text. The book (as well as the Supper) is all things: " a banquet so great and small, . . . so joyous and choleric, . . . so tragic and comic that [you will become] heroic and humble, . . . sophist with Aristotle, philosopher with Pythagoras. . . ." Thus, through Cusa's doctrine of the *Minimum* and *Maximum* and the negative theology of his *De docta ignorantia*, we are led to the Cusan reconciliation of opposites.

It is important to note, moreover, that this reconciliation of opposites (e.g., "so Florentine for its leanness *and* Bolognese for

its fatness" [our italics]) entails unification. The opposites become the same thing. If Bruno begins the *Supper* by stressing the
ascent to Unity and reconciliation into Unity, the object of the
dialogue reflects the Brunian rhetorical technique. It is through
the Hermetic understanding of the Eucharist that religious polarities are to become One. What Bruno seems to be saying is that,
whatever doctrinal differences exist between Catholics and Protestants, they can realize their essential unity through the Supper,[48] the very instrument which reconciles Man and God.

In this notion of oneness *via* participation in the divine
essence, Bruno draws not only upon Nicolaus of Cusa but also
upon the late ancient Neoplatonist, Plotinus. According to Plotinian psychology (in the original meaning of that term), the Ideal
Forms in the Real World contemplate each other. In the very act
of this contemplation, moreover, each Form *becomes* the other.
Having itself once inhabited the Intelligible World before its
incarnation in the body, the individual soul can, in an ecstatic
state, re-enter the Intelligible World and reflect upon other
Forms, including other souls. This ecstatic activity thus unites
the soul with other souls. The Plotinian theory thereby concludes
that each soul becomes each of the others. Bruno, drawing upon
this psychology, implies that the Catholic and Protestant who
follow the Hermetic *methodus* toward mystical reflection and
knowledge can realize their mutual divinity and participation in
the mind of God.[49] This realization will end acrimony and
encourage unity on earth.

While he holds this irenic aim, Bruno finds little to praise in
Protestantism. (The Protestants whom he does praise—Sidney *et
al.*—are, to his mind, liberal and receptive to the Hermetic
philosophy in its Brunian formulation; thus they are malleable
to Bruno's purpose.) Bruno abhors the effects of the Reformation
upon English society. The Protestant denial of the efficacy of
good works in the economy of salvation is destructive of social
coherence. Bruno tells us that the fear of eternal punishment for
transgressing the moral law is the main thing that holds society
together, since nothing else will sway the common people.

Allusions to and direct condemnation of the contemporary

corruption of the English social fabric appear throughout the *Supper*, but most especially in the Second Dialogue. It is well to note that Bruno does not blame the "ignorant" London mob for their barbarous behavior, which he likens to the natural behavior of butting and shoving beasts. Rather, he attributes their actions to the effects of the Reformation. He views these effects as "trickling down" from above. This perspective explains his harsh caricature of the two Oxford doctors, Torquato and Nundinio. Oxford University had once been eminent, its scholars on the cutting edge of European scholarship. However, with the inception of the Reformation, the much-vaunted learned community of Oxford had fallen from its pinnacle into an abyss of ignorant pedantry typified by the worst sort of Renaissance Ciceronian Humanism, as well as by a sterile form of Aristotelianism.[50] Bruno reasons that the teachers of the nation have allowed true scholarship (i.e., that scholarship which had flourished in the time of Colet and More, and had been receptive to the "ancient theologians" of the Hermetic tradition) to fall into desuetude, and that the ramifications of this collapse of learning can be seen throughout England.

As we follow the Nolan (Bruno) and his party to Sir Fulke Greville's lodgings, we find the transportation system in the hands of ineffectual oarsmen, the streets in a state of filth and disrepair, and the market-places overrun with men no better than shoving and pushing beasts of burden. The degraded humanity of the inhabitants of London is expressed, moreover, in xenophobia of a degree that endangers the foreign visitor, and the Londoners take every opportunity to imperil the Nolan's life. Even the hangers-on and attendants in the palaces of the nobility are rude and churlish.

These societal effects are, in Bruno's judgment, merely the reflection of the more profound rudeness and ignorance of the Oxford dons. The bestial attributes of the latter result in turn from the Reformation theology of salvation by faith and grace alone. Yet we must not assume therefrom that Bruno was enchanted with the Catholic salvational economy by faith and good works. His distaste for theological subtleties, to which we have already alluded, was probably directed indifferently to all sides of the Reformation debate. His insistence on the necessity of a doctrine of good works seems to us to have stemmed from entirely practical considerations.[51] His pragmatic approach is clearly seen in the Fourth Dialogue, which he begins with a discourse on the Bible. While this discourse attempts primarily to explain why Moses did not teach his people the heliocentric cosmology (which, since he was inspired by God, he must have known), Bruno argues that the purpose of the Bible (and thus of the vulgar religion) is to establish moral law, which alone can rein in the base impulses of ignorant peoples. Implicit in this argument is the notion that religious moral law is enforced by the threat of eternal perdition. The effectiveness of this threat (as well as of the obverse promise of eternal reward for a life of virtue) depends upon the theology of salvation by faith and good works.[52] The masses, then, need a legislative religion, and this is what England effectively lacked.

From this broad indictment of English morals, learning and religion, Bruno excluded those who were at the summit of English court society. After his arduous journey through London streets and straits, the Nolan enters Greville's house and finds his way to an upstairs banquet room. There, above the fumes of the reeking mob in the streets, Bruno meets with true gentlemen (save, of course, for Nundinio and Torquato who are present to debate with Bruno).[53]

Immediately upon joining them, Bruno recalls for us the purpose of the Supper. Being men of "higher tables," the courtiers of the Sidney circle eschew the "ceremony of the cup." This ceremony is nevertheless described by Bruno in nauseating detail. The cup being passed around, each person sips and leaves particles of food, hair and other delicacies on its rim. In the performance of this distasteful ritual, Bruno says, all the participants become one, each mingling his residues with the others'. We recognize in this strange practice a caricature of communion in both kinds, that is, the Protestants' Lord's Supper. Bruno's deeper meaning can also be seen: participants in this ceremony strive for community, but what is achieved is merely a physical interchange and union of drossy matter. Thus the Eucharistic feast, understood in the common fashion, is a sterile liturgy, yielding at most the basest form of union. We are thus prepared to hear the Nolan's disquisition on the true nature of the Eucharist, the way in which it concords with the natural universe, and its benefits to mankind.

Before we turn to this subject, which really occupies the remainder of the *Supper,* it is well to consider further the background and frame of mind of the guests at the Supper. We have seen that they are men of the "higher tables" where the ceremony of the cup is no longer practiced; among them may be Sir Philip Sidney. Presumably, then, those assembled to hear the debate between Bruno and the Oxford doctors are associated with the Sidney circle. More to the point in terms of the subject matter, they are associated with the Dee circle, for Sidney and others mentioned in the dialogue (such as Walsingham) either were students or friends of Dee, or employed Dee to tutor their children.[54] As friends of John Dee, they had all been exposed to irenic Hermetism. Though they were intellectuals, they were not members of the decrepit and Puritanical Oxford community, and Bruno thus assumed that their religious views were tolerant and latitudinarian. Their lack of sectarian dogmatism is symbolized by the absence of the ceremony of the cup—the Anglican communion in two kinds. (This use of a single metaphor at several levels is a central ingredient of Bruno's style.)

Sidney, Greville, and their friends were familiar with the writings of Hermes Trismegistus and of the other religious philosophers in the supposedly very ancient Hermetic tradition.[55] Whether they were hearing Bruno himself at the supper or reading the *Supper,* these courtiers could therefore be expected to comprehend readily the Hermetic core of Bruno's arguments as well as to understand the metaphoric, poetic, and hieroglyphic allusions employed by the Nolan. These, then, were the true gentlemen whom Bruno addressed, praised, and hoped to enlist in his grand design, which extended from the Hermetic Eucharist to Anglo-French religious and political union.

What better way to persuade these Hermetic adepts than by

presenting the argument in the guise of a discussion of Copernican heliocentricity? As we have already noted, the sun was a powerful symbol in the Hermetic literature. One of the members of the Dee-Sidney circle, Thomas Digges, had already made Copernicanism a respectable and fashionable topic of discussion. The audience thus made receptive, Bruno proceeds in the Third and Fourth Dialogues to debate with Doctors Nundinio and Torquato on the Copernican theory—that is, the Copernican theory as recast Hermetically by Giordano Bruno.

The reader of the *Supper* (like the gentlemen who meet the Nolan outside his residence to escort him to the banquet) has been prepared in the First Dialogue for Bruno's interpretation of Copernicanism. There, the Nolan establishes the importance of Copernicus and places him in historical perspective. Bruno tells us that Copernicus has revived the heliocentric vision of the universe. In so doing, he has not only restored and made respectable the ancient and true teachings of the Greek astronomer Aristarchus but also, unwittingly, the teachings of Hermes Trismegistus and his followers in the Hermetic tradition.[56] We should stress Bruno's view that Copernicus unintentionally helped to resurrect the Hermetic philosophy from the disrepute into which it had fallen due to medieval darkness.

Even though Bruno ridicules the writer of the spurious preface to *De revolutionibus*,[57] for suggesting that Copernicus' book advanced heliocentricity merely as a hypothesis useful for astronomical calculations, his praise of Copernicus is qualified. Bruno lauds "that German" for his contribution to astronomy, but he sees Copernicus as limited by his "mathematical more than natural reasoning." It is this limitation which prevented Copernicus from attaining a true feeling for infinitude, Bruno avers, and it is just this intuition which separates the Nolan from Copernicus.

This view of Copernicus is crucial, for upon it hinges not only Bruno's exposition of Copernicanism but also his attempt to use Copernicanism as a hieroglyph for the Unity which he hopes to advance. When Teofilo assesses the contribution of Bruno, he says:[58]

... [H]ow shall we honor [the Nolan] who found the way to ascend to the sky, compass the circumference of the stars, and leave at his back the convex surface of the firmament? .... Now behold the [Nolan] who has surmounted the air, penetrated the sky, wandered among the stars, passed beyond the borders of the world, [who has] made to vanish the imaginary walls of the first, eighth, ninth, tenth spheres, and the many more you could add. . . .

Bruno has added infinitude to the heliocentric theory and, by so doing, has completely transcended Copernicus. The sun is no longer at the center of the universe, but is only one of infinitely many local centers.

But how does Bruno evaluate this, his supreme achievement? It certainly does not occur to him to claim that his insight was gained by what we would call "scientific" thinking. Rather, Bruno's self-assessment suggests that an "ethical Ego" has been responsible for his intuition of infinity. Cassirer has, we believe, validly perceived Bruno's view of infinitude:[59]

... Giordano Bruno did not look upon the problem of space as exclusively or even primarily a problem of cosmology or natural philosophy, but, rather, as a question of *ethics*. . . . Bruno never affirms the infinity of space by basing himself on the simple testimony of empirical or mathematical vision. He considers sense and intuition as such to be incapable of leading to the true concept of infinity. Rather, we grasp the infinite with the same organ with which we grasp our own spiritual being and essence: the principle of its knowledge is to be sought nowhere but in the Ego, in the principle of self-consciousness. If we want to penetrate the true essence of the infinite, . . . we must perform a free act and a free upward movement of the mind to raise ourselves to it.

We agree with Cassirer that there is a relationship in Bruno's thought between ethics and infinity. Indeed, we argue further that the implications Bruno derives from infinitude are closely related to questions of ethics, especially to what Bruno considered the ultimate ethical question—Unity. It is, moreover, highly satisfying esthetically that a cosmology which upholds an infinite universe and innumerable stars/planets can lead back to the theme of Unity; this possibility is inherent in and emerges from Bruno's holism.[60]

We have already alluded to Bruno's discussions of geological change and their potential for transformation into arguments which dissolve politico-religious polarities. Throughout the final three dialogues of the *Supper,* the same method is used to transform disquisitions on astronomical and optical phenomena into implicit proofs of the essential unity of high-minded Protestants and Catholics. Let us see how Bruno accomplishes this.[61]

While Bruno argues on behalf of an infinite number of worlds, each one a solar system, he stresses that each star/planet is an "animal," that is, an ensouled being. Each of these celestial bodies is similar to the earth, though not exactly the same.[62] If one perceives the animal celestial bodies as analogous to earthly men, he comes to realize that, for all their minor individual differences, all men share the same generic characteristic of having a soul. This soul, because of the Plotinian psychology explained above, partakes of divinity. This is the first step toward demonstrating Unity through multiplicity.

The second step in this process can be seen in Bruno's optical arguments. In one of these, for example, he attempts to prove that two luminous bodies, separated by an opaque body, are not hindered in their ability to illuminate one another. His proof depends again on infinity: remove the two luminous bodies increasingly far from each other, and the opaque body (which remains stationary between them) ceases to be an obstacle to the exchange of light. Infinitely or indeterminately separated, the two luminous bodies experience a mutual and reciprocal illumination. Once again we find the case being made for Unity: the two luminous bodies exchange and share their (divine) light, in much the same way as Marsilio Ficino's doctrine of Platonic love holds that lovers exchange and share their souls through rays emitted from and projected into the pupils of their eyes. In both Ficino's physiological theory and Bruno's optical argument, two become one.[63] The metaphor contained in this argument from optics is not exhausted, as the opaque body represents the Eucharist which need not impede the relationship between Protestant and Catholic or between Man and God. We will refer to this again, but we must first extend the theme of Unity through sharing, by looking at other examples of Bruno's physics. At the end of the Third Dialogue Bruno discusses whether, on a ship in motion, an object dropped from the masthead of the ship will fall straight down to the foot of the mast, or whether it will be left behind.[64] This is a curious and difficult thought experiment, especially since the figure to which the argument refers (Figure 6) contains none of the geometrical notations mentioned in the text. In addition, the text refers to a man standing on the shore, who throws another object at the ship and later drops the object from above the mast as the ship passes below; but neither he nor the man on the masthead is portrayed in the engraving. Still more curious is the fact that Bruno stipulates that the experiment works only if the ship does not pitch; yet the ship in the figure is far from shore on a stormy sea. All this would suggest that Bruno did not intend the illustration to operate simultaneously with the physical argument, but that he intended it to supplement and *complete* the textual argument.

Despite the discrepancies between figure and text, Bruno arrives at the correct conclusion. If the ship does not pitch, the object dropped from the masthead does land at the foot of the mast. Along the way, Bruno tells us that the man on the shore, who throws an object directly at the moving ship,[65] will miss his mark.

The main point to be made here is that Bruno reaches this conclusion, which is consistent with and necessary for his purposes, in a way which is coincidentally and fortuitously correct from the standpoint of modern physics. Our assertion is not made out of picayune desire to deny Bruno his due as a physicist. Rather, the total context of Bruno's argument forces us to this conclusion, which is also consistent with the general character of Bruno's methodology. Recall the ship engraving with its lack of notation, geometric or pictorial, relating to the textual description of the experiment. These discrepancies are not casual, nor are they unintended, for the engraving has a very precise meaning. Yates has shown that this engraving is interpretable within the iconographic traditions of the sixteenth century. The two flames issuing from the yardarms of the ship represent the star deities Castor and Pollux, the Twins, who stand for spiritual calm.[66] Clearly, then, the ship experiment in the text is another example of the holistic approach which allows Bruno to translate back and forth between the corporeal and incorporeal worlds and phenomena.[67]

While one cannot always set forth precise and complete interpretations of the implications of Bruno's arguments (indeed, the possibility of doing so would be in conflict with Bruno's fundamental esoteric attitudes), the following expansion of his meaning is probably fairly close to the mark. When Bruno speaks of the men on the shore and on the masthead, he is creating two distinct "systems" (to use modern scientific terminology). In his static system, the man on the shore does not strike the target at which he aims. The man on the ship, on the other hand, operates within a dynamic system (and is moving with it). This dichotomy between the two men seems intended to show the shore-bound man as a Ptolemaic geocentrist and, in the context of the *Supper*, a pedantic, Puritanical Protestant, whose sacraments are, in Bruno's view, dead. In like manner, the man on the ship is a Hermetic Copernican, one who finds life and motion everywhere. What is really important for Bruno is that the man on the moving ship can hit his mark "naturally," without special effort. On the contrary, Bruno says, the man on the shore, even if he could drop the object from a point over the mast, would find that the object would not fall to the foot of the mast.

Why is the one able to do what the other cannot? Because, Bruno goes on, what is important is the "impressed force" that directs the motion. This assertion, which on the face of it is a serious attempt to explain the physical phenomenon according to medieval impetus theory, immediately calls to mind both the Platonic explanation of local motion and Bruno's comments, elsewhere in the *Supper*, about the movement of iron to the magnet and of straw to amber.[68] We venture to suggest that for Bruno the "impressed force" is an image for the soul or divine spark within each living being. Indeed, Bruno and Plato both tell us that motion is caused by, and is impossible without, the soul. The Hermetically inclined man on the top of the mast finds that the object he drops will reach its appropriate end, for his soul directs his actions more efficiently and productively than those "Mercuries and Apollos" who preach predestination and teach Ptolemaic astronomy.[69]

This brings us to the ship engraving, wherein the above-mentioned dichotomy is reprised and transcended. The flames on the rigging refer, as we have said, to the star deities Castor and Pollux. The Twins, in turn, represent spiritual calm. The ship is in a storm-tossed sea which calls to mind the political and religious turbulence of the 1580s. The wind god in the engraving is less easy to explain. While he may signify the underlying spiritual causes of this disturbance (as we once thought), we are now inclined to the view that he represents the *spiritus mundi* which prevents the ship from pitching, as the wind in the sails steadies a wave-tossed ship.[70]

The man on the masthead with the well-directed aim thus reflects, in the realm of physical phenomena, the calming effects of Castor and Pollux. As we can now understand, the ship figure is an emblem. The Twins are the Hermetically inclined courts of France and England which will, in their unity,[71] calm the troubled European waters. Significantly, this reference to Unity and calm follows a disquisition by Bruno on the highest mountains. He discounts from his consideration such mountain ranges as the Alps and Pyrenees. Instead, he asserts that these ranges are merely parts of a much higher mountainous region, that is, the whole of France. So, too, is the island of Britain a mountain, the summit of which, if it reaches the tranquil zone of the air, "proves that [it] is one of those highest mountains and is perhaps in the region of the happiest living creatures." Bruno then cites the assertion (which he wrongly attributes to Alexander of Aphrodisias) that "Mount Olympus displays, in the ashes of the sacrifices, the condition both of a very high mountain and of the [calm] air lying above the extremes and limbs of the earth."[72]

It is curious to find Bruno claiming that Mount Olympus is

one of the highest mountains. Bruno presumably knew that, even among only the European peaks, Olympus has nowhere near the status of a "very high mountain." But Bruno is not classifying it according to the criteria of geographical measurement but, rather, according to those of myth and metaphysics. Mount Olympus was the abode of the gods. Moreover, on the metaphysical plane, Mount Olympus is the scene of a legendary occurrence. According to legend, a man who had written in the ashes of sacrifices offered on its summit returned the following year to discover that the writing in the ashes had remained intact.

It is thus with Mount Olympus, obviously a symbol of spiritual calm, that those great "mountains," England and France, are equated. To be more precise, Bruno asserts that Britain, if its summit reaches the region of quiescent air, might be said to be "one of those highest mountains and . . . in the region of the happiest living creatures." Bruno has recently come to England from France; because of the Neoplatonic-Hermetic intellectual outlook of the Academy surrounding Henri III,[79] the latter is beginning to reassemble its several mountains to form a single, very high "mountain." The same prospect is offered to England, if its courtiers, at the summit of British society, will likewise reach into the highest regions. England and France will then be twins, and thus one.[74] They will attain this state if they heed the Hermetic lessons that Bruno is teaching them.

Moreover, there is a tacit allusion to the gods' regimen of nectar and ambrosia in Bruno's use of the example of Mount Olympus, the "region of the happiest living creatures." Mythologically, ambrosia and nectar were the truest food and drink, and man's culinary ideal of felicity has always been seen as the striving to emulate that diet. But, in the Christian context, the truest food and drink are the Eucharistic bread and wine.[75] Thus, Bruno apparently refers obliquely to a Hermetic understanding of the Eucharist; one that the liberal English Protestant and the liberal French Catholic can both accept.

The imagery of undisturbed sacrificial ashes, highest mountains, and the Eucharist points back to the theme of *The Ash Wednesday Supper*. The linking of spiritual calm and the Eucharist to the celebration of Ash Wednesday portends the inception of a period of profound moral and religious renewal. The Lenten season is traditionally the time of sacrifice and self-assessment, leading up to the Good Friday and Easter celebrations of the redemption of Mankind. Such traditional and portentous imagery is entirely in keeping with what Bruno saw as his messianic mission. These metaphysical and theological symbols are complemented in Bruno's thought by the natural hieroglyphs of the Copernican system and infinity.

The Copernican theory was fraught with significance, according to Bruno, for two basic reasons. First, the centricity of the Sun symbolically meant to Bruno the dawn of a new age of Egyptian (or Hermetic) Catholicism. On the one hand, Bruno's cosmology denies hierarchies of celestial spheres and asserts the uniformity of space. But on the other hand, the Sun, that most potent of all natural religious symbols, assumes its proper place at the center of our solar system (just as in the other innumerable worlds there are central suns); it stands for divinity which all men can see and whose spiritual light reaches all men.[76]

Second, the Copernican theory also teaches that the earth moves. Bruno extends this doctrine by saying that since all stars and planets are "animals," they all have souls, life, movement. The infinite universe with its innumerable worlds is alive. Stars and planets are alike: they have souls, they share divinity. When these teachings are realized by the *illuminati*, these savants will be prepared to bring to earth the spiritual calm exemplified by the undisturbed sacrificial ashes of Mount Olympus. Their efforts will be successful, just as the physical ship experiment was successful, because of the spiritual, impressed force which directs their enterprise. Indeed, the Hermetic *oculati*—or *magi*—have, as Bruno tells us in the First Dialogue, more potent powers than their Ptolemaic-Puritan opponents who disbelieve in a totally animate universe: the former can heal, for they have and know how to use the healing "hellebore" of the Copernican hieroglyph. They can unite Protestant and Catholic through the Eucharist.[77]

Since Bruno saw the Eucharist as the most divisive element

of the theological debates and religious divisions of his time, his mission to end the troubles in religion began with his efforts to unite the courtiers of London and Paris in their understanding of the Eucharist through the Copernican theory in its Brunian manifestation. In the *Supper*, Torquato asks Bruno if he is sailing to Anticyra, that is, if he is mad. Bruno answers that he is indeed on a mission; he is sailing to the land of the Protestant madness of salvation by faith alone. He brings a hellebore—the Copernican system—to heal their madness. Torquato asks Bruno where the apogee of the sun is. Bruno responds that it is anywhere it pleases him to imagine. Bruno continues by asking: "How many are the sacraments of the Church? It [the sun] is about the twentieth degree of Cancer, and the opposition is about the one-hundred-tenth degree of Capricorn, or above the bell-tower of St. Paul's."[78] Yates points out that the sun is in Cancer in the summer, in Capricorn in winter, and she rephrases Bruno's seemingly inane rejoinder to read, "Is it summer or winter, light or dark, in England?[79] It is summer if the English court accepts the peaceful overtures of the Sun King,[80] Henri III, the solar lion of the Prefatory Epistle; it is summer if the liberal English Protestants repudiate the dead excrements of their Supper and embrace the living, animistic Eucharist of Hermetic Catholicism. As Yates says, paraphrasing Bruno, "Is the earth a dead and inanimate thing, or does it move? Is the Sacrament of the Altar a dead external sign, or does it really contain the divine life? These two questions are inseparable in Bruno's mind."[81]

As the universe is universally animated by God, so too is the sacrament. By taking the sacrament, men can share in the same animistic forces which cause the universe to move. Thus Bruno interprets the Eucharist in its relationship to the Copernican theory. If even the earth moves (because it is an ensouled being), then the Eucharist is alive, animated by the impressed force of God's *spiritus*. All men of good will can accept this definition of the Eucharist, and, if they do, the various confessional formulations of the Sacrament are transcended. Men are thereby united on a higher plane.

It is at this point that the opaque body in the optical

experiment referred to above fits into Bruno's larger scheme. That opaque body is the Eucharist, which presently hinders communication of divine light between men and between Man and God. But when men back away from the endless quarrels about the meaning of the Sacrament, they can bask in that divine light. The opaque body, reduced to a point, thus becomes a conduit of, rather than a hindrance to, the unity of men. The Hermetic, Brunian understanding of the Eucharist, the true ceremony of the cup, involves a deeper commingling of essences than that allowed by either the Protestant or the traditional Catholic definitions of the Supper; Bruno's communion is an active "two-way" process, consistent with the Brunian view of the immanence of divinity in Man. As such, it transcends the passive "one-way" communion of the narrow believers on both sides of the Catholic-Protestant gulf.

The message of *The Ash Wednesday Supper* becomes clear. The universe is infinite with an infinite number of worlds. So, too, there are innumerable men, worlds themselves, since every man is a microcosm. Though different, they are all similar, for they all share divinity, and they are united in the Being of the Divine Mind.

The earth moves. The universe is alive. So, too, are men animated by the divine spark which flows from man to man and from God to Man through the no-longer baleful nexus of the Eucharist. In infinity, multiplicity and motion, there is unity and the coincidence of opposites. Thus is brought to its ultimate fruition the Cusan doctrine.

One cannot emphasize too much the powerful eclecticism that informs Bruno's presentation of his religious mission to England, as it is seen in *The Ash Wednesday Supper*. He is preaching a Hermetic, "Egyptianized" Christianity which is close, he thinks, to the pristine font of divine Revelation, the *Corpus Hermeticum*. Christianity is derived in a diluted form from Judaism, which itself derived epigonically from the Hermetic teachings, and Bruno is attempting to reintroduce those original "Egyptian" elements which have been lost or corrupted. (The reappearance of the heliocentric theory was to Bruno a sign that the times were ripe for this rebirth of the true religion of the Golden Age.) In his approach to the English courtiers, Bruno draws upon ideas which they understood to be linked to the golden Hermetic past: the powerful, magical symbol of the Sun and the concept of universal correspondences and animism which were the bases of the efficacy of Hermetic astral magic. To complement this philosophical-theological approach, Bruno used physical arguments which the Elizabethans recognized as having been current prior to the Protestantization of Oxford: Buridan's impetus theory and Albert of Saxony's theory of earth movement. Such theories had been discussed at the Universities of Oxford and Paris in that earlier, Prereformation period during which there had been a prolonged and fruitful collaboration and interchange of ideas between Paris and Oxford. The very choice of his physical arguments stressed the links and the unity of interests between Paris and London. What Bruno did was to present these familiar physical theories and to "elucidate" their (to him) deeper spiritual, religious and political meanings; thus, he at once both metaphorically and spiritually tied the past and present intellectual links between England and France to the Hermetic tradition and to his Hermetic message.

Since Bruno was drawing upon ideas widely and openly discussed in the two capitals by their court intellectuals, he did not need to argue exhaustively or to maintain a close correlation between his physical arguments and the figures which illustrated them. (Several deviations are noted in the text.) Indeed, too close a linkage between figure and text might have distracted the reader from the mystical meanings which Bruno was drawing from the physical arguments.[82] Thus, unlike the modern reader who attempts to read Bruno as a scientist, the late sixteenth-century reader would not have been disturbed by the discrepancies.

There is no doubt that Bruno's intended audience, those select few in England who read Italian (and who were, in Bruno's view, the *oculati*) understood his message. As we have said, Bruno always claimed that he had gone to England on a mission for the French king. Although it does seem that he arrived in England with letters of introduction from Henri III, it is difficult for the historian to know whether Bruno was really an accredited message-bearer or whether his messianism prompted him to portray himself in that role. Bruno's use of the ship engraving, with its strong associations with the Valois monarchy, supports the view that his mission was official, and that part of that official message is contained in *The Ash Wednesday Supper*.[83] In any case, we do know that at the time Bruno was in London both England and France were threatened by Spain—Henry III by the Spanish-backed Catholic League led by the Guises, and Elizabeth by the plans for the Armada. We also know that in 1584 relations between France and England were very cordial.

This period of cordiality was brief. When in March 1584 the presumptive heir to the French throne, the Duc d'Alençon, became very sick (he died on 12 June), the Guisards supported Cardinal Charles de Bourbon as the successor to Henri III. Henri, however, favored the Huguenot leader Henri de Navarre. On 14 June 1584, just after Alençon died and Henri had openly supported the eventual succession of Navarre, Elizabeth conferred upon Henri III the Order of the Garter. About the same time, Ragazzoni, Papal Nuncio in France, reported rumors that Henri III would form a league with Elizabeth or, at least, that some understanding existed between them. The moment was fragile, for by Spring 1585 it seemed that Henri had been abandoned by many important French cities, by the principal nobles and by the "best" soldiers. On 7 July 1585 Catherine de Médicis, acting on her son's behalf, came to terms with the Catholic League and with Guise and Bourbon. By the terms of the Treaty of Nemours, Henri III completely submitted to the humiliating demands of the League.[84]

In October Bruno left London with Mauvissière. Bruno's mission to England thus coincided, to say the least, with a period of flirtation between France and England. It is in this context that one must view the seemingly strange interest of Bruno's Inquisitors in his relations with Henri III, Henri IV and Elizabeth.[85]

Only by reading *The Ash Wednesday Supper* in the light of the religious and political struggles of the period as well as in the context of the hopes, dreams, and death throes of the Valois monarchy, can one begin to appreciate its richness. For all that Bruno's thinking was tied to the political and religious squabbles of the time, one can see in their context how his genius transcended them to produce a work of lasting appeal.

Notes to the Introduction

1. There is a variant to this myth: that, while Bruno attempted to defend Copernicus, his defense was scientifically inept. The moral is also slightly different: that Bruno was a bad scientist and therefore dangerous to the early modern scientific enterprise. Both views share a misperception of Bruno.

2. Giordano Bruno, *La Cena de le ceneri*, a cura di Giovanni Aquilecchia (Turin, 1955).

3. Giordano Bruno, *Dialoghi italiani*, con note da Giovanni Gentile, terza edizione a cura di Giovanni Aquilecchia (Florence, 1972); and Giordano Bruno, *Opere italiane*, ed. Giovanni Gentile (Bari, 1925-7).

4. *The Portable Rabelais*, ed. and trans. S. Putnam (New York, 1946).

5. John Florio, *A Worlde of Wordes* (1598) in *Anglistica & Americana*, CIV (New York and Hildesheim, 1972).

6. On Bruno's life, see V. Spampanato, *Vita di G.B.*, 2 vols. (Messina, 1921); *Documenti della vita di G.B.*, ed. V. Spampanato (Florence, 1934); D. W. Singer, *G.B., His Life and Thought* (New York, 1950); and F. A. Yates, *Giordano Bruno and the Hermetic Tradition* (London and Chicago, 1964).

On Bruno's use of mnemonics, cf. F. A. Yates, *The Art of Memory* (London, 1966), pp. 199-319.

7. Bruno's satire in the *Supper* easily alienated those who were affronted by his attack on Oxford as well as by his scathing description of the London populace. More importantly, however, was the anger the *Supper* stirred up by its criticism, albeit implicit, of Sir Fulke Greville who failed to send a carriage to take Bruno to the banquet (see *Supper*, pp. 110-11 and 225. Cf. F. A. Yates, *John Florio* (New York, 1968), pp. 98-107.

8. On Henri III, see A. L. Martin, *Henry III and the Jesuit Politicians* (Geneva, 1973).

9. See F. A. Yates, *The French Academies of the Sixteenth Century* (London, 1947), passim.

10. Ibid., pp. 225-8, 231-2, and 234.

11. Cf. F. A. Yates, "Giordano Bruno's Conflict with Oxford," *Journal of the Warburg and Courtauld Institutes*, II (1938-9), pp. 227-42.

12. Bruno was mocked for his Italian pronunciation of Latin; he was also

THE ASH WEDNESDAY SUPPER

criticized for quoting from Marsilio Ficino's *De vita coelitus comparanda* rather than from Copernicus' *De revolutionibus*. See R. McNulty, "Bruno at Oxford," *Renaissance News*, 13 (1960), pp. 300-305.

13. Laski's visit was a misfortune for Bruno in an ironic way. On his return from Oxford to London, Laski stopped to visit the famous Hermetic savant John Dee at Mortlake, his country seat. Laski was so impressed with Dee that he invited him to his court in Poland, and Dee was absent from England for many years. Of all the intellectuals of influence in England, Dee was certainly the one whose attitudes would have disposed him to be most receptive to Bruno's ideas. Had Dee remained in England, Bruno's life might have been very different. On Dee, see P. J. French, *John Dee: The World of an Elizabethan Magus* (London, 1972).

14. The others are, in probable order of composition: *De la causa, principio e uno* (1584; Eng. trans., "Concerning the Cause, Principle and One," in S. Greenberg, *The Infinite in G.B.* [New York, 1950]); *De l'infinito universo e mondi* (1584; Eng. trans., "On the Infinite Universe and Worlds," in Singer, *op. cit.*); *Lo spaccio della bestia trionfante* (1585; Eng. trans., A. D. Imerti, "The Expulsion of the Triumphant Beast" [Rutgers, N.J., 1964]); *De gli eroici furori* (1585; Eng. trans., L. Williams, "The Heroic Enthusiasts," 2 vols. [London, 1887-9], and P. E. Memmo, "The Heroic Frenzies" [Chapel Hill, N.C., 1965]); and *Cabala del Cavallo Pegaseo* (1585; "The Cabala of the Horse Pegasus").

15. For a discussion of these realignments, see p. 52.

16. It is true that Bruno's friend and associate John Florio spent the rest of his life in England. But Florio had several advantages. (1) He was English born (a point he brought up as often as possible); (2) he was infinitely more tactful and agreeable than Bruno; (3) he was indubitably Protestant; (4) he never wrote on explicitly political matters, or identified himself strongly with any controversial view; and (5) there is reason to believe that during his tenure in the household of Mauvissière he worked as a spy for Walsingham, the Queen's High Secretary. See Yates, *John Florio*. Florio plays a minor role in *The Ash Wednesday Supper*; see the Second Dialogue, esp. n. 6.

17. The fostering by the Elizabethan court of an imperial, even Universalist, ideology may have long prevented Bruno from recognizing the pragmatic core of Elizabethan policy. Cf. F. A. Yates, *Astraea: The Imperial Theme in the Sixteenth Century* (London, 1975), pp. 29-120.

18. Documents relating to Bruno's hearings before the Venetian and Roman Inquisitions may be found in V. Spampanato, ed., *Documenti della vita di G.B.* and in A. Mercati, *Il sommario del processo di G.B.* (Vatican City, 1942). See also F. A. Yates, "The Religious Policy of G.B.," *Journal of the Warburg and Courtauld Institutes*, III, 3-4 (1940), pp. 204-5.

19. On the Calabrian Revolt, see Yates, *GB&HT*, pp. 363-5; on the political *quid pro quo* with Spain, see A. M. Patterson, *The Infinite Worlds of G.B.* (Springfield, Ill., 1970), p. 197, and U. Ranieri, *La bella in mano al Boia, una storia inedita di Perugia nel Seicento* (Milan, 1965), pp. 30-3, 73-9, and 162-8.

We have recently argued in an article, entitled "Galileo and the Long Shadow of Bruno," *Archives internationales d'histoire des sciences*, 25/97 (1975), pp. 223-46, that one of the underlying reasons for the prosecution of Galileo in 1633 was his being misperceived as a "resurrected Bruno," and that he

too was offered as a symbolic victim, in similar political and religious circumstances, for the purpose of stamping out utopian political movements.

20. Cf. Patterson, *The Infinite Worlds*, Appendix B.

21. 1896; reprinted by Dover, New York (no date); Vol. I, p. 15.

22. A reputed portrait of Bruno is frequently reprinted in books or
encyclopedia articles about Bruno. We are indebted to Dr. Yates, who has
pointed out to us that it is a sentimentalized nineteenth-century version of a
(probably) seventeenth-century engraving, which must have emerged entirely
out of the imagination of the unknown artist.

23. Cf. Yates, "Religious Policy," passim.

24. Cf. Yates, *GB&HT*, pp. 211-29, for a discussion of Bruno's *Spaccio* and
its allusions to Henri III.

25. See Yates, *John Florio*. Florio made his living mainly by teaching
Italian, and was the author of two fine Italian-English dictionaries as well as of
several conversation-grammars and related books. See p. 15 of the Introduction.

26. M. S. Kelly, *The "De mundo" of William Gilbert* (Amsterdam, 1965),
pp. 56-7. See also D. H. D. Roller, *The "De magnete" of William Gilbert*
(Amsterdam, 1959), pp. 71-2. There had been a like interest in the Copernican
theory among the members of the French Palace Academy. This common
French and English interest may have recommended the theory to Bruno as an
entree suitable to his mission.

27. John Dee had praised the Copernican theory for its efficiency in
calculation. As Marsilio Ficino and John Colet had before him, he probably
construed the Sun as a religious symbol, and he probably also saw the Copernican system as pregnant with religious revelation. Digges, the Copernican
exponent, was a pupil of Dee, and the Sidney circle was close to Dee and Digges.
Cf. French, *John Dee*, pp. 97-103 and passim; and A. McLean, *Humanism and
the Rise of Science in Tudor England* (New York, 1972), pp. 133-45.

28. See Yates, *Astraea*, passim.

29. On Postel and the French monarchy, see W. Bouwsma, *Concordia
Mundi: The Career and Thought of Guillaume Postel* (Cambridge, Mass.,
1957), pp. 216ff.

30. See the *Supper*, pp. 87ff.

31. For Bruno's view of Copernicus, see the *Supper*, pp. 86ff; for his view of
Aristotle, see   p. 217.

32. Witness the comment attributed to Alfonso the Wise of Leon and
Castile: "If the Lord Almighty had consulted me before embarking upon the
creation, I should have recommended something simpler." (Quoted in I. B.
Cohen, *The Birth of a New Physics* [Garden City, N.Y., 1960], p. 45.)

33. This was the view of Pope Urban VIII, who prescribed the "medicine
of the end" for Galileo's *Dialogue* as a disclaimer of objective reality for the
Copernican system. As Urban put it, one must not necessitate God. See G. de
Santillana, *The Crime of Galileo* (Chicago, 1955), Ch. VIII.

34. See the *Supper*, pp. 139ff.

35. S. Drake, "Impetus Theory Reappraised," *Journal of the History of
Ideas*, 36/1 (1975), p. 29.

36. *Supper*, p. 82.

37. Here "conservation" must be construed in the sense of an unchanging state.

38. *Supper*, pp. 221ff.

39. *Supper* p. 221-2.

40. That is, motion other than natural motion, impressed by an outside source; e.g., the motion of a ball in the hand of the thrower.

41. *Supper*, pp. 206-8.

42. Cf. P. O. Kristeller, *Eight Philosophers of the Italian Renaissance* (Stanford, Cal., 1964), p. 138: "... Galileo could have read Bruno long before the latter was condemned, and the resemblance between certain passages in Galileo and Bruno that deal with the place of the earth in the universe is so great that it may not be incidental after all."

43. According to the dialogue, the supper was held in the residence of Sir Fulke Greville; however, Bruno later told the Inquisitors that it was held in the French Ambassador's residence on 14 February 1584. If the supper was at least in part a Eucharistic feast, as Yates and we suspect, this latter place would be more plausible; in Elizabeth's time, the Catholic Mass could be held only in the homes of foreign Catholics resident in London.

44. This sense of *cena* parallels the meaning of the French *la cène*: the Last Supper of the Lord and His disciples, and its liturgical commemoration.

45. That Bruno considered the question of the nature of the Eucharist as that most urgently in need of solution is attested to by his comments, after his return to Paris from London in 1585, to Guillaume Cotin, the librarian of the Abbey of St. Victor in Paris. He told Cotin that the "troubles" in religion were traceable to the insidious subtleties of theologians in discussing the sacraments and, in particular, the Eucharist. He noted that SS. Peter and Paul had known nothing of such subtleties, and that they had only known that *"hoc est corpus meum."* Cf. Yates, *GB&HT*, p. 230.

46. These are the positions, respectively, of the Roman Catholics, Lutherans, Calvinists, and Zwinglians.

47. Cf. Ernst Cassirer, *The Individual and the Cosmos in Renaissance Philosophy*, M. Domandi, transl. (Philadelphia, 1972), Ch. 1, for a detailed discussion of the Cusan doctrines of the *Minimum* and *Maximum*, as well as those of the reconciliation of opposites and *docta ignorantia*.

48. This point is also made in the Prefatory Epistle. After listing what the Supper is not, after listing *minima* and *maxima* (wherein he shows that the Supper is at once both polarities), Bruno says: This is the Ash Wednesday Supper.

49. According to the Plotinian scheme, Ideas contemplating each other retain their distinctness; however, they are not separate. In the same way, Bruno's exposition of this view retains the distinctiveness of Catholic and Protestant even as they realize their unity. But the cause of such distinctions (e.g., differences in theological subtleties) will not impede the consummation of an earthly union, just as it does not impede the incorporeal union. (On Plotinian psychology, cf. A. H. Armstrong, *An Introduction to Ancient Philosophy* [London, 1968], p. 185.)

50. Whether this was in fact the case may be debated by modern scholars. Bruno's criticism of Oxonian Humanism is similar to Pico della Mirandola's

critique of Ciceronian Humanism and the defense of Scholastic "barbarity" in his letter to Ermolao Barbaro (referred to in n. 29, Pref. Epist.). Cf. Yates, *GB&HT*, pp. 167-8.

51. We have already mentioned the importance Bruno placed on the life-giving interactions of all things with all others. Evidently, a doctrine which imposes the necessity of good works for one's fellow man is strongly concordant with such a universal mutual interaction.

52. Many Protestant theologians were aware—or were made aware by their critics—that salvation by faith and grace alone could undermine public morality. If men are predestined to Heaven or Hell, the argument ran, there is no necessity (save that, as Luther and Calvin said, of glorifying God—which is, practically speaking, lacking in effective necessity) to live uprightly. Since grace is irresistible, there is no way to lose salvation; nor are the reprobate able by any means to gain it. Consequently, Protestant divines tended to "theologize like Augustine and to preach like Pelagius" (as Jurieu retrospectively said in the seventeenth century). In this way, they could remain true to classical Protestant theology, and at the same time inhibit the masses from libertinism. However, this Protestant form of religious pragmatism put the Protestant theologians on the horns of a dilemma. By holding out Hell as a threat contingent upon the malefactions of men (while still preserving a predestinarian theology), they cast God in the worst possible light; men were to be punished for actions for which they were not ultimately responsible. Cf. D. P. Walker, *The Decline of Hell* (Chicago, 1964), passim.

53. We might note, however, that Bruno does not give unqualified praise to the gentlemen who were present; he portrays them as chattering while he was speaking.

54. Cf. French, *John Dee*, pp. 126-7.

55. The *Corpus Hermeticum* (or *Hermetica*) actually dates from the third century A. D. The definitive, correct dating was not achieved until 1614, when Isaac Casaubon pricked the Hermetic bubble. Besides Hermes Trismegistus himself, the Hermetic tradition included a sequence of legendary and real figures such as Orpheus, Zoroaster, Pythagoras, Plato, Lucretius, the late-ancient Platonists, Dionysius the Areopagite, and certain medieval and Renaissance philosophers.

56. It is probably not the case that the *Corpus Hermeticum*, attributed to Hermes Trismegistus, actually upheld heliocentricity as a physical reality. More to the point, however, the *Hermetica* place great emphasis on astral magic, the Sun having paramount importance in this magical system. Plato, though not a heliocentrist, also cast the Sun in a central role. In the episode on the cave in the *Republic*, for example, the Sun is used as a metaphor for the Good. In the early seventeenth century, another Hermetist, Tommaso Campanella, placed the temple of the Sun at the center of his utopian City of the Sun, and the sun-worshippers of this city practiced astral magic. This does not necessarily mean that Campanella accepted the physical reality of Copernicanism as Bruno did. In any case, Campanella became an ardent though inconstant defender of Galileo. (The *Corpus Hermeticum* has been edited and translated into French by A. D. Nock and A.-J. Festugière: Paris, 1945 and 1954 [4 vols.]; republished 1972.)

57. Bruno calls him an "arch-Ass." Kepler correctly identified Osiander as the author of the Preface in 1609. Osiander also changed several chapter headings and added *"coelestium orbium"* to the title.

58. *Supper*, pp. 88ff.

59. Cassirer, *The Individual and the Cosmos*, p. 188. Regarding Bruno's non-scientific perception of infinity, Cassirer quotes Bruno's *De l'infinito universo e mondi*. Dial. I. *Opere italiane*, ed. Gentile, p. 307: *"Non è senso che vegga l'infinito, non è senso da cui si richieda questa conclusione, perchè l'infinito non può essere oggetto del senso: et però chi dimanda di conoscere questo per via di senso, è simile a colui che volesse veder con gl'occhi la sustanza e l'essenza: et chi negasse per questo la cosa, perchè non è sensibile, o visibile, verebe a negar la propria sustanza et essere."* We might add that Bruno would have found infinity discussed in Nicolaus of Cusa, and that, also, the Doctrine of Plenitude necessitates God's creation of an infinite universe.

60. That this view is also a central aspect of the esthetic of modern science is, we believe, one of the strongest links between Bruno's mysticism and modern science. This point is obscured by the reticence of modern scientists with respect to explicit esthetic discussion. But the esthetic drive is no less pervasive in the one than in the other.

61. We will make no attempt to "explain" all of Bruno's physical arguments; a few examples will suffice to clarify his approach. On the scientific arguments in the *Supper*, see L. S. Lerner and E. A. Gosselin, "Was Giordano Bruno a Scientist?: A Scientist's View," *American Journal of Physics*, 41/1 (1973), pp. 24-38; and idem, "Giordano Bruno," *Scientific American*, 228/4 (1973), pp. 86-94.

62. Bruno says, for example, that many of them are populated with beings who are in some cases better, in others worse than the inhabitants of the earth. Cf. *Supper* p. 90.

63. Bruno's argument has still another layer of meaning. Since man has divinity within himself (cf. *Supper*, p. 91), Bruno's argument also applies to the relationship between Man and God; the opaque body cannot hinder the sharing of divine light between Man and God. (This again parallels Ficino's doctrine of Platonic Love, since Ficino argued that no relationship between lovers is dignified and "heavenly" unless God forms a triad with the lovers; cf. P. O. Kristeller, *The Philosophy of Marsilio Ficino* [Gloucester, Mass., 1964], pp. 276-88).

Bruno also discusses the reciprocal passage of divine light between God and Man in his arguments in the *Supper*, pp. 146-8 and 143-4. There, a luminous body, at an infinite distance, can illuminate an entire sphere. Bruno seems to refer implicitly to the medieval argument about whether it is possible that there be human life at the Antipodes. (See the first of the articles cited in n. 61.) If we think of the antipodal people as being adversaries (cf. *Supper*, p. 96), illumination of an entire sphere by a luminous body suggests that both Catholics and Protestants are recipients of divine light, and that thus again, they are one.

64. *Supper*, pp. 162-5. This experiment may actually have been performed about 1576 by Thomas Digges who in any case obtained the correct result. (Cf. A. Koyré, *Metaphysics and Measurement*) [Cambridge, Mass., 1968], pp. 124-5; F. R. Johnson and S. V. Larkey, *Huntington Library Bulletin*, 5

(1934), pp. 92-3 and, for Digges' experimental results, p. 99. Just as in the broader case of the Copernican theory, Bruno draws and builds upon a scientific question of current interest among the Dee-Sidney circle.

65. Which in the text is on a river rather than at sea.

66. F. A. Yates, "The Emblematic Conceit in G.B.'s *De gli eroici furori* and in the Elizabethan Sonnet Sequences," *Journal of the Warburg and Courtauld Institutes*, VI (1943), pp. 109-10. Yates has recently shed more light on this emblem; see her *Astraea*, pp. 135-7, 163, 166, 168 and plates 19b, 23c, and 23d. She shows that the ship emblem in a variant form had been used atop an arch celebrating the entrance of Charles IX into Paris in 1571 (after the conclusion of the Treaty of Saint-Germain in 1570, which had temporarily ended the French religious wars). The ship is the symbol of Paris and, by extension, France. In 1571 Castor and Pollux stood for Charles IX and his brother Henri, who guided the ship of state across the troubled waters of French domestic strife. Bruno uses this emblem in 1584. Certainly, as Yates suggests, the ship stands for a message of peace from the French King to England. However, Yates does not relate the emblem to the physical argument in the text nor does she explain what persons the two flames represent. (The flames are intended to represent St. Elmo's fire, which symbolizes Castor and Pollux.) Charles IX was dead; thus the Twins must be England and France, or more precisely, Elizabeth and Henri III. This of course fits in with our interpretation.

67. In *Lo spaccio della bestia trionfante*, Bruno raises Henri III to the celestial world, where the reform of the world (which follows the reform of the heavens in the *Spaccio*) is to devolve upon him.

68. *Supper*, p. 207.

69. Cf., for example, *Supper*, p. 96.

70. It is conceivable that Bruno intends the wind god to represent himself. Given his messianic streak, it would not have been illogical for Bruno to have used a self-portrait to represent the *spiritus-magus* who brings spiritual calm to Europe.

71. Again we see the implementation of a form of Plotinian psychology. Though they are two, the Twins are one, born simultaneously from the same mother: they are distinct, but not separate, in the Divine Mind.

72. *Supper*, pp. 161.

73. Cf. Yates, "Religious Policy," p. 203.

74. Just before this discussion of "highest" mountains, Bruno has shown that Aristotle divined earth movement. The Oxford doctors, Nundinio and Torquato, have not, however, been willing to rise from the level of rationalism to the heights of contemplation (which of course the highest mountains also represent). Yet, once Bruno's auditors and readers do become willing to ascend these heights, then the Hermetically-induced unity of England and France can be achieved. Thus, it makes perfect sense that Bruno follows this discussion of highest mountains and Mount Olympus with that of the ship experiment and of Castor and Pollux. Cf. Yates, *French Academies*, 112-3 and 115, n. 4.

75. Cf. John VI:54, 56.

76. See n. 64, above.

77. Hélène Védrine, in *La Conception de la nature chez G.B.* (Paris, 1967), minimizes Bruno's Hermetism and magic. We believe that she misconstrues

Bruno's thought. Especially in the case of magic, she goes to great lengths to show that Bruno's treatises on magic were merely theoretical, and that he did not practice magic. This point of view, with its ancillary criticism of Yates, is beside the point, we think. One does not have to assert that Bruno actually practiced magic in the more mundane sense of the word; rather, one should realize that Bruno considered magical both the Hermetic understanding of the world and the ability to translate the belief in the animate universe into ethically unifying action vis-à-vis the incontinent political behavior of his day.

78. *Supper* p. 189.

79. Yates, "Religious Policy," p. 189.

80. When Henri's favorite, Duc Anne de Joyeuse, was married to the Queen's half-sister, Marie de Lorraine, in 1581, the "Magnificences" for the Joyeuse wedding portrayed Henri as the Sun King. Cf. Yates, *Astraea*, p. 164.

81. Yates, "Religious Policy," p. 188.

82. In all probability Bruno cut the figures in the *Supper* himself. Cf. Yates, *GB&HT*, p. 320, n. 4; and Yates, *Astraea*, p. 168, n. 3.

83. As in modern diplomacy, several levels of "officialness" were in use. Even if Henri III himself sent Bruno on an explicit mission, he would probably have found it advisable to be deliberately vague as to the level of official backing possessed by his emissary on what was, from his standpoint, a highly speculative line of endeavor.

84. Cf. Martin, *Henry III*, pp. 121, 134, 141-2. However, Henri followed the terms of the treaty only loosely: instead of joining with the Catholic League in a war against Henri de Navarre, the King sent emissaries to try to convert him. By 1586 Henri III was again free enough from Guisard-League control to express openly his dislike of Spain and to resume his friendship with England. (In 1588, for example, he refused to allow the Spanish Armada to provision in French ports.) He also continued to abide by his obligations under the Treaty of Soleure to protect Calvinist Geneva. (Cf. ibid., p. 170.)

85. Thus, although it is difficult to discern from the surviving records of Bruno's trial just how seriously the charge of advocating the movement of the earth figured in his condemnation, it seems clear that Bruno could not in the final analysis recant his Copernicanism. It was an integral, though metaphorical, part of his religious and political programme, with the latter's projected role for these intended universal monarchs. To have rejected Copernicanism would have entailed recantation of his doctrine of the Eucharist and of his central aim of religious irenicism. Cf. Yates, *GB&HT*, pp. 354-5.

The Ash Wednesday Supper

La Cena de le ceneri

LA
CENA DE
le Ceneri.

DESCRITTA IN
CINQVE DIALOGI, PER
quattro interlocutori, Con tre con-
siderationi, Circa doi
suggettj.

Jordanj Brunj Nolanj

All' unico refugio de le Muse. l' Illustriss. Michel
di Castelnouo. Sig. di Mauuissier, Concressalto, et
di Ionuilla, Caualier del ordine del Re Chrianiss. et
Conseglier nel suo priuato conseglo. Capitano di
50. huomini d'arme, Gouernator et Capitano di
S. Desiderio. et Ambasciator alla sere-
niss. Regina d' In-
ghilterra.

p. Ballesdens. p

L' vniuersale intentione e' dechia-
rata nel proemio.
1584.

Courtesy Bibliothèque Nationale, Paris

THE
ASH WEDNESDAY SUPPER

DESCRIBED IN
FIVE DIALOGUES, BY
four interlocutors, with three
reflections, on two
subjects

To the sole refuge of the Muses: the most illustrious Michel
de Castelnau, Lord of Mauvissière, Concressant,[1] and
of Jonville,[2] Knight of the order of the Most Christian King[3] and
Councillor in his Privy Council; Captain of
fifty men-at-arms, Governor and Captain of
St.-Dizier,[4] and Ambassador to Her
Most Serene Highness the Queen of
England.

The general purpose is made manifest
in the preface.
1584.

Notes to the Title Page

1. The name Concressant is sometimes given as Concressaut. Since Fr. *saut* = Fr. *sault* = It. *salto,* Bruno's *Concressalto* is a reasonable translation into Italian. The matter is confused, however, by the fact that there is also a place named Concressault, with which Mauvissière had no connection.

2. Bruno has *Ionvilla.* This is almost certainly the modern Joinville.

3. I.e., the *Ordre du Saint Esprit.*

4. Bruno has *S. Desiderio.* The town is named after St. Dizier (or Didier), Bishop of Langres (martyred A.D. fifth century). There are several French saints named Dizier; the name is usually rendered into English as Desiderius.

To the Malcontent

If by cynical tooth you are pierced,
Curse yourself, O barbarous dog;[1]
Who vainly flaunt at me your cudgel and sword,
Beware, lest you incense me.

Because you wrongly attack me to my face,
I slash your hide and rip you up;
And if, perchance, my body falls to earth
Your infamy shall be inscribed in marble.[2]

Go not naked to steal honey from the bee;
Nor bite what might be stone or bread;
Nor go unshod when sowing thorns.

Do not despise, O fly, the spider's web;
O mouse, pursue not frogs;
Flee foxes, O spawn of fowl.

And believe in the Gospel
Which fervently admonishes that
Those who sow the seeds of error
Reap from this, our field, Remorse.

---

1. There is a play on words here between "cynical" (It., *cinico*) and "dog" (Spanish, *perro*). "Cynic" derives from the Greek "doglike" (*cyniços*), which supposedly characterizes the sneer of the cynic.
2. We have taken some license here. Lit., "written in diamond" (*nel diamante scritto*).

PREFATORY EPISTLE

PREFATORY EPISTLE

Dedicated to the most illustrious and excellent
Lord of Mauvissière[1]
Knight of the King's Order and Councillor of his Privy
Council, Captain of fifty men-at-arms, Governor-General of
St.-Dizier and Ambassador of France to England.

Now behold, Sir, this book is not a banquet of nectar for Jove the Thunderer, signifying majesty; not a protoplastic one for man's desolation;[2] it is not the banquet of Ahasuerus for a mystery;[3] not that of Lucullus[4] for fortune, nor that of Lycaon for sacrilege;[5] not that of Thyestes for tragedy;[6] not that of Tantalus for torment;[7] not that of Plato for philosophy;[8] not that of Diogenes[9] for poverty; not that of leeches for a trifle; not that of the archpriest of Pogliano for Berni's satire;[10] not that of Bonifacio Candelaio for comedy.[11] But this is a banquet so great and small, so professorial and studentlike, so sacrilegious and religious, so joyous and choleric, so cruel and pleasant, so Florentine for its leanness and Bolognese for its fatness, so cynical and Sardanapalian,[12] so trifling and serious, so grave and waggish, so tragic and comic that I surely believe there will be no few occasions for you to become heroic and humble; master and disciple; believer and unbeliever; cheerful and sad; saturnine and jovial; light and ponderous; miserly and liberal; simian and consular; sophist with Aristotle, philosopher with Pythagoras;

See page 74 for Notes to the Prefatory Epistle.

laugher with Democritus and weeper with Heraclitus.[13] I mean that after you have sniffed with the Peripatetics, supped with the Pythagoreans, drunk with the Stoics, there will still be something left over for you to suck with him who, showing his teeth, smiled so pleasantly that his mouth touched both ears. Indeed, by breaking the bone and extracting the marrow,[14] you will find something that would make a dissolute of St. Colombino, Patriarch of the *Gesuati*,[15] would petrify any market-place, make monkeys split their sides with laughter, and break the silence of any graveyard.

You may well ask me: what symposium, what banquet is this? It is a supper. What supper? Of ashes.[16] What does "supper of ashes" mean? Has it perhaps taken place before? Can one properly say at this point: *cinerem tamquam panem manducabam?*[17] No, but it is a banquet which begins after sunset on the first day of Lent, which our priests call *dies cinerum* and, sometimes, day of memento.[18] What is the object of this banquet, this supper? Not only to consider the mind and accomplishments of the most noble and well-born Sir Fulke Greville,[19] in whose eminent house we met; not only to consider the honorable customs of those most urbane gentlemen who were present as spectators and listeners, but mainly to see what Nature can do in creating two ghastly harridans, two dreams, two ghosts, two quartan agues.[20] While the historical meaning of all this is being sifted and then tasted and chewed, we shall draw appropriate topographies of a geographical, ratiocinative and moral order, and then make speculations of a metaphysical, mathematical and natural order.

Argument of the First Dialogue

Thus you will see two subjects set forth in the first dialogue, together with the reason for their names (should you wish to understand it); *second*, for their sake, the binary scale of numbers will be celebrated; *third*, the laudable features of the rediscovered and restored philosophy will be brought forth; *fourth*, it will be

shown how praiseworthy is Copernicus; *fifth,* the fruits of the
Nolan philosophy will be set forth, along with the difference
between this and other ways of philosophizing.

Argument of the Second Dialogue

In the second dialogue you will see: *first,* the original occasion for the supper; *second,* a description of journeys and voyages, which will be judged by all to be more poetic, and perhaps
allegorical, than historical; *third,* one plunges confusedly into a
moral topography, so that it seems that, looking here and there at
everything with Lynceus' eyes,[21] and not stopping too much
along his walk, he contemplates the great structures [of the
universe] while, at the same time, he stumbles over every bit of
stone, every pebble.[22] In doing this, he acts just like a painter for
whom it is not enough simply to portray a story, but then, in
order to fill up the canvas and to bring his picture into conformity with nature through his art, he also paints stones, mountains, trees, fountains, rivers, and hills; here he shows a royal
palace, there a forest, here a stretch of sky, and in that corner the
half-disk of the rising sun, and one by one a bird, a pig, a deer, an
ass, a horse. But it is enough to show of this animal only the head,
of that one only the horn, of another only the hind quarter, of this
only the ears, of that the whole; and he portrays each one with a
gesture and manner peculiar to him, so that the person who looks
and judges can attach substance to the image[23] with greater
contentment. In the same manner are you to read and visualize
what I have to say. *Finally,* this blessed dialogue concludes with
the arrival at the dining room, with being welcomed graciously
and seated ceremoniously at the table.

Argument of the Third Dialogue

You will see the third dialogue divided into five parts,
according to the propositions of Doctor Nundinio. Of them the

first deals with the necessity of being bilingual.[24] The *second* explains the purpose of Copernicus, resolves a most important doubt concerning celestial phenomena, shows the folly of studying perspective and optics in order to establish the size of luminous bodies, and offers concerning all this a new, resolute and most certain doctrine. The *third* demonstrates the constitution of worldly bodies, and declares the extent of the universe to be infinite, so that it is useless to search for the center or circumference of the universal world, as if it were one of its component bodies. The *fourth* affirms that the material of this world of ours, which is called the globe of the earth, is the same as that of the worlds which are the bodies of other stars; and that it is childish to have believed and to believe otherwise. It further affirms that those worlds are so many intellective animals, and that they have on them many and innumerable simple and complex beings which grow and understand, no less than we see them to live and grow on the surface of this earth. The *fifth*, which is brought about by an argument presented by Nundinio at the end, shows the vacuity of the two great tenets, and other similar ones, by which Aristotle and others were so blinded that they did not see the movement of the earth to be true and necessary; and they were so hamstrung that they could not [even] believe it possible; but once this movement is granted, many secrets of nature are uncovered which have been hidden until now.

Argument of the Fourth Dialogue

You will have at the beginning of the fourth dialogue the means for responding to every theological argument and difficulty, as well as the means for showing that this philosophy conforms to the true theology and is worthy of the favor of the true religions. After this, a person will be introduced who knows neither how to dispute nor how to question to the point, in order to offer material about which Smith will ask questions and Teofilo will answer. By virtue of his impudence and arrogance, he appears to the most ignorant as being more learned than

Doctor Nundinio, but you will see that all the presses in the world would not suffice to extract a single drop of juice from what he says. But in reality, this is a subject for the boasts of Prudenzio and the caprices of Frulla. I truly regret the existence of this part of the dialogue.

Argument of the Fifth Dialogue

The fifth dialogue is added, I assure you, for the sole purpose of concluding our supper in a less sterile manner. Here, *firstly*, the most appropriate dispositions of the bodies in the ethereal region will be set forth, showing that that which is called the eighth sphere, the heaven of the fixed stars, is not in fact a heaven in which those bodies which appear to shine are equidistant from the center; but rather, that those bodies which appear near to each other are actually more distant from one another in length and breadth than they are from the sun and the earth. *Secondly*, that there are not just seven errant planets merely because we have always believed this to be the case, but, by the same token, there are countless others which the ancient and true philosophers[25] justly called *aethera*, meaning "runners,"[26] because it is these bodies which truly move, and not the imaginary spheres. *Thirdly*, that such motion necessarily derives from an internal principle as if from its proper nature and soul; this truth destroys many fantasies both about the motive effect[27] of the moon on the waters and on other kinds of humors and about other natural things which seem to derive the principle of their motion from an external efficient [cause]. *Fourthly*, this dialogue resolves those doubts, doubts which are nurtured on the stupidest reasoning about the gravity and levity of bodies, and shows that all natural motion tends to be circular, either about its own center or about some other center. *Fifthly*, it is shown to be necessary that this earth and other similar bodies move not with one, but with many different motions; and that these can be neither more nor less than four simple ones which determine a compound motion; this part shows what are the motions of the earth. *Lastly*, the addition

71

of other dialogues in the future is promised, to provide that which is lacking to the fulfillment of this philosophy; and the dialogue concludes with an adjuration by Prudenzio.

You will be astonished that such great things will be completely explained so succinctly. Then, if on occasion you see lighter subjects presented, which must raise fears of being subjected to the haughty censorship of Cato,[28] do not worry, since such Catos would be blind and mad indeed if they could not discover what is hidden under these *Sileni*.[29] So many diverse subjects must be put together that they do not appear to constitute a single topic,[30] but appear here like a dialogue, here a comedy, here a tragedy, here poetry, and here rhetoric, here praise, here vituperation; here demonstration and teaching; here we have now natural philosophy, now mathematics, now morals, now logic; in conclusion, there is no sort of knowledge of which there is not here some fragment. Consider, Sir, that the dialogue is historical and, while occasions, movements, passages, meetings, gestures, affectations, discourses, propositions, answers, subjects and blunders are reported, all of them subjected to the rigors of judgment of four men, there is nothing that will not be set forth for some reason. Consider also that not one word will be superfluous, for everywhere there will be things of no little importance to reap and unearth; and perhaps [there will be] more where less is apparent. As for what appears on the surface, those who gave the occasion for presenting the dialogue,[31] and perhaps a satire and comedy, had reason to become more circumspect when measuring men with the rule with which velvet is measured and when weighing souls with a steelyard. Those who, as spectators or readers see how others become touched in the head, will have means of becoming wise and of learning at their expense. Those who are wounded or crushed will perhaps open their eyes and see their poverty, nudity, and indignity. Even if they will not admit their errors, they will try to correct and cover themselves; if not for love's, at least for shame's sake. If you think our Teofilo and Frulla lash too sternly and too heavily the backs of those they have subdued, do consider, Sir, that these beasts do not have such tender skin; and even if the strokes were doubled a hundred times, they would pay no heed or would think them a maiden's caresses. And I would not want to be deemed blameworthy for the fact that on such trifles and such inadequate grounds as are offered to me by these doctors, I desired to amplify such grave and worthy propositions; I am sure that you can catch the difference between seizing a thing for a foundation and taking it for expediency. For indeed the foundations must be proportionate to the size, condition, and nobility of the edifice, but the incidentals can be of all sorts, for all sorts of effects; since the smallest sordid things are the seeds of great and excellent things; trifles and follies give birth to great counsels, judgments, and inventions. I need not stress, since it is obvious, that errors and crimes have often provided the occasion for the establishment of exalted rules of justice and virtue.

If in this portraiture, it seems that the colors do not correspond perfectly to life, and the lines do not appear to you exactly as they should, you should know that the fault is a result of the fact that the painter could not examine the portrait from those aspects and distances to which artists are accustomed; since, besides the fact that the canvas or field was too close to his face and eyes, it was not possible to take the least step backward, nor to place himself to one side or the other without fear of making the leap that the son of the famous defender of Troy made.[32] Nevertheless, take this portrait for what it is, where there are those two, those hundred, those thousand, all of them;[33] it is not my intent to reeducate you in what you already know, nor to add water to the swift river of your judgment and genius. But rather, it is a common thing, that even though we are familiar with things in their more perfect living form, we are not on that account accustomed to disparage their portrait and representation. Besides, I am certain that your generous spirit will weigh more heavily the affectionate gratitude with which this book is offered, than the book itself. This is dedicated to you, who are closer to and show yourself more propitious and more favorable to our Nolan than others, and for this reason are a more worthy object of our homage in this clime, where faithless, conscienceless merchants easily become Croesi,[34] and penniless, virtuous men without difficulty become *Diogenes*. To you [it is dedicated] who with such munificence and liberality have welcomed the Nolan under your roof and into a place more eminent than your home;[35] so that, if this land, instead of sending out a thousand surly giants, were to produce as many Alexanders, you would see more than five hundred coming to pay court to this Diogenes who, by the grace of the stars, does not have anyone else but you to make the sun rise for him,[36] even if (in order not to make him poorer than that cynical rogue) it [the sun] sends some direct or reflected ray into that hole of which you know.[37] To you this book is dedicated, who in Britannia represent the eminence of so magnanimous, great and powerful a King,[38] who from the most noble bosom of Europe makes the uttermost corners of the earth resound with the voice of his fame; that King who, when he roars[39] with rage like a lion from a deep den, strikes dread and mortal terror into the other predatory powers of these forests; and who, when he is calm and in repose, sends forth such a blaze of open-hearted and courteous love as kindles the near tropic, heats the frozen Bear and dissolves the harshness of the arctic wastes turning under the eternal sway of proud Boötes.[40] *Vale.*[41]

Notes to the Prefatory Epistle

1. Michel de Castelnau, Marquis de Mauvissière (1520-1592), and ambassador of the King of France in London. Bruno lived in his household during his stay in London. See the Introduction, pp. 18-20.

2. protoplastic . . . desolation: that is, the banquet of Adam, whose eating of the forbidden fruit led to the Fall of Man.

3. The banquet of Ahasuerus was the beginning of Esther's and the Jews' ascendancy in Persia. The "mystery" is probably an allusion to the Jewish feast of *Purim* which celebrates this event. Cf. Esther, passim.

4. Licinius Lucullus, the conqueror of Mithridates, renowned for his great wealth and luxury.

5. Lycaon, a mythical king of Arcadia, profaned Jove's altar by offering the god human sacrifices.

6. Brother of Atreus, who set before him as food the flesh of his own son.

7. Tantalus, king of Phrygia, stole the secrets of the gods. He was punished in Hades, where he stood chin-deep in water under an overhanging fruit tree. The water and the fruit receded from him, remaining just out of reach, whenever he attempted to satisfy his thirst or hunger.

8. Plato . . . philosophy: Bruno here refers to Plato's *Symposium* which is set at a banquet.

9. Cynic philosopher (413-327 B.C.). He was born in Sinope, but passed most of his life in Athens. He eschewed all worldly goods, despised social conventions, and lived in a barrel.

10. archpriest of Pogliano [*sic;* read: Povigliano]: mentioned in Francesco Berni's (1477-1535) *A messer Jeronimo Fracastoro veronese.*

11. Cf. Bruno's comedy *Il Candelaio* (Paris, 1582), in which Bonifacio is the protagonist.

12. Sardanapalus is the Greek form of the name Ashurbanipal, the greatest king of Assyria (reigned 669-626 B.C.). The magnificence of his mode of life led the Greeks to take him as the archetype of luxurious effeminacy. He was said to have burned himself together with his wives and treasures, rather than face death alone.

13. Heraclitus: the pre-Socratic philosopher who took flux as the law of all being ("You cannot step twice into the same river."). His celebrity in the Renaissance was due to the discovery and publication of the writings of Sextus Empericus, a controversialist of A.D. second century who, in order to demonstrate the contradictions of dogmatic philosophers, put together a great deal of information about, and fragments of, the teachings of the various schools. Heraclitus was among the ancient philosophers he discussed.

14. Cf. Rabelais, *Gargantua and Pantagruel,* Author's Prologue, Book I: " . . . by careful reading and frequent meditation, you should break the bone and suck the substantific marrow—that is to say, the meaning of the Pythagorean symbols which I employ—in the certain hope that you will be rendered prudent and valorous by such a reading; for in the course of it you will find things of quite a different taste and a doctrine more abstruse that shall reveal to you most high secrets and astonishing mysteries in what concerns our religion, as well as the political state and economic life." Quoted with slight changes from *The Portable Rabelais,* Samuel Putnam, ed., Viking, New York, 1946, pp. 49-50. The strong parallelism of the texts suggests that Bruno is covertly referring his reader to Rabelais' more explicit expression of purpose. However, in the absence of proof that Bruno was familiar with Rabelais' work, this should be regarded as speculation only. Cf. n. 29, below.

15. St. Colombino is Giovanni Colombini (1304? - 1367) who founded the *Gesuati* (also called "the Poor of Christ and the Pope") in 1367. He maintained perfect chastity in married life. (The *Gesuati* were to be suppressed in 1668 by Pope Innocent IX.)

16. See the Introduction, pp. 46-8, for a discussion of the multiple implications of this sobriquet.

17. Cf. Psalm CI:10: "I ate ashes for bread,"

18. That is, Ash Wednesday.

19. Greville (1554-1628) was the gentleman in whose house the supper was

supposedly given (though there is evidence that the dinner really was held at Mauvissière's residence). He had a long and distinguished political career, and was elevated to the peerage as Lord Brooke in 1620. He is remembered today mainly for his poetry.

20. two ghastly harridans . . . two quartan agues: these terms refer to Doctors Nundinio and Torquato, who will oppose the Nolan's philosophy in the dialogues. The epithets come from a sonnet by Berni, wherein the Archbishop Andrea Buondelmonti is satirized. (A quartan ague is a type of malaria in which the fever peaks every four days.)

21. Lynceus, one of the Argonauts who searched for the Golden Fleece, was famed for the sharpness of his eyes; cf. the later Roman Accademia dei Lincei, made famous by Galileo.

22. The structural inconsistency of this sentence is in the original.

23. It., *istoriar (come dicono) la figura;* lit., "historize (as one puts it) the image."

24. It., *la necessità de l'una e de l'altra lingua.*

25. A reference to the philosophers in the Hermetic tradition. On Bruno's relationship to the Hermetic tradition, cf. F. A. Yates, *Giordano Bruno and the Hermetic Tradition* (Chicago, 1964).

26. It., *corridori.* Cf. Plato, *Cratylus* 410 B (also Aristotle, *De caelo* I, 4; *Meteorologica* I, 3, where Plato's false etymology of *"corridori"* is retained). The derivation is actually from *aithein,* to kindle or burn. The use of this false etymology was not unique to Bruno, but was current in his time; one sees it also, for example, in the work of the syncretist philosopher Agostino Steuco *(Ennarationum in Psalmos, Tomus secundus [of his Operą omnia] qui est primus Psalmorum liber* [Paris, apud Michaëlem Sonnium, 1577.]; foll. 69v.-70r.): *"Is, ut dixi,* error veterum fuit, *qui caelum suspicientes,* lumina eius Deos esse crediderunt, *eaque ut Deos coluerunt. Et si Platoni credimus,* inde nomen Dei *apud Graecos ductum* est ἀποτγθεειν, *id est a currendo. . . ."* (Emphasis ours.) Cf. the *Supper,* p. 206.

27. It., *moto attivo.* Florio gives "a . . . cause of stirring of any thing" for *moto,* and this seems more meaningful in context than "active motion."

28. Marcus Porcius Cato (234-149 B.C.), famous as a severe and priggish judge of Roman morals.

29. This alludes to the well-known passage in Plato's *Symposium* (215 A) where Socrates is compared by Alcibiades to the statues of Silenus displayed in the workshops of sculptors. Ugly on the surface, these *Sileni* contained, within, precious images of deities. Socrates also is ugly without, but within he is the epitome of Beauty and Wisdom.

This imagery (like those of the sucking of the marrow, and of the mysteries contained in the work—cf. n. 14) was a popular literary conceit, used also by Rabelais in his *Gargantua* (Author's Prologue; cf. transl. cit. and *Oeuvres de François Rabelais,* A. Lefranc, ed., I [Paris, 1913], pp. 4-12.) As Lefranc points out, Rabelais' sources for his use of the Silenus conceit could have been one or more of the following: G. Pico della Mirandola, *Letter to Ermolao Barbaro* (cf. Pico, *Opera omnia,* I [Basel, 1572], p. 354); Erasmus, *Sileni Alcibiadis* (Paris, 1527), passim, (as well as Erasmus' *Enchiridion* and *Praise of Folly*); and Guillaume Budé, *De studio litterarum recte et commode instituendo* (Paris,

1532). Rabelais' sources for the use of such terms in his Prologue as "Pythagorean mysteries" (which were employed as a device to pique the reader's interest with the promise of esoterica to follow) are from an Italian tradition, found in the heroic-comic poets (e.g., Pulci and Berni; cf. *Morgante maggiore*, Ch. XXVII, st. 4, and *Orlando innamorato*, Ch. XXV, 5 & 6). The precise source of Rabelais' image of the dog, bone and marrow is less easy to pin down. However, in the *Republic*, 376 A-B, Plato satirizes the Cynics by comparing them and their philosophizing to dogs who growl at (and presumably bite) strangers, but who calm themselves before friends. (Cf. also *Schol. in Arist.*, ed. Brandis [Berlin, 1836], 23^b 16 & ff.) It is possible that Rabelais built upon the passage in Plato (and on that in the *Scholia*) to arrive at his dog-and-bone conceit. Or it may simply have been a commonplace of the time.

Since the Silenus and "mysteries" conceits were ready at hand in sources that were as available to Bruno as to Rabelais, it cannot be proven that Bruno had read and was here imitating Rabelais. The same point bears, with less certitude, on the bone-and-marrow imagery.

On the other hand, although there is no external proof that Bruno knew French, internal evidence in the *Supper* suggests that he may have had a reading ability in the language. See below, n. 58 in the notes to the Fourth Dialogue, where it is shown that Bruno was quite familiar with certain ideas from the *Discours philosophiques* of Pontus de Tyard—more so than he was with Copernicus. (It is of course possible that he gained his knowledge of Tyard's rendition of a crucial passage in *De revolutionibus* from conversations with Tyard himself. Likewise, he may have learned something of Rabelais' Prologue from conversations in Latin or Italian with French friends.)

Thus, whether Bruno drew on Rabelais remains an open question. We have not, however, found the marrow-and-bone image in analogous form anywhere else. The possibility remains that Bruno, like Rabelais, was drawing on the *Republic*. For although Plato (and the *Scholia*) do not mention a bone and marrow in their disquisitions on the Cynics, the imagery follows rather logically from the comparison of the Cynics to dogs who growl at strangers and welcome friends (or bones). That Bruno was dwelling on Plato appears plausible when we remember that he mentions Cynics (and even the "cynical bite") several times in the Proemial Poem, and elsewhere.

30. It., *scienza*.

31. those . . . dialogue: Bruno refers here and in the following passage not only to Nundinio and Torquato but also, by implication, to the Aristotelian professors at Oxford University before whom Bruno had spoken and by whom he had been ridiculed. (See the Introduction, p. 18.) Cf. Yates, *GB&HT*, Index, *sub* "Oxford, Bruno and."

32. the son . . . of Troy: Astyanax, the son of Hector and Andromache, who was thrown from a tower by Odysseus after the reduction of Troy.

33. where there are . . . all of them: The exact meaning of this phrase is unclear in the Italian (". . . *ove son que' doi, que' cento, que' mille, que' tutti;*"). It may refer to the deviations of the portraiture from reality, or perhaps to the two professors, Nundinio and Torquato, the other characters in the dialogue, and the populace of London which is described in the Second Dialogue.

34. *Croesi* is the plural of Croesus; hence, rich men.

35. welcomed the Nolan . . . than your home: Not only did the French ambassador lodge Bruno in his London residence, but he and the Nolan became close friends. Hence, Bruno says that "you welcomed me into your home, and more importantly, into your heart."

36. Alexanders . . . make the sun rise for him: allusion to the well-known episode of the visit paid by Alexander the Great to Diogenes at a time when the latter was "at home" in his barrel; cf. n. 9, above. Alexander asked the philosopher if there was any favor he could do for him. "Yes," replied Diogenes, "you can move, for you are blocking my sunlight."

37. That is, Diogenes' barrel; figuratively, England.

38. The King of France, Henri III, whom Bruno describes as a "beneficent solar lion." Henri is portrayed, in a similar celestial appearance, in Bruno's *Lo Spaccio della bestia trionfante (The Expulsion of the Triumphant Beast)*. Cf. Yates, *GB&HT, sub nom.* "Henri III."

39. It., *freme.* The primary definition given by Florio is "roars" or "roars like a lion," which is obviously more appropriate than the modern meaning, "quivers."

40. A northern constellation containing the bright star Arcturus, whose rising and setting was supposed to portend tempestuous weather.

41. Farewell.

First Dialogue

Dialogo Primo.

Interlo-cutori. { Smitho.
Theophilo Philofopho,
Prudentio pedante.
Frulla.

Arlauan ben latino ? THE.
Si. SMI. Galant'huomini ?
THE. Si. SMI. Di buona
riputatione? THE. Si. SMI.
dotti ? TH. Affai competen
temente. SMI. Ben creati,
cortefi,ciuili ? TH. Troppo
mediocremente.SMI.Dot-
tori? TH. Meffer fi, Padre fi,Madonnafi, Madefi ;
credo da Oxonia. SMI. Qualificati? TH. Come
non ? huomini da fcelta, di robba lunga, ueftiti di
uelluto ; un de quali hauea due cathene d' oro lu-
cente al collo : et l' altro (per Dio)con quella preti
ofa mano(che contenea dodeci anella in due dita)
fembraua vno ricchiffi mo gioielliero,che ti cauaua
gl' occhii et il core,quando la uagheggiaua. SMI.
Moftrauano faper di greco ? TH. Et di birra etiam
dio. PRV. Togli uia qnell' etiamdio pofcia é vna
absoleta

By permission of the Houghton Library, Harvard University

FIRST DIALOGUE

Interlocutors: Smith; the philosopher Teofilo; the pedant Prudenzio; and Frulla.[1]

SMI. Did they speak Latin well?

TEO. Yes.

SMI. Were they gentlemen?

TEO. Yes.

SMI. Of good reputation?

TEO. Yes.

SMI. Learned?

TEO. Competent enough.

SMI. Well-bred, obliging and polite?

TEO. Not sufficiently.

SMI. Doctors?

TEO. Yes, for 'tis "yes sir," "yes father," "yes milady," "yes," "yes"; graduated from Oxford, I think.

SMI. Qualified?

TEO. Certainly. Distinguished, long-robed[2] men, dressed in velvet: one wore two sparkling chains of gold around his neck, and the other, by God, seemed a very rich jeweller; twelve rings were so disposed on two fingers of his precious hand that, when your admiring gaze fell on it, it gouged out your eyes and heart.

See page 100 for Notes to the First Dialogue.

SMI. Did they seem to know Greek?

TEO. And beer, eftsoons![3,4]

PRU. Don't use that "eftsoons." It is an ancient and obsolete expression.

FRU. Keep quiet, Sir. He is not speaking to you.

SMI. What did they look like?

TEO. One looked like the constable of the giantess and the ogre; the other looked like the *amostante*[5] of the Goddess of Reputation.

SMI. They were two then?

TEO. Yes, because it is a mystic number.

PRU. *Ut essent duo testes.*[6]

FRU. What do you mean by *"testes"*?[7]

PRU. Witnesses, judges of the Nolan's adequacy. *At me hercle,*[8] why did you say, Teofilo, that the number two is mystic?

TEO. Because, as Pythagoras says, two are the primary coordinations, finite and infinite, curved and straight, right and left, and so on. Two are the kinds of numbers, even and odd, one of them male and the other female. Two are the Cupids, superior and divine, inferior and vulgar. Two are the acts of life, reason and emotion. Two are their objects, Truth and Good. Two are the kinds of motions: straight, by which bodies tend to conservation, and circular, by which they conserve themselves.[9] Two are the essential principles of things, substance and form. Two, the specific differences of substance, rare and dense, simple and compound. Two, the contrary and active first principles, heat and cold. Two, the first parents of the things in nature, the sun and the earth.

FRU. In line with the purpose of the aforesaid series of two, I shall set forth another binary scale. The beasts entered the ark two by two and then disembarked two by two.[10] Two are the coryphaei of the celestial signs: Aries and Taurus.[11] Two are the kinds of beasts of burden:[12] horse and mule.[13] Two are the animals made in man's image and likeness: the monkey on the earth and the owl in the sky. Two are the false and honored relics of Florence in this country: the teeth of Sassetto and the beard of Pietruccio.[14] Two are the

animals that the prophet called more intelligent than the
people of Israel: the ox, because he knows his owner, and
the ass, because he can find his master's stable.[15] Two were
the mysterious mounts of our Redeemer: the she-ass and
the colt,[16] symbolizing the old Hebrew and the new gentile
believers. Two are the names, derived from them, which
formed the cognomens of the secretary of Augustus: Asinius and Pollio.[17] Two are the kinds of asses: domestic and
wild. Two, their most common colors: gray and black.
Two are the pyramids on which the names of these two and
other similar doctors must be written and consecrated to
eternity: the right ear of Silenus' horse, and the left ear of
the antagonist of the god of gardens and vineyards.[18]

PRU. *Optimae indolis ingenium, enumeratio minime con-
temnenda!*[19]

FRU. My dear Messer Prudenzio, I glory in the fact that you
approve my statements, you who are more prudent than
Prudence itself, so that you are *prudentia masculini gener-
is.*[20]

PRU. *Neque id sine lepore et gratia.*[21] Then, *isthaec mittamus
encomia. Sedeamus, quia, ut ait Peripateticorum princeps,
sedendo et quiescendo sapimus;*[22] so we will protract till
sunset our tetralogue about the success of the colloquy of
the Nolan with Doctor Nundinio and Doctor Torquato.[23]

FRU. I would like to know what you mean by "tretalogue."

PRU. I said *tetra*logue: *id est, quatorum sermo,* in the same way
that dialogue means *duorum sermo,*[24] trilogue, *trium sermo,* and so on for pentalogue, heptalogue, and others
which are improperly called dialogues; some may claim
that the sense of the word is derived from *diversorum logi;*
but it is improbable that the Greeks, who invented this
word, meant the first syllable *"di" pro capite illius latinae
dictionis "diversum."*[25]

SMI. For mercy's sake, Maestro, let's drop these grammatical
lucubrations and come to our subject.

PRU. *O saeclum!*[26] It seems to me you take little account of
words.[27] How are we going to start a good tetralogue if we

do not know what tetralogue means and, *quod peius est*,[28] if we think it is a dialogue? *Nonne a definitione et a nominis explicatione exordiendum*, as our Arpinate[29] teaches?

TEO. You, Messer Prudenzio, are too prudent. Let's drop, I pray you, these grammatical discourses and reckon our discourse a dialogue since although we are four persons, we will be two in the matter of proposing and answering, discoursing and listening.

Now, O Muses, come to inspire me as I make a beginning and return to the subject! I am not addressing you, Muses who speak with flowery and grand verse in Helicon,[30] for I suspect ye will complain about me in the end when, having made so long and wearisome a pilgrimage, having crossed such dangerous seas, and having tasted such savage customs, ye would quickly be obliged to return home barefoot and naked because here in England there are no fish for Lombards.[31] I omit the fact that not only are ye foreigners, but, moreover, ye are of that race of whom a poet said:

No Greek was ever devoid of malice.[32]

Besides, I cannot fall in love with something which I do not see. Others, others have enchained my soul. To you others, then, I speak, ye who are graceful, kind, mild, tender, young, beautiful, delicate, blond, fairskinned with rosy cheeks, full lips, divine eyes, breasts of enamel, and hearts of diamond; for you I devise so many thoughts in my mind, gather so many affections in my soul, conceive so many passions in my life, pour so many tears from my eyes, exhale so many sighs from my breast, and in my heart kindle so many flames: To you, Muses of England, I say: inspire me, breathe on me, warm me, ignite me, distill and resolve me into liquor, make me into juice and make me utter not a small, feeble, narrow, short and succinct epigram, but an abundant, broad vein of lengthy, fluent, grand and steady prose, whence my rivers will not be fed as from a narrow stream but as from a capacious channel.

And thou, my Mnemosine,[33] who art hidden under thirty seals and shut up in the bleak prison of the shadows of Ideas,[34] harmonize a little in my ear.

Some time ago, two men came to the Nolan on behalf of a royal retainer in order to inform him [the Nolan] how much he [the retainer] longed for his conversation on [and thus his exposition of] Copernicus and other paradoxes in his new philosophy. To which the Nolan replied that in judging and determining he saw through neither the eyes of Copernicus nor those of Ptolemy, but through his own eyes. As to the observations, however, he thought that he owed much to these [two] and to other diligent mathematicians who successively, from time to time, adding light to light, had laid down sufficient principles to lead us to such wisdom as could have been brought forth only after many not insignificant stages. He added that these men are in effect interpreters who translate words from one language to another; but then there are others who penetrate into the sense, and they are not the same ones. Or, they [the former] are like country folk who report the circumstances and shape of a battle to a captain who was absent; it is not they who understand the proceedings, the reasons and the art by which the victory had been gained, but he who has experience and better judgment of the military art. So, to the Theban Manto[35] who saw but did not understand, Tiresias, the blind but divine interpreter, said:

> *Visu carentem magna pars veri latet,*
> *Sed quo vocat me patria, quo Phoebus, sequar.*
> *Tu lucis inopem gnata genitorem regens,*
> *Manifesta sacri signa fatidici refer.*[36]

In the same way, what could we judge, if the many and diverse verifications of the appearances of the superior or surrounding bodies[37] had not been proclaimed and presented to the eyes of reason? Certainly, nothing. Nevertheless, having rendered thanks to the gods, the bestowers of gifts, who proceed from the first and infinite omnipotent light, and having exalted the scholarly works of these noble

85

spirits, we recognize without any reservation that we must open our eyes to what they have noted and seen; but we do not grant what they have conceived, understood, and determined.

SMI. Please tell me, what opinion have you of Copernicus?

TEO. He was a man of deep, developed, diligent and mature genius; a man not second to any astronomer before him except in order of succession and time; a man who, in regard to innate intellect,[38] was greatly superior to Ptolemy, Hipparchus, Eudoxus and all others who followed in their footsteps.[39] This estate he attained by freeing himself from a number of false presuppositions of the common and vulgar philosophy, which I will not go so far as to term blindness. Yet, Copernicus did not go much further [away from the common and vulgar philosophy] because, being more a student of mathematics than of nature, he could not plumb and probe into matters to the extent that he could completely uproot unsuitable and empty principles and, by resolving perfectly all the difficulties in the way, free both himself and others from numerous empty enquiries and fix their attention on constant and sure things.

In spite of this, who will ever be able to praise sufficiently the greatness of this German[40] who, having little regard for the stupid mob, stood so firmly against the torrent of beliefs and, although almost destitute of vital reasons, took up again those despised and rusty fragments that he was able to get from the hands of antiquity, refurbished them, and assembled and fastened them together again with his mathematical more than natural reasoning.[41] In this way, he brought the cause, which had been ridiculed, despised and vilified, to be honored, praised, [to be] more credible than its opposite and most certainly more serviceable and expeditious for theoretical and calculative purposes. So this German, even though he did not have sufficient means to be able to defeat completely, conquer, and suppress falsehood beyond all resistance, nevertheless stood firm in determining in his mind and avowing openly that it must in the end be necessarily concluded that this globe moves with respect to the universe, rather than that it be possible for the totality of innumerable bodies, of which many are known [to be] more splendid and greater [than the earth], to look to the earth as the center and basis of their circles and influences (in spite of nature and reason which suggest the contrary, with most perceptible motions). Who, then, will be so rude and discourteous toward the labors of this man as to forget how much he accomplished, and not to consider that he was ordained by the gods to be the dawn which must precede the rising of the sun of the ancient and true philosophy,[42] for so many centuries entombed in the dark caverns of blind, spiteful, arrogant, and envious ignorance? Who, marking what he could not do, would place him among the common herd who are moved and guided by, and throw themselves headlong after, the voice of a brutish and ignoble fancy[43] sounding at their ears? Who would not rather count him among those who, with happy genius, have been able to raise themselves and stand erect, most faithfully guided by the eye of Divine Intelligence?

And now, what shall I say of the Nolan? Perhaps it is not appropriate for me to praise him, since he is as close to me as I am to myself. [But] certainly, no reasonable man will blame me for praising him, since it is not only fitting but sometimes also necessary, as the lucid and learned Tansillo said so well:

> Even though, for a man who longs for regard and
> honor,
> Speaking much of himself is not seemly,
> Since the tongue of one whose heart fears and loves
> Does not merit faith in its words,
> Sometimes, nevertheless, it seems fitting
> That another person preach his fame
> And speak in his favor: so that
> He gets the profit without the blame.[44]

87

Besides, if there be one so fastidious that he would not under any circumstances suffer praise of his own merits, or the like, he should know that sometimes [praise] cannot be separated from those merits and their fruits. Who will blame Apelles for saying to those who ask him, that the work he displays is his own? Who will reprove Phidias[45] for responding to those who ask, "Who is the creator of this magnificent sculpture?" that it is he himself? Now, then, in order to make you understand the present argument and its importance, I propose to you a conclusion which soon will appear very plain and simple. If the ancient Tiphys[46] is praised for having invented the first ship and crossed the sea with the Argonauts:

> *Audax nimium, qui freta primus*
> *Rate tam fragili perfida rupit,*
> *Terrasque suas post terga videns,*
> *Animam levibus credidit auris;*[47]

if, in our own times, Columbus is glorified as the one of whom it was foretold long ago:

> *Venient annis*
> *Saecula seris, quibus Oceanus*
> *Vincula rerum laxet, et ingens*
> *Pateat tellus, Tiphysque novos*
> *Detegat orbes, nec sit terris*
> *Ultima Thule;*[48]

[if these men are so praised,] how shall we honor this man [the Nolan] who has found the way to ascend to the sky, compass the circumference of the stars, and leave at his back the convex surface of the firmament? The helmsmen of explorations[49] have discovered how to disturb everybody else's peace, [how to] violate the native spirits[50] of the [diverse] regions, [how to] mingle together that which provident nature had kept separate; [how] by intercourse to redouble defects and to add to old vices the new vices of other peoples, with violence to propagate new follies and to plant unheard-of insanities where they did not before exist, so that he who is strongest comes to conclude that he is wisest. They showed new ways, instruments and arts for tyrannizing and murdering each other. The time will come when, in consequence of all this, those men,[51] having learned at their own expense (through the way things turn out), will know how to and will be able to return to us similar and even worse fruits of such pernicious inventions.

> *Candida nostri saecula patres*
> *Videre procul fraude remota.*
> *Sua quisque piger littora tangens,*
> *Patrioque senex fractus in arvo*
> *Parvo dives, nisi quas tulerat*
> *Natale solum, non norat opes.*
>   *Bene dissepti foedera mundi*
> *Traxit in unum Thessala pinus,*
> *Iussitque pati verbera pontum,*
> *Partemque metus fieri nostri*
> *Mare sepostum.*[52]

The Nolan, in order to cause completely opposite effects, has freed the human mind and the knowledge which were shut up in the strait prison of the turbulent air. Hardly could the mind gaze at the most distant stars as if through some few peepholes, and its wings were clipped so that it could not soar and pierce the veil of the clouds to see what was actually there. It could not free itself from the chimeras of those who, coming forth with manifold imposture from the mire and pits of the earth (as if they were Mercuries and Apollos descended from the skies), have filled the whole world with infinite folly, nonsense and vice, disguised as so much virtue, divinity and discipline. By approving and confirming the misty darkness of the sophists and blockheads, they extinguished the light which made the minds of our ancient fathers divine and heroic. Therefore human reason, so long oppressed, now and again in a lucid interval laments her base condition to the divine and provident Mind that ever whispers in her inner ear, responding in suchlike measures:

> Who will mount for me, O Madonna, to the sky,
> And bring back thence my lost wisdom?[53]

Now behold, [54] the man [the Nolan] who has surmounted the air, penetrated the sky, wandered among the stars, passed beyond the borders of the world, [who has] effaced the imaginary walls of the first, eighth, ninth, tenth spheres, and the many more you could add according to the tattlings of empty mathematicians and the blind vision of vulgar philosophers.[55] Thus, by the light of his senses and reason, he opened those cloisters of truth which it is possible for us to open with the key of most diligent inquiry; he laid bare covered and veiled nature, gave eyes to the moles and light to the blind, who could not fix their gaze and see their image reflected in the many mirrors which surround them on every side; he loosed the tongues of the dumb who could not and dared not express their entangled opinions, [and] he strengthened the lame who could not make that progress of the spirit which base and dissoluble matter cannot make. He makes them no less present [on them] than if they were actual inhabitants of the sun, of the moon, and of the other known stars; he shows how similar or different, greater or lesser are those bodies which we see far away, in relation to the earth which is so close to us and to which we are joined; and he opens our eyes to see [truly] this deity, this our mother [the earth] who feeds and nourishes us on her back after having conceived us in her womb to which she always receives us again, and he [leads us] not to think that beyond her there is a material universe[56] without souls, and life and even excrement among its corporeal substances.

In this way, we know that if we were on the moon or on other stars, we would not be in a place very different from this—and maybe in a worse place, just as there may be other bodies quite as good and even better in themselves and in the greater happiness of their inhabitants.[57] Thus we will know so many stars, heavenly bodies, deities numbering many hundreds of thousands, who take part in the ministry and the contemplation of the first, universal, infinite, and eternal Mover. Our reason is no longer imprisoned by the fetters of the eight, nine, or ten imaginary mobiles or movers. We know that there is naught but one sky, one immense ethereal region where those magnificent lights keep their proper distances in order to participate in perpetual life. These blazing bodies are the ambassadors who announce the excellent glory and majesty of God. So we are led to discover the infinite effect of the infinite cause, the true and living sign of infinite vigor; and we have the knowledge not to search for divinity removed from us if we have it near; it is within us more than we ourselves are. In the same way, the inhabitants of other worlds must not search for divinity in our world, for they have it close to and within themselves, since the moon is no more heaven[58] for us than we for the moon. We can thus put to a much better purpose what Tansillo almost certainly said jokingly:

> If you do not seize the good that is near you,
> How can you find the good which is far away?
> It seems to me a great mistake to despise yours,
> And to long for what is in others' hands.
> You are like him who abandoned himself
> Desiring in vain his own image:[59]
> You are like the hound who fell into the river,
> Seeing what his own shadow held in his mouth.[60]
>   Forget the shadows and embrace the truth;
> Do not exchange the present for the future.
> I do not despair of having something better;
> But, by living more happily and calmly,
> I rejoice in the present and hope of the future
> And so I get double satisfaction.[61]

With this, one man, even alone, can and shall triumph and, in the end, will have the victory and will triumph over the general ignorance. There is no doubt that the matter will thus be determined: not through the multitude of blind and deaf witnesses, of insults and empty words, but by the force of well-regulated sense, which must needs succeed in the end; because, in fact, all the blind are not worth one who sees, and all the fools cannot replace one wise man.

PRU. *Rebus et in censu si non est quod fuit ante,*
Fac vivas contentus eo, quod tempora praebent.
Iudicium populi nunquam contempseris unus,
Ne nulli placeas, dum vis contemnere multos.[62]

TEO. This is most prudently said with respect to the conventions and the common rules and practice of polite conversation, but not with respect to the apprehension of truth and the rules of contemplation, of which the same wise man said:
Disce, sed a doctis; indoctis ipse doceto.[63]
And again, what you say concerns a doctrine suitable for the many; thus it is advice regarding the multitude: For this burden is not for the shoulders of everyone, but for those, like the Nolan, who can bear it, or at least can move it toward his ends without experiencing perilous difficulty, as Copernicus was able to do. Moreover, those who possess this truth should not communicate it to every sort of person unless they want to wash the ass's head, as the saying goes, or see what swine can do with pearls,[64] or gather from their study and labor such fruits as rash and stupid ignorance, along with conceit and incivility (its eternal and faithful companions) are wont to produce. Thus we[65] are apt to become teachers of the ignorant and illuminators of those blind men who are not bereft of sight through natural impotence or lack of intelligence and discipline; rather, they are called blind only because they do not observe and reflect, being devoid only of action and not of ability as well. Of these there are some so malicious and perfidious that out of a certain slothful envy they become angry and puff themselves up with pride against him who seems willing to teach them. For they are believed to be—and, what is worse, they believe themselves to be—learned doctors,[66] [and] he dares to show that he knows what they do not know. Consequently, you will see them inflamed and enraged.

FRU. As happened with the two barbarous doctors of whom we

will speak. One of them, no longer knowing what to answer and to argue, stood up as if he wanted to finish [the argument] with a budget of adages by Erasmus; with raised fists, he yelled: *"Quid? nonne Antyciram navigas?*[67] *Tu ille philosophorum protoplastes, qui nec Ptolomaeo, nec tot tantorumque philosophorum et astronomorum maiestati quippiam concedis? Tu ne nodum in scirpo quaeritas?"*[67] and other propositions worthy of being resolved on his back with those double staves, called *bastoni*, with which porters are accustomed to take the measurements for the packsaddles for asses.[69]

TEO. Let's leave these propositions for now. There are other [ignoramuses] who, because of some credulous folly, stubbornly wish to remain in the darkness of what they have once learned badly, fearing that seeing will change them for the worse.

    Of another kind are the happy and talented minds on whom no honest study is lost: they do not judge rashly, they have free intellect, clear sight, and are children of heaven. While they are not inventors themselves, they are estimable examiners, investigators, judges and witnesses of Truth. From these men the Nolan has won, wins, and shall win assent and love. These are most noble spirits who are capable of listening to him and discoursing with him. Because, in truth, no one is worthy of contending with him in these matters; if someone is not prepared to agree with him completely, through not having sufficient [mental] capacity, he should at least agree with him about many great and important things, and should acknowledge that what he cannot know as absolutely true, certainly appears as most probable.

PRU. Be that as it may, I am loath to depart from the opinion of the ancients, because, as the wise man says, in antiquity there is wisdom.[70]

TEO. And in many years there is prudence, as the saying continues. If you understood correctly what you said, you would see that from your principle can be inferred the contrary of what you think. I mean that we arc older and have greater age than our predecessors; I mean, in that which has to do with certain judgments about the matter we are discussing. The discernment of Eudoxus,[71] who lived soon after the rebirth of astronomy (if indeed it was not reborn in him), could not be as mature as that of Calippus,[72] who lived thirty years after the death of Alexander the Great; as years were added to years, so observations could be added to observations. For the same reason, Hipparchus[73] must have known more than Calippus, since he had noted the observations concerning celestial mutations made up to one hundred ninety-six years after the death of Alexander the Great. Menelaus, the Roman geometer, knew more than Hipparchus since he observed the motions[74] four hundred sixty-two years after Alexander's death. Even more must Mahomet Aracensis[75] have seen one thousand two hundred two years after that death. One thousand eight hundred forty-nine years after Alexander's death, Copernicus, almost in our time, has seen the most of all. But what of those others who, notwithstanding that they lived later, were no more discerning than those who came before? What of the greater part of those who are of our own time but who have not, on that account, more wit? This comes about because the former did not, and the latter do not, relive the lives of others. And, what is even worse, the former and the latter both lived like corpses in their own years.[76]

PRU. Say what you please; drag the matter off in your own merry way however you like; I am still a friend of antiquity. As for your opinions and paradoxes, I do not believe that so many men of such wisdom were ignoramuses, as you and other friends of novelty think.

TEO. Well, Master Prudenzio, if this vulgar opinion of yours is as true as it is old, certainly it was false when it was new! Before this philosophy which suits your brain arose, there existed the philosophy of the Chaldeans, of the Egyptians, of the magi, of the Orphists, of the Pythagoreans and of

94

others who spring readily to mind[77] [and] who better suit
our head;[78] from them first rebelled frivolous and empty
logicians and mathematicians who were not so much
enemies of Antiquity as strangers to the Truth. Let us put
aside, then, the question of the old and the new, seeing that
there is no new thing which cannot be old[79] and there is no
old thing which has not been new, as your Aristotle rightly
noted.

FRU. If I don't speak, I shall surely burst and die. You have said
"your Aristotle," speaking to Master Prudenzio. Do you
know in what sense I understand Aristotle to be his, *id est,*
that he is a Peripatetic? (If it please you, let us put this little
digression in parenthetically.) Once, at the door of the
archiepiscopal palace of Naples, there were two blind
beggars, one of whom said he was a Guelph, the other a
Ghibelline; thereupon, they started beating each other so
cruelly with their staves that, if they had not been pulled
apart, I don't know how the matter would have ended. But
a decent citizen approached them and said: "Come here,
you two blind rogues. What's a Guelph? What's a
Ghibelline? What does it mean to be a Guelph or a
Ghibelline?" In truth, one of them had no idea what to
answer or what to say, while the other replied: "Signore
Pietro Costanzo,[80] my master of whom I am very fond, is a
Ghibelline." Exactly of this sort are many Peripatetics who
get angry and heated for Aristotle, and declare that they are
completely on his side; they want to defend the doctrine of
Aristotle; they are enemies of those who are not friends of
Aristotle; they want to live and die for Aristotle, but they do
not understand even the titles of the books of Aristotle. If
you want me to show you one of them, here he is—the man
to whom you said "your Aristotle," and who from time to
time flashes you an *Aristoteles noster, Peripateticorum
princeps,* a *Plato noster, et ultra.*[81]

PRU. I have little regard for your regard, [and] I do not at all
esteem your esteem.

TEO. Please do not interrupt our talk again.

SMI.   Go on, Messer Teofilo.

TEO.   Your Aristotle noticed, I say, that what happens to all things, happens no less to different opinions and ideas; in fact, to evaluate philosophies according to their antiquity is like trying to decide which came first, night or day. That upon which, then, we must fix the eye of consideration is whether we are in the daylight with the light of truth above our horizon, or whether it is in that of our antipodal adversaries. Are we in the dark, or are they? And, in conclusion, are we, who make a beginning of the renewal of the ancient philosophy, in the morning which makes an end to the night, or are we rather in the evening which ends the day? And certainly this is not difficult to decide, even if we judge hastily by the fruits of the two different kinds of contemplation.

   Now, let us see the difference between the former and the latter.[82] The former are moderate in life, expert in medicine, judicious in contemplation, unique in divination, miraculous in magic, wary of superstition, law-abiding, irreproachable in morality, godlike in theology, and heroic in every way.[83] All this is shown by the length of their lives, their healthier bodies, their most lofty inventions, the fulfillment of their prophecies, the substances transformed by their works, the peaceful deportment of their people,[84] their inviolable sacraments, the great justice of their actions, the familiarity of good and protecting spirits, and the vestiges, which still remain, of their amazing prowess. I leave to the judgment of anyone of good sense the consideration of the fruits of the latter.

SMI.   Now, what will you say if most of our contemporaries think quite the opposite, especially as to doctrine?

TEO.   I'm not surprised; because, as is common, those who lack understanding think they know more, and those who are complete fools think they know everything.

SMI.   Tell me, how can one correct them?

FRU.   Take away their heads and replace them with others.

TEO.   Take away (by some manner of argumentation) their reckoning of [their] knowledge, and by pointed arguments dispossess them as much as possible of this foolish opinion, in order to make listeners of them; the teacher having first made sure that they have capable and able intellects. According to the custom of the Pythagorean school and our own, I will not give them leave to take the role of interrogators or disputants before they have heard the whole course of philosophy; because, if the teaching is perfect in itself and has been completely understood by them, it will purge all doubts and clear away all contradictions. Beyond this, should one discover a more polished intellect, he can then see what more there is to add, remove, correct, and change. At this point, he will be able to compare these principles and conclusions to other contrary principles and conclusions; and thus rationally to agree or disagree, ask and answer. For it is impossible to know how to doubt and to inquire purposefully, and with profitable system, about any art or field of knowledge, if one has not first listened. One will never be a good examiner and judge of an issue if he has not first informed himself about the matter. Therefore, when learning proceeds by degrees, proceeding from stable and confirmed principles and foundations to the structure and [the] perfection of things which can be discovered through it, the listener must remain silent and, before having completely heard and understood, must believe that with the progress of learning, all difficulties will cease. The *Efettici* and Pyrrhonists[85] have another method: professing that it is not possible to know anything, they are always asking questions and looking without ever finding. No less unhappy are those spirits who want to discuss even the clearest things, wasting as much time as can be imagined; and those who, in order to appear learned or for other base pretexts, want neither to teach nor to learn, but only to oppose and to contest the truth.

SMI. I have a scruple about what you have said, since there is an innumerable multitude of those who presume to learning and esteem themselves worthy of being constantly listened to, as you [can] see from all the universities and academies which are packed with these *Aristarchi*[86] who would not concede a zero to the Almighty Thunderer Jove. Those who study under them will, in the end, have gained nothing more than to have advanced themselves from ignorance, which is a privation of truth, to thinking and believing that they know, which is madness and a kind of falsity. You see, then, what these listeners have gained: taken from the ignorance of simple negation, they are put into the ignorance of wrong inclination, as they say. Now, how can I be sure that, expending so much time and effort, and losing the opportunity for better studies and occupations, I shall not (as is wont to happen to the majority of the others) infect my mind with pernicious follies rather than gain knowledge? How shall I, who know nothing, be able to distinguish between dignity and indignity, between the poverty and wealth of those who consider themselves wise and are thought to be so? I see clearly that we are all born ignorant and readily believe that we are ignorant; we grow and we are educated in the discipline and habits of our home. No less do we hear censure of the laws, rituals, faith and customs of those who are our adversaries and strangers to us, than they of us and our affairs. By dint of some natural nourishment the roots of zeal for our own things are planted in us no less than in those many and diverse others for theirs. How easily has it become incorporated into custom for our people to deem it an offering to the gods, when they have subdued, slain, conquered, and murdered the enemies of our faith; no less than all the others [will do] when they have done the same things to us. And with no less fervor and conviction of certitude do the latter thank God for having the light, through which they expect eternal life, than do we render thanks for not being in their blindness and darkness. To these convictions about religion and faith are added convictions about knowledge. Either because of the teaching of those who guide me, parents and pedagogues, or because of my whim and fancy, or because of the reputation of some doctor, I will count myself to have profited under the arrogant and blissful ignorance of a horse with no less satisfaction of my mind, than anybody else [has] under a lesser ignoramus or even a scholar. Do you not know how powerful is the habit of believing and being brought up on certain opinions since childhood, in shutting off the most obvious things from the understanding? It is no different with those who are accustomed to eating poison, whose health at length not only feels no injury but further has even converted it into a natural food, so that the antidote itself becomes lethal. Now tell me, with what art will you, more quickly than someone else, win the ear of a person in whose mind there is perhaps less tendency to listen to your propositions than to those of a thousand others?

TEO. It is a gift of the gods if they guide you and destine you to cross paths with a man who is not so much esteemed as a true guide but in truth is such a one, and [if the gods] illuminate your inner spirit to choose what is best.

SMI. But one usually follows the common opinion, so that in case of error he will not be without general approval and companionship.

TEO. A thought most unworthy of a man! It is for this reason that wise and sublime men are so rare. And this is the will of the gods, since what is common and general is neither esteemed nor considered valuable.

SMI. I believe indeed that the truth is known by few, and that things of great value are mastered by very few. But I am perplexed that [the] many things which ought not be valued, which are worth nothing and can be [even] greater follies and vices, are so seldom found among the small number of select men (whose number is perhaps not much more than one man).[87]

TEO. Yes, but in the end it is safer to seek the true and the proper outside the mob, because it [the mob] never contributes anything valuable and worthy. Things of perfection and worth are always found among the few. If perfect and worthy things were exceptional and belonged to exceptional men, anyone, although he could not discover them by himself, could at least come to know them; and these things would be precious not so much by way of cognition as in simply possessing them.[88]

SMI. Let us then drop these discussions and pause a bit to hear and consider the ideas of the Nolan. It is surely enough that he has gained such a great reputation that he is worth listening to.

TEO. This would satisfy him. Now you will see how mighty his philosophy is in taking care of and defending itself, [as well as] in baring the emptiness and revealing the fallacies of sophists and the blindness of the common and vulgar philosophy.

SMI. With this object in mind, since it is now night, we will return tomorrow at the same hour and consider the encounters and the doctrine of the Nolan.

PRU. *Sat prata biberunt; nam iam nox humida caelo praecipitat.*[89]

END OF THE FIRST DIALOGUE

Notes to the First Dialogue

1. Because *Smith* is such a common name, this character has not been identified with any certainty. He has been tentatively identified either with a John Smith (to whom was dedicated Claudius Hollyband's [pseudonym for a Frenchman in London, Desainliens] *The italian Schoolmaister Containing rules for the perfect pronouncing of th'italian tongue, with familiar Speeches and certain Phrases taken out of the best Italian authors, and a fine Tuscan*

histoire called Arnald and Lercenda [London, 1575]) or a William Smith (a poet and disciple of Edmund Spenser, who published a pastoral poem, *Chloris, or the Complaint of the passionate despised Shepherd*). Cf. Lewis Einstein, *The Italian Renaissance in England* (New York, 1902), p. 101; and J. Lewis Mc Intyre, *Giordano Bruno* (London, 1903), pp. 36-37.

Teofilo presents Bruno's philosophy. The name means "dear to God," which is the same meaning as the name *Philoteus* which Bruno put before his own name in his *De compendiosa architectura et complemento Artis Lullii* (Paris, 1582) and again in his *Recens et completa ars reminiscendi* (London, 1583). Bruno uses the name Teofilo or Filoteo in a number of his dialogues.

Prudenzio is the too prudent pedant; because of his excessive prudence, he constantly interjects learned quibbles and trifles.

Frulla is a frivolous character who is introduced to laugh at and to foil Prudenzio. In the first draft of the *Cena*, he is introduced as Smith's servant. Literally, *frulla* means "a snap of the fingers," hence, a trifle.

2. They wore doctoral robes.

3. It., *eziandio*. "Eftsoons" is the most archaic of the translations given by Florio.

4. There is a pun here. *Saper di greco* in Smith's question can signify either "to know Greek" or "to taste Greek wine." Teofilo's response implies that the latter meaning is the more appropriate one.

5. Arabian civil rank corresponding to viceroy.

6. Probably a legal phrase meaning "there must be two witnesses." He refers to Doctors Nundinio and Torquato, who are the subjects of these opening remarks.

7. Frulla is making a pun on the double meaning of *testes* as "witnesses" and "testicles."

8. But, by Hercules. An oath used by Terence and Cicero.

9. See the Introduction, p. 31.

10. Cf. Genesis VI: 19 and VIII: 16 ff.

11. Aries and Taurus are the spring constellations. The vernal equinox occurs when the sun is in Aries, and this begins the astrological year.

12. Lat., *nolite fieri*.

13. Cf. Psalm XXXI: 9: *"Nolite fieri sicut equus et mulus, quibus non est intellectus."*

14. Joking allusion to two Tuscans living in England, Tommaso di Vincenzio Sassetto and Pietruccio Ubaldini. *Sassetto* means "pebble" and *pietruccio* "little rock;" thus the duality.

15. Cf. Isaiah I: 3: *"Cognovit bos possessorem suum, et asinus praesepe domini sui: Israel autem me non cognovit, et populus meus non intellexit."*

16. Cf. Matthew XXI: 5, 7 and Zach. IX: 9. For an explanation of why Bruno calls the she-ass and the colt "mysterious," see Yates, *GB&HT*, pp. 259-260, and John M. Steadman, "Una and the Clergy: The Ass Symbol in *The Faerie Queene*," *Journal of the Warburg and Courtauld Institutes*, XX (1958), pp. 134-136. The explanation is deeply esoteric; since the references cited above deal with Bruno's discussion of the she-ass and the colt in his *Cabala del Cavallo Pegaseo* (London, 1585), it is problematic whether he intended such deep meanings in the passing reference here (and especially since it is the inconsequential Frulla who is speaking).

17. It., *Asinio e Pullione. Pullione* "derives" from the Latin *pullus* ("colt," "young ass"). Asinius Pollio was a friend of Augustus, founder of the first library in Rome, and author of a history, now lost, of the civil war between Caesar and Pompey.

18. Silenus' horse was an ass, and the adversary of Priapus, the god of orchards, was also an ass. University professors, such as Nundinio and Torquato, therefore deserve two ears of an ass.

19. Wit of great talent, you have made an outstanding statement!

20. You are prudence of the masculine species, that is, the archetype of prudence. This is an allusion to Aristotle, *Generation of Animals*, trans. A. I. Peck (London, 1953), 728 A, 17ff., where he states that the male is the typical and excellent form of the human species, while the female is but an imperfect male.

21. And not without elegance and grace.

22. Let us leave off these encomiums. Let us sit down, because, according to the leader of the Peripatetics [Aristotle], in sitting and resting we come to wisdom.

23. These are the two Scholastic professors who will finally appear in the Third Dialogue. In Italian, Torquato means "wearing a necklace"; Nundinio means "chatterbox" or "barker at a circus."

24. We are in the midst of a quibble over words, their meanings, and their appropriateness; a tetralogue is supposedly a discussion among four interlocutors, a *"duorum sermo"* is one between two people, and so forth. Prudenzio's etymology is nonsense; the word "dialogue" means "discourse," not "discourse between two persons."

25. for the beginning of the Latin word *"diversum."*

26. Egad!

27. It., *buone lettere*.

28. what is worse.

29. Is it not necessary to begin with the definition and the explanation of the noun? Cf. Cicero, *De officiis* I, 2, 7. ("Our Arpinate" is Cicero.)

30. Helicon is a mountain in Boeotia, sacred to Apollo and the Muses. The Muses are sometimes called the Heliconiades; Teofilo is here addressing the Greek Muses.

31. Fra Giovanni da Vercelli, the General of the Dominicans, paying a visit incognito to a friary in Germany, the better to judge its condition, was badly treated by the prior, who gave him only a few boiled vegetables to eat while the friars were eating fish; in northern Europe, Italians were often called "Lombards." Hence this quotation. The legend would have been familiar to Bruno, who was a Dominican.

32. Fusion of two lines by Pulci in his *Morgante maggiore* (XVIII: 175 and XXI: 138).

33. The goddess of Memory. Bruno wrote two treatises on the mnemonic art; for a discussion of them, see F. A. Yates, *The Art of Memory* (London, 1947), Chapters IX, XI-XIV.

34. In his arcane philosophy, Bruno repeatedly dwells on the concepts of seals and shadows. In fact, his treatise *On the Thirty Seals (Triginta sigillorum explicatio)* is a guide to understanding the elaborate emblems he invented in order to hide his teachings from vulgar eyes (a topic which he also dealt with in

his book *On the Shadows of Ideas* [*De umbris idearum*]). For a discussion of these books and their contents, cf. Yates, *GB&HT, sub nom.* "Giordano Bruno," in the Index.

35. Daughter of Tiresias, a prophetess.

36. Seneca, *Oedipus*, vv. 299-300, 505-506 (295-296, 301-302): Much of the truth is concealed from him who is without sight, But anywhither my country and Phoebus call me, I will follow. You, daughter, guiding a father in need of light, Report the sure signs of the divinatory sacrifice. (Tiresias was the famous blind soothsayer of Thebes, counsellor of Oedipus.)

37. I.e., those above and around the earth.

38. It., *giudizio naturale*.

39. Ptolemy, Hipparchus, and Eudoxus all espoused the geocentric theory of the universe.

40. Copernicus was from Thorn (now Tirun) in Polish Prussia. There has existed throughout modern times an unseemly and pointless squabble as to his nationality, even among historians who should know better. The notion of nationality was quite different in the Renaissance than it is today; Copernicus spoke German as his native language, but owed allegiance to the King of Poland. While Bruno here refers to Copernicus as a German, he participated in 1583 in a famous debate on the Copernican theory at Oxford. The debate was held in honor of the Polish Prince Albert Laski, and the subject was presumably chosen with Laski's nationality in mind. See the Introduction, p. 18.

41. It., *discorso*.

42. See below, n. 78.

43. It., *fide*.

44. Luigi Tansillo, *Vendemmiatore*, stanza XXIX. Bruno often quotes from the works of Tansillo, a poet and friend, who died in 1568, and for whom Bruno retained a life-long admiration. Bruno made him an interlocutor in his *De gli eroici furori*.

45. Apelles was a distinguished Greek painter of the time of Alexander the Great. Phidias was a famous sculptor, contemporary with Pericles, who made the celebrated statue of Jupiter Olympius.

46. Tiphys was the pilot of the Argo, the ship that carried Jason and the Argonauts in search of the Golden Fleece.

47. Seneca, *Medea*, vv. 301-304: Too audacious was the man who first violated the treacherous waves with fragile raft and, seeing his native shores recede behind him, committed his life to the capricious winds.

48. Seneca, *Medea*, vv. 378-382 (375-79): Time will come when the Ocean will open the barriers of the world and a new land will appear and another Tiphys will discover new worlds and Thule will not be the end of the world any more. (Thule is an island in the extreme north of Europe; according to some, it was Iceland, and, to others, Mainland, one of the Shetland Islands.) This passage was often quoted in the literature of the voyages of discovery. Cf. L. E. Huddleston, *Origins of The American Indians* (Austin, Tex., 1967), pp. 25-6.

49. It., *gli Tifi*, the pluralized form of *Tifi* (Tiphys), the Argo's pilot; hence *gli Tifi* are the helmsmen of any explorative expeditions.

50. It., *patrii genii*, intended in the figurative sense of "native talents," or perhaps "penates."

51. I.e., those to whom our follies were communicated through navigation and commerce.

52. Seneca, *Medea*, vv. 329-339: Our fathers lived in an age of innocence, devoid of falsehood. Each of them, quietly enjoying his own shore, getting old in his father's field, rich in his poverty, knew no other riches than those produced by the land. The Thessalian wood [the Argo] destroyed the wise laws of the world and the judicious separation of its shores; the sea suffered the scourge of oars and it, formerly separated from us, became frightful to us.

53. Ariosto, *Orlando furioso* XXXV, 1.

54. The following passage, up to the quotation from Tansillo, is partly paraphrased and partly translated by Bruno in his *Acrotismus seu rationes articulorum physicorum*, in *Opera latine conscripta*, ed. F. Tocco, I (Naples and Florence, 1879), i, 66-67.

55. Bruno's characterization of his achievements here is strikingly similar to Lucretius, *De rerum natura* I, 72ff.

56. It., *corpo.*

57. It., *animali;* Bruno of course means "ensouled beings."

58. Note the play on heaven and divinity.

59. Reference to Narcissus who, enamored of his reflection in a pond, attempted to embrace it and drowned.

60. I.e., you are like Aesop's hound who looked into the river while holding a bone in his mouth; he saw the bone reflected in the water, and fell into the river, losing his bone, when he vainly tried to get the reflected one.

61. Tansillo, *Vendemmiatore*, stanzas XVIII and XIX.

62. *Disticha Catonis* III, 11, and II, 29, in Baehrens, *Poetae lat. min.*, III, 228 & 226: If affairs and possessions are altered, Live contentedly with what the present offers you. Never alone despise the judgment of the people, Lest you please no one, while you would despise the mob.

63. *Disticha Catonis* IV, 23, in Baehrens, *ed. cit.*, p. 232: Learn, but from learned men; as for the unlearned, teach them.

64. Cf. Matthew VII: 6: *Neque mittatis margaritas vestras ante porcos.*

65. Bruno means "they," i.e., those who communicate the truth indiscriminately.

66. It., *dotti e dottori.* The pun is lost in English.

67. What? Do you want to sail to Anticyra? (Anticyra, a town in Phocis, was one of the most important markets of hellebore, which ancient physicians considered as the specific drug against mental diseases. *"Antyciram navigas,"* therefore, really means "Are you crazy?"). Cf. Erasmus, Chiliade I, Centuria VIII, No. 52 of the *Adagia* (Paris, Chevillot, 1579; col. 255). Although Bruno despised pedantic Humanists (as is shown in his treatment of Prudenzio), he held Erasmus in great esteem. For example, in his *Artificium perorandi (Op. lat.* II, iii, 376) he called Erasmus *"princeps humanista."* (Bruno's spelling here is *Antyciram.*)

68. You, you presumptuous "first man" of philosophers, don't you concede anything to Ptolemy or to so many of the greatest philosophers and astronomers? Are you not seeking a knot in a riddle?

69. In other words, Frulla is saying that such inanities should be resolved by a beating worthy of dumb asses.

70. Job XII: 12: *In antiquis est sapientia et in multo tempore prudentia.*

71. Eudoxus was a Greek astronomer and disciple of Plato.

72. Calippus was a Greek astronomer and friend of Aristotle. The system of the celestial spheres derived from the observations and calculations of Eudoxus and Calippus, who argued that the observed irregular motions of the sun, moon and planets were compound motions made up of the regular rotations of a nest of concentric spheres, rotating at different speeds and in different directions, each with its poles fixed somewhere in the surface of the larger one immediately outside it. The work of these two astronomers greatly influenced Aristotle's vision of the universe.

73. Hipparchus was a celebrated astronomer of Nicaea.

74. It., *la differenza de moto.*

75. Mahomet Aracensis is the Arabic astronomer, al-Battânî. He came from ar-Raqqah, whence his Latinized, adjectival last name [H]Aracensis. Bruno has taken this list of astronomers from Copernicus, *De revolutionibus* III, 2: *Historia observationum comprobantium inaequalem aequinoctiorum conversionumque praecessionem.* (Bruno misquotes Copernicus when he says that Menelaus lived four hundred sixty-two years after Alexander's death; Copernicus has four hundred twenty-two years.)

76. Cf. Seneca, *De brevitate vitae,* Chs. 14: 1-2; 12: 7-9; 15: 5.

77. It., *di primo memoria.*

78. Teofilo refers here to the Hermetic tradition in philosophy, to which Bruno himself belonged. Mixing philosophy, astrology and magic, this tradition was said to have begun with Hermes Trismegistus in Egypt; the tradition then passed to the ancient Chaldeans (to whom we owe astrological studies); thence to the mythical Orpheus who composed the *Orphic Hymns,* thence to Zoroaster, Pythagoras, Plato, Plotinus and the late ancient Neoplatonists; finally, in the Renaissance to Marsilio Ficino, Pico della Mirandola, Cornelius Agrippa and Giordano Bruno (not to mention Tommaso Campanella and Robert Fludd). Mistakes abound in this genealogy. For example, Hermes (or Mercurius) Trismegistus, the supposed contemporary of Moses (Bruno says he lived before Moses) perhaps never lived. In any case the *Hermetica* attributed to him are certainly of late Alexandrian origin, dating from the time of the Neoplatonists and the Gnostics (i.e., the second to the fourth century A.D.). This correct dating of the *Hermetica,* accomplished by Isaac Casaubon in 1614, accounts for the heavily Platonic and Neoplatonic tone of the Hermetic corpus.

79. Cf. Ecclesiastes I: 9.

80. A comrade-in-arms of Giordano Bruno's father.

81. Our Aristotle, leader of the Peripatetics, . . . our Plato, and more.

82. I.e., the Hermetists and the Aristotelians.

83. It., *in tutti effeti eroici.* According to Florio, *heroico* can mean "noble" or "magnanimous" as well as "heroic." For Bruno, "heroic" does not have the same sense at all as in modern English or Italian. It refers to the soul made divine and heroic, and can be compared to the concept of the *furor* of passionate love. He suggests that the Hermetic philosopher aims at the Hermetic gnosis: "the Magus man, who was created divine, with divine powers, and is in the process of again becoming divine, with divine powers." (Quoted from Yates, *GB&HT,*

p. 281; cf. also John C. Nelson, *Renaissance Theory of Love* [New York, 1963], Chs. III & IV; Hélène Védrine, *La Conception de la nature chez Giordano Bruno* [Paris, 1967], passim.)

84. See the Second Dialogue below for a description of the savagery of the London mob, a result of the inferior philosophy of their betters in the universities.

85. *Efettici* are "irresolute"; they were the followers of the ancient Sceptic Pyrrho (*ca.* 365-275 B.C.). The Pyrrhonian Sceptics suspended judgment and assent on any proposition or statement; though Truth exists, it cannot be known. Pyrrhonian Scepticism became quite popular in the sixteenth century, especially among Michel de Montaigne and his followers who used this philosophy as a means of bringing religious peace to war-torn France (cf., for example, Montaigne's *Defense of Raymond Sebond;* R. H. Popkin, *History of Scepticism from Erasmus to Descartes* [New York, 1960]).

86. Followers of Aristarchus, the distinguished critic of Alexandria, who scrutinized the verses of Homer with special severity and contended that many of his verses were spurious. Hence *Aristarchi* means "severe critics."

87. This is a very difficult passage both to understand and to translate. In Italian it reads: *Credo bene, che la verità è conosciuta da pochi, e le cose preggiate son possedute da pochissimi; ma mi confonde, che molte cose son poche, tra pochi, e forse appresso un solo, che non denno esser stimate, non vaglion nulla e possono esser maggior pazzie e vizii.*

88. This passage is also obscure in meaning. In Italian: *Bene, ma in fine è più sicuro cercar il vero e conveniente fuor de la moltitudine, perché questa mai apportò cosa preziosa e degna, e sempre tra pochi si trovorno le cose di perfezione e preggio. Le quali, se fusser solo ad esser rare ed appresso rari, ognuno, benché non le sapesse ritrovare, almeno le potrebbe conoscere; e cossi non sarebbono tanto preziose per via di cognizione, ma di possessione solamente.*

89. Vergil, *Eclogae* III, iii and *Aeneid* II, 8-9: The meadows are watered enough; the dewy night is already descending from the sky.

Second Dialogue

The Nolan agrees to debate at Greville's house on Ash Wednesday, 109—No one comes for the Nolan at the appointed time, 110—He is summoned in the evening, 110—A slow and perilous voyage on the Thames, 111—A muddy street, 113—Twenty-two steps from home, 115—Decision to go on, 116—The virtue of perseverence, 117—The power of princes shown in their arbitrary acts, 117—Praise of Queen Elizabeth, 119—Of her Council, 119—Of Cecil, Dudley, Walsingham, and Sidney, 119—Baseness of the common people of England, 120—Their violent hostility to foreigners, 121—The four classes of servants, 122—Bestiality of the lower classes, 123—The Nolan resumes his perilous journey, 126—Incivility of Greville's hangers-on, 126—Arrival in the dining hall, 126—Confusion as to precedence, 126—Ceremony of the cup, 126

SECOND DIALOGUE

TEO. Then Sir Fulke Greville[1] said to him: "Messer Nolan, give
me the reasons, if you please, why you think the earth
moves." The Nolan answered that he could not give any
explanation since he did not know Greville's capacity for
understanding him, or the extent of his knowledge; he was
therefore afraid of emulating those who recite their arguments before statues or go and talk to the dead. Rather, he
wished Greville to make known the reasons which led him
to believe that the earth is stationary and, in this way, to
demonstrate what he knew; because, according to the acu-
ity and power which his mind would show in presenting
his reasons, his doubts could be resolved. The Nolan added
that, because of his desire to prove the imbecility of contrary ideas by using the very principles which seem to
confirm them, it gave him no little pleasure to find his
interlocutors prepared for this enterprise, and they would
always find him ready to respond. In this way, he would
show the superior strength of the foundations of his own
philosophy, compared to the vulgar philosophy, by employing the opportunity to answer and clarify.

   This answer pleased Sir Fulke very much and he said:
"You do me a great favor. I accept your proposal and will
set aside a day when people may raise objections, so that
you will doubtless lack no opportunity to set forth your

See page 128 for Notes to the Second Dialogue.

case. Wednesday week, that is, Ash Wednesday, you are invited with many gentlemen and learned persons, so that after eating we may discuss a variety of fine matters." "I promise you," said the Nolan, "that I will not fail to be present at that or any like occasion where I might have similar opportunities, for there is no obstruction subject to my power which can frustrate my desire to understand and to know. But, I pray you, do not invite ignoble, ill-bred persons, unlearned in such speculations." (And he was certainly justified in this reservation, for he had met many doctors of this country with whom he had discussed learned matters, and he had found their methods more like those of peasants than could be wished for.) Sir Fulke replied that the Nolan had nothing to fear; the people he intended to invite were most mannerly and learned. Thus, everything was agreed upon. Now, the appointed day having come, help me, O Muses, to recount [what happened]!

PRU. *Apostrophe, pathos, invocatio, poetarum more.*[2]

SMI. Listen, please, Messer Prudenzio!

PRU. *Lubentissime.*[3]

TEO. The Nolan, having waited till after lunch[4] and having received no news, thought that the gentleman had, in the course of his other occupations, forgotten or had not been able to arrange the matter. And, without thinking any more of it, he went for a walk and visited some Italian friends. Coming home later, after sunset . . .

PRU. Already had wheeling Phoebus turned his back on our hemisphere and [turned] his flaming face to illuminate the antipodes.

FRU. Please, Magister,[5] I beg you to go on with the story because your manner of recounting gratifies me marvellously.

PRU. O, that I knew the story!

FRU. Then, in the name of the Devil, shut up!

TEO. Later that evening, coming home, he found in front of his house Messers Florio and Gwynne,[6] who had been looking for him a long time. Seeing the Nolan approach, they said:

"Please be so kind as to hurry without wasting any more time, for many knights, gentlemen and doctors are awaiting you, and among them there is one with the same last name as yours,[7] who is a ready speaker in discussion." "Well," said the Nolan, "we cannot do ourselves any harm. Only in one way are we inconvenienced; I had hoped that we would have this affair in sunlight, but I see that we will dispute by candlelight." Messer Gwynne explained that some knights who had wanted to be present could not come to lunch, so they had come for supper. "Well then," said the Nolan, "let's go. Pray God He will be with us along our way in this black night, in these perilous streets."

Now, although we[8] were on the right road,[9] we thought to do better and shorten the way. We turned toward the Thames to find a boat to take us toward the Palace. We reached Lord Buckhurst's[10] palace pier, and from there we called out "oars," that is "boatmen,"[11] but we waited so long that we could have, in the same space of time, made the entire journey on foot and performed some errands along the way. At last two boatmen answered from afar; with infinite slowness, as if they were going to their own hanging, they reached the bank. Then, after many questions and answers about whence, where, and why, and how and how much, they brought the prow of the boat up to the last step of the pier. One of the two men, who looked like the ancient ferryman of the Tartarean realm,[12] offered his hand to the Nolan, and the other one, who I think was the son of the first although he seemed to be about sixty-five, took care of us who followed. And, suddenly, even though there was no Hercules, no Aeneas, nor Rodomont, the king of Sarza,[13]

> *gemuit sub pondere cymba*
> *Sutilis, et multam accepit rimosa paludem.*[14]

Hearing this music, the Nolan said: "Please God, let this man not be Charon; I think this is the boat called the rival of the *lux perpetua*;[15,16] certainly it rivals Noah's Ark in

111

antiquity, and by my faith it is surely a relic of the Flood."
Every part of the boat trembled under your touch and even
the slightest movement echoed throughout the whole boat.
"Now I understand," said the Nolan, "how it could be that
the walls of Thebes, if I remember correctly, were vocal[17]
and sometimes sang as if to some melody. If you do not
believe it, listen to the accents of this boat, which whistles
like a choir of fifes blown by the waves that pour in
through the multitude of cracks and splits on all sides."[18]
We laughed, but God knows how.

> ... Hannibal, seeing his troubled empire
> Molested by Fortune,
> Laughed among the sorrowing, weeping people.[19]

PRU.   *Risus Sardonicus.*[20]

TEO.   Inspired by that sweet harmony, [we responded] as does
Love to Disdain, to the weather and the seasons, and we
accompanied these sounds with our songs. Messer Florio,
as if remembering his loves, sang: "Where, without me,
sweet my life."[21] The Nolan responded: "The wretched
Saracen, O feminine mind," and so forth. So, we went on
little by little as much as the boat allowed, which (since
worms and time had reduced it to such a condition that it
could have been used as a cork) seemed with its *festina
lente*[22] to be as heavy as lead, while the arms of the two old
men seemed broken; they stretched their bodies to their
entire lengths while rowing, but succeeded only in making
very slow progress.

PRU.   *Optime descriptum illud "festina,"*[23] relating to the quick
movement of the boatmen's backs; *"lente,"* relating to the
oars which were like the incompetent laborers of the god of
orchards.[24]

TEO.   In this way, proceeding through much time but little space
and not having covered even a third of our journey, we
reached a point just beyond the place called the Temple,[25]
when suddenly our guides,[26] instead of hurrying, turned
the prow toward the bank. The Nolan asked: "What are
they doing? Do they perhaps want to catch their breath?"

112

And his friends interpreted[27] [the boatmen's] answer: That they would go no further, as they had reached their house. We begged them again and again to no avail, as they were of that type of peasant in whose heart are blunted all the darts of the god of love worshipped by the country folk.

PRU. *Principio omni rusticorum generi hoc est a natura tributum, ut nihil virtutis amore faciant, et vix quicquam formidine poenae.*[28]

FRU. There is also another saying referring to every boor:

    Rogatus tumet,
    Pulsatus rogat,
    Pugnis concisus adorat.[29]

TEO. To sum up, they dropped us there and, having paid and thanked them (since in this place you cannot do anything else when such canaille wrong you), we were shown the quickest way to the road.

But now I really need thee, sweet Mafelina, who art the muse of Merlin Cocaio.[30] There was a street which began as a mudhole around which, either by design or by chance, there was no detour. The Nolan, who had studied and lived at schools more than any of us,[31] said: "I think this is a swinish passage; nevertheless, follow me." He had not finished these words when he suddenly fell so deeply into the mud that he could not pull his legs out; and, thus, helping each other, we passed through that stretch of road hoping that that purgatory would not last long. But through an iniquitous and harsh fate, he and we, we and he, found ourselves engulfed in a slimy patch which, as if it were the Orchard of Jealousy or the Garden of Delights, was bounded both hither and thither by high walls; and since there was no light at all to guide us, we could not distinguish the road already passed from the one we had yet to follow; we only hoped that each step would bring the end: ever sinking knee-deep into the liquid mire, we fell toward deep, dark Avernus.[32]

No one could now advise the others; we did not know what to say, but in speechless silence some of us whistled with rage, some whispered, snorting through their lips, some, sighing, stopped for a while, some cursed under their breath and, since our eyes did not serve us, each one's feet guided the others'; each one of us, as if blind, was confused in guiding the others, so that:

> Like him who, long lying and bewailing
> In his hard bed the slothful flow of hours,
> Hopes for some theriac, some spell, powder,
>   draught
> To end the deep pain he feels:
> But when, at length, the poor wretch comes to see
> That every remedy is vanquished by pain,
> Despairing, he acquiesces, and in dying
> Disdains for health to struggle more.[33]

Thus it was with us; after having tried again and again and not having perceived any remedy to our misfortune, we despaired and, ceasing to rack our brains in vain, we resolved to go on wallowing in that deep sea of liquid mud which spread its slow-flowing stream from the bottom of the Thames to its banks.

PRU. What a beautiful conclusion!

TEO. Each one of us had taken the resolve of the tragic blind man of Epicuro:

> When fatal Destiny leads me, blind,
> I let myself go wherever my feet carry me,
> Nor, pitying myself, do I hope for more.
> I will find perforce a ditch, a stumbling block,
>   a stone
> So merciful it will draw me from this struggle
> And hurl me into a deep void.[34]

But, thanks to the gods (since, as Aristotle says, *non datur infinitum in actu*[35]), without incurring any worse misfortune, we found ourselves at last in a slough which, even if it did not yet afford us a bit of dry bank for a pathway, at least showed us more courtesy since it did not foul our feet; and, a little further on, it turned into a gutter, one side of which provided us a stony place to put our feet on dry ground.

Thus with exceeding slowness we proceeded, staggering like drunks, not without danger of breaking this head or that leg.

PRU. *Conclusio, conclusio!*[36]

TEO. To conclude, *tandem laeta arva tenemus:*[37] We thought we were in the Elysian Fields when we reached the main public road; and, from the appearance of the place and recalling whence the accursed detour had taken us, behold, we found ourselves twenty-two steps, more or less, from the spot which we had left in search of the boatmen, and near the abode of the Nolan. O manifold dialectics, O knotty doubts, O importunate sophisms, O captious cavils, O obscure enigmas, O tangled labyrinths, O enchanted sphinxes—Disentangle yourselves or let yourselves be disentangled.

At this crossroad, at this doubtful step,
Ah me, what must I do,[38] what must I say?

We would have gone home from there since Master Mud and Master Sludge had shod us with such boots that we could hardly move our legs. Besides, the rules of odomancy[39] and the series of omens advised us that it would be unwise to continue our journey. The stars, which all lay behind a dark, obscure mantle, leaving the air foggy, impelled us homeward. The hour dissuaded us from going on, and exhorted us to turn back, while the proximity of the [Nolan's] place benignly applauded this exhortation. Chance, which had pushed us this far with one hand, now made the greatest effort in the world with two much stronger wrists.[40] With no less force than a stone is drawn to the center by its intrinsic principle and nature, exhaustion similarly impelled us to the right.[41] In the other direction[42] there would be much toil, travail, and discomfort, which might well lead nowhere. But the worms of conscience said: "If this short journey, not twenty-five steps, has cost you so much, what will be [the price] of the long stretch of road remaining? *Mejor es perder que mas perder.*"[43] From one direction, our common desire bade us not to disap-

point the expectations of those knights and noble gentlemen, while the other direction responded with the cruel
regret that, considering the time, the hour, and the situation, they had not taken the trouble nor thought to send
gentlemen a horse or a boat; so we did not think they would
resent our absence. From hither we were accused of being,
after all, either impolite or like those over-punctilious men
who measure things according to merits and favors and
who are more accustomed to receiving than to paying
courtesy; and [of being] like those base and ignoble men
who would rather lose than win in these matters. From
thither we were excused, since where there is force there is
no reason. From hither the Nolan's particular interest was
attracted, for he had promised he would come, and they
would be able to hang I know not what [reputation] on his
back if he did not; moreover, he has a great desire to see new
customs when he has the chance, to meet intelligent men,
and to acquire, if possible, some new truth and to strength-
en the good habit[44] of knowledge and to become aware of
what he lacks. From thither we were held back by our
common weariness, and by I know not what spirit, which
give certain reasons more true than worthy of repetition.

Who must resolve this dilemma? Whose is it to triumph by this free will? Whom will reason favor? What has
fate determined? Behold, fate, through reason, opens the
door of intellect, enters and forces the decision to continue
the journey. *O passi graviora*,[45] we are told, O pu-
sillanimous, O superficial, inconstant and spiritless men ...

PRU. *Exaggeratio concinna.*[46]

TEO. ... this undertaking is not, is not impossible, however
difficult it may be. The difficulty is such that it leaves the
lazy behind. Common and easy things are for vulgar and
common people; men who are exceptional, heroic and
divine pass along the road of difficulty so that Necessity is
bound to confer on them the palm of immortality. We
came to the conclusion that, even were it not possible in the
end to win the *palio*,[47] we should nevertheless run and

make every effort in a matter of such importance, and contend to the last breath. Not only the victor is praised but also those who did not die as lazy cowards; the latter lay the blame for their loss and death on the back of Fate and tell the world that it is not through their own failing that they lost, but through a twist of fate that they came to such an end. Not only is he who deserved the *palio* worthy of honors, but also those who ran so well that they are indeed worthy and capable of having deserved it, even though they did not win. And blameworthy are they who stop in despair in the middle of their course and do not go on with as much energy and vigor as possible, even though they are the last to cross the finish line. Let perseverence, then, be victorious because, if the travail is so great, the prize will not be mediocre. All valuable things are difficult to obtain. Narrow and thorny is the way of beatitude; perhaps Heaven promises a great thing to come of it:

> . . . *Pater ipse colendi*
> *Haud facilem esse viam voluit, primusque*
> *per artem*
> *Movit agros, curis acuens mortalia corda,*
> *Nec torpere gravi passus sua regna veterno.*[48]

PRU. This is a very pompous climax, which would be appropriate to a matter of greater importance.

FRU. It is proper and in the power of princes to exalt low things which, having been exalted, will be judged worthy and will truly be worthy. And in this, their acts are more illustrious and notable than if they magnified the great, because there is nothing which they believe to be deserving by virtue of its own greatness. Otherwise, superior men would retain their superiority by saying that their position was fitting not because of the favor, kindness and generosity of the prince, but because of justice and reason. So, usually [princes] do not exalt the worthy and the virtuous, because they judge that such men do not have occasion to give them as much thanks as would a poltroon or scummish rogue who had been exalted. Besides, [the latter] have the prudence to show that Fortune, to whose blind majesty they owe so much, is superior to virtue. If sometimes princes exalt an honorable and virtuous man among others, it rarely happens that he keeps that degree for long, since by preferring another man to him, they make him realize how much more authority is worth than merit, and that merit is worth nothing if authority does not tolerate and allow it. You can understand, through this comparison, why Teofilo emphasizes this matter so.[49] However base it may seem, it is nonetheless different from exalting sauces, orchards, gnats, flies, nuts, and other similar things in the mode of the ancient writers; different, also, from the poles, sticks, fans, roots, *gniffeguerre*,[50] candles, bed-warmers, figs, quintans,[51] rings, and other similar things which modern writers praise, which are not only considered ignoble, but are somewhat nauseating. But it is enough to look, among the others, for two men[52] who know the meaning of all this, and from whom we can surely expect great things. Do you not know that when Saul, the son of Kish, was out searching for asses he was about to be deemed worthy of being anointed king of the Israelites? Read, read the first book of Samuel and you will see that that noble personage was more concerned with finding the asses than with being elected king. It even seems that he would not have been satisfied with the kingdom unless he could have found the asses; thus, every time Samuel spoke to him about his coronation, he answered: "And where are the asses? Where are they? My father sent me to find the asses. Don't you want me to find my asses?" In sum, he did not calm down until the prophet told him that the asses had been found, meaning, perhaps, that he could be happy to have that kingdom which was worth his asses and even more.[53] Thus it happens that looking for something sometimes becomes an omen for a kingdom. Heaven, then, promises great things. Now, Teofilo, continue your story: tell us the successes of this search that the Nolan made; let us hear about the rest of his journey.

PRU. *Bene est, pro bene est, prosequere, Theophile.*[54]

SMI. Hurry up, because suppertime draws near. Tell us quickly what happened after you decided to continue the long and troublesome trip rather than to return home.

TEO. Up with the sails and clear the decks, Teofilo, and remember that there is no time right now to speak of the most sublime things in the world! There is no room here to speak of that earthly divinity, of that singular and most exceptional Lady who, from this cold sky near the Arctic parallel serves as a beacon to the whole terrestrial globe: I mean Elizabeth,[55] who in her title and royal dignity is not inferior to any king in the world; in judgment, wisdom, counsel and rule, she is second to no one who holds the sceptre on earth. I leave it to all men to judge what rank she holds among all other princes in her knowledge of the arts and sciences, as well as in her understanding of and facility in all the languages spoken in Europe both by common and learned men. Indeed, if the power of fortune corresponded to and equalled that of her most noble spirit and nature, this great Amphitrite[56] would surely open her mantle and so much enlarge its circumference as to embrace not only Britain and Ireland but another whole globe as well, equal in size to the whole universe:[57] wherefore with fuller meaning, her powerful hand would sustain the globe of a general and whole monarchy.

There are no words to speak of the mature, discreet, and far-seeing Council[58] with whom for twenty-five years and more this heroic soul has made peace and quiet triumph with a wink of her eyes, in the midst of the misadventure of a sea of adversity; [with whom she] has stood firm amid the multitude of powerful billows and swollen waves of the diverse tempests which the haughty and mad Ocean, surrounding her on all sides, has dashed against her with all its might. And, even if I do not personally know them nor expect to know them, I often hear about her most illustrious and excellent knights, one of whom is the Treasurer of the realm,[59] and the other is Robert Dudley,[60]

Earl of Leicester. Their open-handed humanity is well known the world over, and is widely praised and spoken of together with the fame of their Queen and her reign, and they are said to receive, with particular favor, any foreigner not completely devoid of grace and gratitude. Together with the most excellent Sir Francis Walsingham,[61] chief Secretary of the Royal Council, these men who sit near the sun of the royal splendor are able, with the light of their lofty culture, to expunge and dispel the darkness and, with the warmth of loving courtesy, to smooth and polish any rudeness and crudity which is to be found not only among the Britons but also among the Scythians, Arabs, Tartars, cannibals and anthropophagi. You cannot properly describe the polite conversation, the kindness and politeness of the many knights and most noble personages of the realm. Among them is the most illustrious and excellent knight, Sir Philip Sidney,[62] who is so well known, and most particularly to us, first, through his reputation, of which we heard when we were in Milan and France[63] and then personally (now that we are in his own country). His totally unblemished character and his most praiseworthy manners make him so exceptional and singular that it is difficult to find his like among the most exceptional and most singular men either outside or inside Italy.

But now, the bulk of the common people presents itself most importunately before my eyes; they are such a stinkhole[64] that, if they were not mightily well suppressed by the [above-mentioned] others, they would send forth such a stink and such an evil reek as would darken the name of the whole population, to the extent that England could boast a people which in irreverence, incivility, coarseness, boorishness, savagery and ill-breeding would yield nothing to any other people the earth might nourish on its breast.

Leaving aside, now, the many subjects who are worthy of some honor, distinction or nobility, I set before your eyes others who, seeing a foreigner, seem, by God, so many wolves and bears and who, by their grim looks, regard him as a pig would someone who came to take away his trough. This most ignoble lot (to whom this applies) is divided into two kinds, . . .

PRU. *Omnis divisio debet esse bimembris, vel reducibilis ad bimembrem.*[65]

TEO. . . . of which one comprises the artisans and shopkeepers. These, recognizing in some way that you are a foreigner, make faces at you, laugh at you and mock you, make mouth-farts, and call you, in their jargon, a dog, traitor, and foreigner; and to them this last is a very insulting name which entitles the bearer to be the scapegoat for all the wrongs of the world, whether he be young or old, gowned or armored, nobleman or gentleman. If by some misfortune you should happen to touch one of them or lay your hand on your sword, in an instant you will see an army of blackguards gather all along the street. Undoubtedly they come out of the shops, but so quickly that they seem to spring from the earth, even more quickly than (as poets pretend) a multitude of armed men sprang from the dragon's teeth scattered by Jason.

After giving a most honorific and genteel review of a forest of sticks, long poles, halberds, pikes and rusty pitchforks (which, having been given them by the prince for a good purpose, are always poised and ready for this and similar occasions), you will see them hurl themselves on you with coarse fury, without considering whom, why, where and how, and without a word from one to another. Each one of them, giving vent to his innate contempt of foreigners, will draw near you (if he be not hindered by the crowd of others who are trying to carry out the same idea) and with his own bar he will measure your doublet and, if you aren't careful, he will permanently pin your hat to your head. And if a nobleman or a gentleman happens on the scene, even if he is an earl or a duke who is displeased by such villainy, he, doubting that by joining you in the fray

121

THE ASH WEDNESDAY SUPPER

he can help you (even at the cost of harm to himself), will be forced to chafe with anger within and to await on the sidelines the end of the assault (because these ruffians do not respect any person when they have weapons in their hands). Now, at last, when you think it well to seek out a barber[66] and rest your tired and beaten body, you will discover that the very rascals who beat you have become so many policemen and bailiffs who, if they can find a way of pretending that you have touched someone, will make you run, even if your back and legs are broken as badly as you could imagine, as if you wore the winged shoes of Mercury; or were mounted on Pegasus, or straddled the steed of Perseus, or rode the hippogriff of Astolphus or drove the dromedary of Midian[67] or trotted on one of the giraffes of the three Magi. By force of blows, they will make you hurry; they will help you onward with such fierce knocks as will make you prefer the kicks of an ox, an ass or a mule. They will never leave you until they have thrown you into prison; and here, *me tibi comendo.*[68]

PRU. *A fulgere et tempestate, ab ira et indignatione, malitia, tentatione et furia rusticorum . . .*

FRU. *. . . libera nos, domine.*[69]

TEO. Besides these, there is the class of servants. I do not mean the servants of the first surplice[70] who are the gentlemen[71] of barons, who usually do not wear any heraldic device or emblem except when the barons are overly ambitious or when the gentlemen wish to show excessive adulation: among such servants you find politeness.

PRU. *Omnis regula exceptionem patitur.*[72]

TEO. But, excepting some of each sort who are less deserving of such criticism, I am speaking of the other classes of servants, of which some are of the second rank, and all these wear heraldic livery. The masters of the servants of the third rank are not grand enough to give them livery or, perhaps, the servants are deemed unworthy or incapable of wearing it. After the liveried and nonliveried servants are those of the fourth rank who are the servants' servants.

PRU. *Servus servorum non est malus titulus usquequaque.*[73]

TEO. The servants of the first rank are poor and needy gentlemen
who put themselves under the protection of greater men
with the intention of becoming rich or of acquiring honors. They remain under the wings of their principals; for
the most part they are not distinct from their households,
and they follow their lords without indignity; in turn, they
are valued and favored by their masters. Those belonging
to the second rank are bankrupt petty merchants or artisans, or those who have studied how to read (or some
other art), but without any result; they have run away or
have been expelled from some school, shop or tavern.
Those who belong to the third rank are sluggards who have
left a more independent trade in order to escape hard labor:
these can be either aquatic idlers from the boats, or earthly
idlers from the fields. The last ones, of the fourth rank, are a
miscellany of desperadoes who have fallen into disgrace
with their masters, or refugees from storms, or pilgrims, or
the useless and indolent, or those who no longer have
opportunity to steal, or those recently escaped from prison,
or those who aim to cheat whomever comes to pick them
up where they hang out, that is, the columns of the
Exchange and the portals of St. Paul's. In Paris you can
find as many as you want of the same stripe, at the gates of
the Palace; in Naples, at the gates of San Paolo; in Venice,
on the Rialto; in Rome, in the Campo di Flora.[74]

Among the last three classes are those who, in order to
show how mighty they are in their own houses and how
much guts they have, what good soldiers they are, and how
they despise the whole world, [act in the following man-
ner]. Those who do not seem inclined to give way to them,
they shove with their shoulders as if with a galley ram, so as
to spin them right round, and thus to show them how
strong, robust and powerful they are; strong enough, if
need be, to destroy an army. And should they come across a
foreigner, let him yield ever so much room, they are bound
to show him in every way possible what Caesar, Hannibal,

Hector and an ox would do were they to return to fight again. The water carriers don't act simply like asses who (especially when loaded) are pleased to follow a straight line, so that if you don't move they won't either, [and] you must push them aside or they you; but, if you don't keep your wits about you, they will let you feel the points of the iron spouts on their jars. Those who carry beer and ale are even worse; if through your inadvertence they should come upon you in their paths, they will make you feel the weight of the load they are carrying; and they are not only good at carrying things with their shoulders but also at pushing things before them and dragging as it were a cart. These men can be excused because of the authority they have when carrying such a burden, that is, when they are more like horses, mules or asses than men. But I accuse all the others who have a tiny bit of reason, and who are, more than the aforesaid ones, made in the image and likeness of man: after having smiled at you, as if they know you and wish to greet you, instead of saying "good morning" or "good evening," they give you a nasty poke. I accuse, I say, those others who, sometimes pretending to flee or to chase someone or to run to some necessary errand, rush out of a shop and come up behind you or beside you so as to give you the violent thrust of an enraged bull. This is what happened to poor Messer Alessandro Citolino,[75] whose arm they broke and shattered in this way, raising laughter and bringing enjoyment to the whole marketplace; and, when the magistrate came to enquire, he could not discover any indication that such an event had taken place there. So when you feel like leaving your house, beware of doing so without a serious reason, and don't think it will be like going for a stroll around town.[76] Then cross yourself and arm yourself with a cuirass which can stand the test of an harquebus,[77] and prepare to make, of your own accord, as little trouble as possible if you do not wish to suffer the worst by force. But what are you complaining about, poor man? Do you think a butting animal is an ignoble thing?

Don't you remember, Nolan, what you wrote in your book entitled *L'Arca di Noè?*[78] There, when the animals had to arrange themselves, putting an end to the struggle over precedences, do you remember how the ass was in danger of losing the pre-eminence of his seat on the poop of the ark so that he could be a kicker rather than a butter? Which animals represent the nobility of humankind on the fearful Day of Judgment, if not lambs and kids? Such nobility is shown by those virile, courageous and intrepid people who will never be divided among themselves like *oves ab haedis;*[79] they will be distinguished, nevertheless, as are the sires of the lambs from the sires of the kids, as the most venerable, fierce and butting.[80] In the celestial court, the former have a more favorable position than the latter; and, if you do not believe me, you should lift your eyes to the sky and see which one was put at the vanguard of the celestial signs. Which one opens the year with the butt of his powerful horns?

PRU. *Aries primo; post ipsum, Taurus.*[81]

TEO. Who is deemed worthy of coming next in order, after the great captain and first prince of flocks, if not the grand duke of herds, with whom came two pages or Ganymedes, the beautiful twin boys?[82] Think, then, how many people (and what kind) hold supremacy in places other than a rotting ark!

FRU. I could certainly not find any difference between such men and such beasts, except for the fact that the latter butt with their heads and the former shove with their shoulders. But leave these digressions and go back to what happened that night, during the rest of the journey.

TEO. Well, after the Nolan had received about twenty of these violent shoves, particularly at the pyramid near the palace at the junction of three streets,[83] six fine fellows came toward him and one of them gave him such a nice, fat[84] thrust that it was worth ten; it pushed him toward the wall, which gave him a second shove surely worth another ten. "T'ank'ee maister,"[85] said the Nolan. I think he thanked him because he had hit him with his shoulder rather than with the point at the center of his buckler or with the crest on his helmet.

　　This was the last mishap, for soon after, by the grace of St. Fortune, having traveled impassable paths, passed through doubtful detours, crossed swift rivers, left behind sandy shores, forced a passage through thick slimes, overcome turbid bogs, gaped at rocky lavas, followed filthy roads, knocked against rough stones, hit against perilous cliffs, we arrived alive, by the grace of Heaven, at the port, *id est,* at the portal, which was opened as soon as we touched it. When we went inside, we found downstairs a great variety of people and servants who, without stopping or bowing or showing the least sign of respect, showed their contempt by their attitude, and did us the favor of pointing out the door. We went in and found upstairs that they had given us up and sat down to table, after having waited a long time for us. We greeted each other again and again . . .

PRU. *Vicissim.*[86]

TEO. . . . with some small ceremony. (Among others, there was this amusing incident. One of us, who was given the lowest place, thinking that it was the head of the table, wanted, in his modesty, to go and sit where the head was. Consequently, a little while was spent in contention between those who, according to etiquette, wanted him to sit in the lowest place and him who, in humility, wanted to sit in the highest.) At last, Messer Florio sat across from a knight sitting near the head of the table; Sir Fulke to the right of Messer Florio; the Nolan and myself at the left side of Messer Florio; Doctor Torquato at the left of the Nolan, and Doctor Nundinio across from the Nolan.

　　Then, thank God, the ceremony of the cup did not take place. Usually the goblet or chalice passes from hand to hand all round the table, from top to bottom, from left to right, and in all directions with no order but that dictated by rough politeness and courtesy. After the leader of this dance has detached his lips, leaving a layer of grease which could easily be used as glue, another drinks and leaves you a crumb of bread, another drinks and leaves a bit of meat on the rim, still another drinks and deposits a hair of his beard and, in this way, with a great mess, no one is so ill-mannered, tasting the drink, as to omit leaving you some favor of the relics stuck to his moustache. If one does not want to drink, either because he has not the stomach or because he considers himself above it, he need merely touch the cup to his mouth so that he too can imprint on it the morsels of his lips. The meaning of all this is that, since all of them come together to make themselves into a flesh-eating wolf to eat as with one body the lamb or kid or Grunnio Corocotta;[87] thus, by applying each one his mouth to the selfsame tankard, they come to form themselves into one selfsame leech, in token of one community, one brotherhood, one plague, one heart, one stomach, one gullet and one mouth. And this is achieved through certain courtesies and trifles which are the funniest things in the world to see; but it is a most cruel and irksome tragedy if you are a gentleman who finds himself in the midst of it, since you feel obliged to do as the others, for fear of being considered impolite and discourteous; because this constitutes the very height of politeness and courtesy. But, since this custom remained only at the lowest tables, and has disappeared from these others,[88] if not for a certain more venial reason,[89] let's allow them to dine without further observation.[90] Tomorrow, we will speak of what occurred after supper.

SMI. See you later.
FRU. Goodbye.
PRU. *Valete.*[91]

END OF THE SECOND DIALOGUE

Notes to the Second Dialogue

1. The supper supposedly took place in Greville's house on February 14, 1584. But later, Bruno told the Inquisition that it occurred at the French embassy. See the Introduction, n. 43.

2. Apostrophe, pathos, and invocation, in the manner of the poets.

3. Most happily.

4. In fact, Elizabethans ate their heavy dinner (*pranzo*) in the afternoon. We use the modern "lunch" to convey a proper sense of time.

5. Master.

6. John Florio (1533-1625), born in London of a refugee Waldensian family and raised in Italian Switzerland, was the author of two Italian-English dictionaries and a translator of Montaigne's *Essais*. See the Introduction, p. 15 and n. 16. Matthew Gwynne, a physician, philosopher, musician and poet, died in 1627.

The journey begins from the French embassy in Butcher Row, which runs into the Strand near where the Law Courts now stand. The goal of the journey is a lodging of Greville's, apparently near Whitehall.

7. That is, "Brown." Aquilecchia suggests that this may refer to the physician Lancelot Browne.

8. It is not accidental that Teofilo was in the Nolan's party, since they were really the same person.

9. The Strand.

10. Thomas Sackville, Lord Buckhurst.

11. It., "*oares (id est, gondolieri)."*

12. I.e., Hades.

13. That is, the King of the Saracens. Cf. Ariosto, *Orlando furioso* XXVIII, 86-87 and passim. The name is preserved in the English word "rodomontade."

14. Vergil, *Aeneid* VI, 413-414: The ramshackle craft creaked under his weight and let in through its seams great swashes of muddy water.

15. Perpetual light. From the Requiem for the dead.

16. Just as for the Christians the dead go to the next world accompanied by the Requiem, so the Greeks and Romans believed their dead entered Hades by crossing the Acheron.

17. Allusion to the myth of Amphion, who built the walls of Thebes. When he played on his lyre, the stones moved of their own accord and took their places in the wall. It was said that thenceforth the walls remained impregnated with a melodious quality. (It is not surprising that Bruno refers to this myth, for it was popular among the Neoplatonists and Hermetists of the Renaissance. For more information on Amphion and his importance to Renaissance philosophers, see F. A. Yates, *The French Academies of the Sixteenth Century* [London, 1947], Index, *sub nom.*)

18. It.: *Si non credete, ascoltate gli accenti di questa barca, che ne sembra tanti pifferi con que' fischi, che fanno udir le onde, quando entrano per le sue fessure e rime d'ogni canto.* Cf. Vergil, *Aeneid* I, 123. There is a play on words here that cannot be rendered into English: *rime* means both "cracks" and "songs"; *canto* means both "side" and "verse."

128

19. Petrarch, *Rime* CII, 5-7.

20. A sardonic laugh; by extension, one of the classic symptoms of tetanus.

21. Ariosto, *Orlando furioso* VIII, 76. This is the lament of Orlando for the lost Angelica, to which the Nolan answers with the lament of Rodomont, rejected by Doralice, in *Orlando furioso* XXVIII, 117. The juxtaposition of the like sorrows of the two adversaries is a burlesque allusion to the universality of their present misery.

22. Make haste slowly. (This had been the Emperor Augustus' motto.)

23. "Make haste" is an excellent characterization, relating to. . . .

24. Priapus, more correctly the god of gardens and vineyards. The allusion is to the apparently inefficient oscillations peculiar to the sex act, with which Priapus is closely associated.

25. Originally it was the residence of the Knights Templars, in Fleet Street.

26. It., *padrini*. A sarcastic allusion based on the fact that the word literally means "godfathers."

27. As will appear at the beginning of the Third Dialogue, Bruno did not understand English; thus his friends had to translate the words of the boatmen for him.

28. Every kind of rustic people has, first of all, this characteristic: they never do good for virtue's sake and rarely do they do it for fear of punishment.

29. The first line derives from an epigram widely known in the twelfth century; the second and third derive from Juvenal, *Satire* III, 300: If he is questioned, he becomes arrogant; if beaten, he prays; if punched, he even adores.

30. Mafelina is a corruption of the name Melpomene, the Muse of tragedy (cf. Merlin Cocaio, *Il Baldo* I, 13-15, 62-63); Cocaio (Teofilo Folegno, fl. *ca.* 1520) was a parodist and Benedictine who, under the pseudonym of Limerno Pitocco, composed *Orlandino (Little Orlando;* cf. the title *Orlando furioso),* a rather ludicrous, mock-chivalric romance. Under the name of Merlinus Coccaius, he described the wanderings of his fantastic hero-vagabonds in the *Opus macaronicorum.*

31. Bruno is here making it perfectly clear that the mire represents what he sees as the sorry plight of the English universities, and perhaps others as well.

32. Lake Avernus (now Lago Averno), near Cumae, Puteoli and Baiae, was almost entirely surrounded by steep wooded hills, whose deadly exhalations supposedly killed the birds that flew over it; therefore, myth placed the entrance to Hades at Lake Avernus.

33. A sonnet by Tansillo *(Qual uom, che giace, e piange lungamente,* in *Poesie liriche,* ed. Fiorentino, p. 8).

34. First and third tercets of the tragicomedy *La Cecaria* (Venice, 1525) by Marco Antonio Epicuro (1472-1555).

35. No act can have infinite regress, or, Every action must have a first cause.

36. Conclusion, conclusion! [Be done with it!]

37. At last we came to the happy field. (Cf. Vergil, *Aeneid* VI, 744).

38. This is the beginning of Petrarch's *canzona,* "*Che debb'io far? che mi consigli, Amore?*" See F. Wulff, "*La Canzone 'Che debb'io far?' selon les manuscrits autographes de Pétrarque,*" *Lunds Universitets Årsskrift* 38, I, 1 (1902), pp. 1-24, which contains, in addition to the poem, a critical discussion of two Vatican MSS of it.

39. The art of foretelling the way.

40. It., *pulsi.* Florio defines *polso* as "the mooving of the arteries called the pulse." Since Bruno has just used the phrase, "pushed us . . . with one hand," it makes sense to extend the imagery by translating *pulsi* as "wrists," where one usually takes the pulse. See the OED for examples of similar metonymic use in English.

41. I.e., toward the Nolan's residence.

42. I.e., to the left, away from the Nolan's house and toward Greville's palace.

43. Spanish saying: Better to lose than to lose more.

44. It., *abito:* equivalent to the Latin *habitus,* a quality indwelling in the mind or soul.

45. Vergil, *Aeneid* I, 199: Comrades, . . . worse than this have you suffered.

46. Beautiful exaggeration.

47. The *palio* was a banner awarded the victors at races in Italy; such a race is still held annually in Siena.

48. Vergil, *Georgics* I, 121-124: Jove himself desired that agriculture should be harsh and he forced man to till the soil with art, stimulating mortal spirits with the spur of trouble, and he did not allow his reign to become torpid with profound lethargy.

49. That is, the decision to go on.

50. Persons who send other persons to war in their stead.

51. Malarial fevers.

52. Reference to Doctors Nundinio and Torquato who will appear in the following dialogues.

53. Cf. I Kings IX & X.

54. It is good, it is for the good to continue, Teofilo.

55. Elizabeth I (reigned 1558-1603).

56. The wife of Neptune and goddess of the Ocean. Bruno applied this appellation to Queen Elizabeth again in his *De gli eroici furori,* which was dedicated to Sir Philip Sidney. This cognomen is part of the cult of Elizabeth which flourished among the courtiers and court poets. Elizabeth was also called a goddess *(diva Elizabetta)* and Astraea (the virgin goddess of Justice who had lived on earth during the Golden Age). Bruno sees the Queen as Amphitrite, the Ocean, who is the source of all numbers; thus she is a monad, a spiritual being who reflects within herself the whole universe in all its multiplicity. During his "English period" Bruno made Elizabeth an essential element of his Egyptian-Neoplatonic-magical religious reform, whose aim was the contemplation of the divine in all things, the searching out of the Unity behind the multiplicity of appearances, from which Unity emanate all Ideas. Elizabeth, therefore, is that Amphitrite, that One and that Universal Monarch who, he believed, would aid him in establishing (and who would govern) the reformed Hermetic world. Cf. Yates, *GB&HT,* pp. 288-290; ibid., "Queen Elizabeth as Astraea," *Journal of the Warburg and Courtauld Institutes,* X (1947), pp. 80-81; ibid., *Astraea,* pp. 29-87.

57. Which, according to Bruno, is infinite.

58. It., *Conseglio.* There is an ambiguity here. It could refer to Elizabeth's wisdom; however, internal logic and evidence suggest that Bruno intends reference to Elizabeth's advisers who helped form her political wisdom.

59. William Cecil, Lord Burghley (1520-1598).

60. Robert Dudley (1532?-1588), Earl of Leicester and favorite of Elizabeth.

61. Sir Francis Walsingham (1536-1590) was Secretary to Queen Elizabeth.

62. He was the nephew of Dudley and a brilliant poet in the Petrarchan style. He was born in 1554 and died in battle in 1586. He belonged to the circle of the Elizabethan magus, John Dee; thus, he also praised and protected Bruno, who dedicated to him his *Lo Spaccio della bestia trionfante* and *De gli eroici furori*. For Sidney's relations to Dee and the Hermetic movement, cf. P. J. French, *John Dee: The World of an Elizabethan Magus* (London, 1972), pp. 98-99, 119-121, 127-129, 132-138.

63. Sidney probably visited Milan in 1578.

64. It., *sentina*. Florio gives "a sinke, a jakes, a privie, a common shore, a heape of filth, also a companie or filthie pack of lewd base rascals, a pack or heape of mischiefes, a place where rascals and whores meet."

65. Every division must have two parts, or be reducible to two parts.

66. I.e., a barber-surgeon.

67. Cf. Judges VI: 3-5 & Isaiah LX: 6.

68. I commit myself to thy protection.

69. From the lightning-bolt and the storm, from rage and disdain, from evil, temptation and the anger of the boors, O Lord deliver us. (Cf. *Breviario*, Litany of Lent: *Ab ira et odio et omni mala voluntate, libera. . . . A fulgere et tempestate libera nos, Domine.*) This is a mild burlesque of the Lenten liturgy.

70. It., *cotta*. The surplice was a mark of distinction worn by those who assisted at the altar; it came to signify by extension the various orders of courtiers whose servants were distinguished by their livery. Figuratively, then, *cotta* means "rank."

71. I.e., "gentlemen's gentlemen" or upper-level servants.

72. Every rule has its exception.

73. "Servant of the servants" is not always a bad title. (This is an ironic and pointed allusion to the title, *servus servorum Dei*, used by the popes. Prudenzio observes that if the servants of the fourth rank are the "servants of servants" in the way that the pope is, their title and condition should not be belittled.)

74. In modern Italian, *Campo dei Fiori;* curiously enough, this was the square in which Bruno was burned at the stake in 1600, after his trial and condemnation by the Roman Inquisition for heresy and apostasy.

75. Italian man of letters, who embraced the Reformation in 1565 and immigrated to Geneva and then to London. He is perhaps mentioned by Bruno because he like Bruno was the author of mnemonic works (*Tipocosmia* and *Luoghi*).

76. In Italian towns it was customary and comparatively safe for a gentleman to stroll at his leisure. Bruno is again demonstrating the barbarous nature of the London mob, whose low moral state, in Bruno's view, may be laid at the door of the Reformation and the sterile, pedantic Aristotelian learning at the universities.

77. A cuirass is a kind of chest and back armor; the harquebus (or arquebus) is an obsolete portable firearm, having a matchlock operated by a trigger and supported for firing by a hook.

78. *Noah's Ark,* a work written by Bruno not later than 1572, which is now

lost. It was probably a symbolic exposition of moral philosophy in the style of his *Cabala del Cavallo Pegaseo* (London, 1585).

79. Sheep from goats. Cf. Matthew 25: 32: *Et congregabuntur ante eam omnes gentes, et separabit eos . . . sicut pastor segregat oves ab haedis.*

80. These Londoners are like goats (more so than sheep), not kids, because of their adult and superior strength in butting.

81. Aries [the Ram of the zodiac] comes first; after him, Taurus [the Bull of the zodiac].

82. Gemini is the third sign of the zodiac.

83. I.e., at Charing Cross.

84. Bruno uses the Spanish word *gorda* here.

85. It., *Tanchi maester.* The Nolan knows no English.

86. Again.

87. A suckling-pig whose Last Will and Testament was a schoolboy's joke of long standing.

88. The nauseating custom just described is now practiced only by men of lower stature and breeding than those courtiers with whom the Nolan is about to sup.

89. This is probably a veiled allusion to the fact that the "ceremony of the cup" is intended as theological satire. See n. 90, below.

90. This burlesque is intended as a criticism of the Protestant practice of communion in two kinds, and more generally as an opening attack on what Bruno regards as the pernicious and divisive squabbles among the various Christian sects over the precise meaning of the Eucharist. He stresses the fact that enlightened gentlemen are above such quarrels. (It is also possible that the supper Bruno attended was really an Ash Wednesday communion service; internal evidence at this point indicates that the service followed the Roman Catholic custom of partaking only of the bread; this would be all the more plausible if, as Bruno later told his Inquisitors, the supper was really held at the residence of the French ambassador. Cf. Introduction, n. 43.

91. Keep in good health.

THIRD DIALOGUE

THIRD DIALOGUE

TEO. Now Doctor Nundinio, having put his person to rights, shaken his back a bit, placed both hands on the table, looked quickly all round, readied his tongue in his mouth, lifted his eyes to heaven, drawn a shadow of a smile from his teeth, and [having] spat once, started in this way:

PRU. *In haec verba, in hosce propupit sensus.*[1]

First Proposition of Nundinio

TEO. *"Intelligis, domine, quae diximus?"*[2] And he asked the Nolan if he understood English. The Nolan answered no, and he spoke truthfully.

FRU. So much the better for him; otherwise he would have heard more things disagreeable and worthless than not. There is much avail in being deaf in truth on those occasions when one would prefer to be deaf by choice. I would be easily convinced that he understands [English], although, not caring to answer the uncivil questions which the unmannerly multitude ask at every meeting, and wanting rather to philosophize about the customs of those who approach him, he pretends not to understand.[3]

PRU. *Surdorum alia natura, alii physico accidente, alii rationali voluntate.*[4]

TEO. Do not think that of him; because, even though he has

See page 165 for Notes to the Third Dialogue.

135

spent nearly a year in England,[5] he understands no more than two or three of the most commonly used words, which he knows to be greetings. But he does not know the individual meaning of any one of them; so that he would not be able to use even one of them correctly, if he wanted to.

SMI. What does it signify, that he has so little intention of learning our language?

TEO. There is nothing which obliges or inclines him to do so, as those worshipful gentlemen with whom he usually converses all know how to speak Latin, French, Spanish or Italian.[6] Knowing that English is used only on this island, they would consider themselves savages if they knew no language other than their mother-tongue.

SMI. Not being able to speak more than one language is a contemptible thing, not just for well-born Englishmen, but for every other people as well. Nevertheless, in England, as indeed in other countries (such as Italy and France, to be sure) there are many gentlemen of this sort, with whom those who do not speak the local language cannot converse without the anguish which derives from the need for interpreting.

TEO. It is true that there are still many who are gentlemen only by pedigree; it is to their advantage as well as ours that they are neither understood nor seen.

Of the Second Proposition of Nundinio

SMI. What did Doctor Nundinio say next?

TEO. "Then," he said in Latin, "I propose to interpret to you what we are saying: We must believe that Copernicus was not of the opinion that the earth moves, since this is unseemly and impossible, but that he attributed motion to it rather than to the eighth heaven, for ease in calculations."[7] The Nolan said that, if Copernicus said that the earth moves for this reason alone and no other, his understanding was very slight and insufficient. But it is certain that Copernicus meant what he said as he stated it and proved it with all his might.

SMI. Do you mean that they foolishly tossed forth such a judgment of Copernicus' opinion, which cannot be gleaned from any of his propositions?

TEO. Know that Doctor Torquato gave birth to this assertion; of all [the works] of Copernicus (although I can believe he had paged through them from cover to cover), he remembered only the names of the author, the book, and the printer, the place where it was printed, the year, and the number of quires and pages; and because he was not ignorant of grammar he understood a certain prefatory epistle which was added by I know not what ignorant and conceited ass.[8] [The latter] (as if he wanted to support the author by excusing him, or for the benefit of other asses who, finding greens and small fruit, would not put down the book without having eaten) gives this advice to them before they begin reading the book and considering its opinions:

"Since the fame of the new hypotheses of this work (according to which the earth moves and the sun stands still and fixed at the center of the universe) is already widespread, I do not doubt that some learned men" (he rightly said "some," of whom he might be one) "feel themselves very much offended, deeming this a starting-point for throwing into confusion the liberal arts, until now so well and so long set in order. But if they care to consider the matter more closely, they will find that the author [Copernicus] is not worthy of blame, since it is proper for astronomers to formulate diligently and skillfully the true order[9] of celestial motions. Since for various reasons they cannot find the true causes of the latter [motions], it is permissible to feign and fashion them as they please by [means of] geometrical principles, through which it is possible to calculate past and future motions. For this reason, these hypotheses do not need to be true or even probable.[10] Thus must the hypotheses of this man be considered, unless there be someone so ignorant of optics and geometry that he believes that the distance of forty degrees and more, which Venus attains in moving away from the sun to one side or the other, is brought about by its movement in the epicycle. Were this true, who is so blind that he cannot see that the consequences would go against all experience: that the diameter of the star [i.e., Venus] would appear four times, and its body more than 16 times[11] greater when it is closest, in the opposite of the apogee [i.e., perigee] than when it is at its farthest, and is said to be in apogee? There are still other hypotheses which are no less awkward than this, but which it is not necessary to discuss." And at the end he concludes: "Let us then assay these hypotheses only for their wonderful and inventive ease of calculation, for if someone takes them as true, he will leave this discipline more foolish than if he had never entered it."[12]

Now see what a fine doorkeeper he is! Consider how nicely he opens the door and has you enter into participation in that most honorable knowledge, without which the ability to compute and calculate and practice geometry and perspective are nothing more than pastimes for ingenious madmen. Consider how faithfully he helps his master!

For Copernicus it did not suffice just to say that the earth moves, but he also affirmed and asserted it in his dedicatory letter to the Pope.[13] In this he wrote that the opinions of philosophers are very far from those of the common mob [whose opinions] are unworthy of being followed and most worthy of being avoided, since they are contrary to truth and right thinking. And he gave many other indications of his view. Notwithstanding which, he agreed firmly with the opinion held in common by those who understand this philosophy and those who are pure mathematicians, that [even] if his hypotheses were displeasing on account of apparent drawbacks, it was proper that he [nevertheless] be conceded the liberty of supposing the motion of the earth, in order to make demonstrations more solid than those made by the ancients, just as they had been free to imagine many sorts and patterns of circles for the purpose of demonstrating the phenomena of the stars. It is impossible to gather from these words that he doubted what he had constantly asserted, and would prove in the first book, where he adequately responds to the arguments of those who hold the contrary [view], performing the task not only of a mathematician who supposes, but also of a physician[14] who demonstrates, the movement of the earth.

But in truth it signified little for the Nolan that the aforesaid [motion] had been stated, taught, and confirmed before him by Copernicus, Niceta Syracusus the Pythagorean, Philolaus, Heraclitus of Pontus, Hecphantus the Pythagorean,[15] Plato in his *Timaeus*[16] (where the author states this theory timidly and inconstantly, since he held it more by faith than by knowledge), and the divine Cusanus in the second book of his *On Learned Ignorance*,[17] and others in all sorts of first-rate discourses. For he [the Nolan] holds [the mobility of the earth] on other, more solid grounds of his own. On this basis, not by authority but through keen perception and reason, he holds it just as certain as anything else of which he can have certainty.

SMI. That's fine. But, if you please, what argument is it that that doorkeeper[18] to Copernicus brought forth—for it appears to have more than a little verisimilitude (even if it is not true)—according to which Venus should vary as much in size as it varies in distance?[19]

TEO. That idiot, who so mightily feared that one could be driven mad by the teaching of Copernicus! I cannot imagine how he could have raised more absurdities than by stating with such solemnity and persuasive conviction that those who believe that [the earth moves] are grossly ignorant of optics and geometry. I would like to know what optics and geometry that beast means, [which] show only how excessively ignorant he himself and his teachers are of true optics and geometry. I would like to know how it is possible to deduce the reckoning[20] of the propinquity and remoteness of luminous bodies from their size and, conversely, how it is possible to deduce the proportional variation of size of like bodies from their distance and propinquity. I would like to know by what principle of perspective or of optics we can definitely establish the correct distance, or the greatest and smallest difference, from any variation of diameter. I would like to know if we are wrong in concluding as follows: [that] we cannot establish the true size or distance of a luminous body from its apparent size, because just as the same rule does not apply for an opaque as for a luminous body, so the same rule does not apply for a less luminous body and a more luminous body and another very luminous body; by means of which [rule] we could judge their size or their distance. [An object] the size of a man's head cannot be seen at two miles' distance, but a much smaller lamp or some similar fiery object can be seen without much variation (though there is [some] variation) up to [a distance of] sixty miles. For example, it is often possible to see the candles of Valona[21] from Otranto in Puglie, between which lands lies the great expanse of the Ionian Sea. Anyone of good sense and reason knows that if the lamps were twice as bright, they would be seen at a distance of one hundred forty miles as they are now seen at a distance of seventy miles, without any difference in [their] size; if they were three times as luminous, [they would be seen] at [a distance of] two hundred ten miles; if four times as luminous, at two hundred eighty miles, calculating every time the same addition of proportion and degree; since maintaining the effect of the same diameter and size of a body depends more on the quality and innate strength of the light than on the size of the body.[22] Do you wish it thus, O wise opticians and experts in perspective, that if I see that a light at a distance of one hundred *stadia*[23] is four inches in diameter, the same light, at a distance of fifty *stadia*, be eight inches in diameter; at a distance of twenty-five, sixteen; at a distance of twelve and one-half, thirty-two, and so on until the light, being very near, will have whatever size you can imagine?[24]

SMI. From what you are saying it would not be possible to prove on the basis of geometrical reasoning that the opinion of Heraclitus of Ephesus is wrong (though it is), according to which the size of the sun is that which appears to our eyes;[25] Epicurus held the same theory in his *Epistle to Sophocles*,[26] and in the eleventh book of *De natura*, as Diogenes Laertius[27] mentions, he says that, so far as he can judge, the size of the sun, of the moon, and of the other stars is the same as appears to our senses, because, he says, if they lost size with distance, they would lose color[28] even more; and certainly, he says, we must not judge those luminaries in a different way than those which are close to us.

PRU. *Illud quoque epicureus Lucretius testatur quinto "De natura" libro:*[29]

> *Nec nimio solis maior rota, nec minor ardor*
> *Esse potest, nostris quam sensibus esse videtur.*
> *Nam quibus e spaciis cumque ignes lumina*
>   *possunt*
> *Adiicere et calidum membris adflare vaporem,*
> *Illa ipsa intervalla nihil de corpore libant*
> *Flammarum, nihilo ad speciem est contractior*
>   *ignis.*
> *Lunaque sive Notho fertur loca lumine lustrans,*
> *Sive suam proprio iactat de corpore lucem,*
> *Quicquid id est, nihilo fertur maiore figura.*
> *Postremo quoscumque vides hinc aetheris ignes,*
> *Dum tremor est clarus, dum cernitur ardor eorum,*
> *Scire licet perquam pauxillo posse minores*
> *Esse, vel exigua maiores parte brevique,*
> *Quandoquidem quoscumque in terris cernimus*
>   *ignes,*
> *Perparvum quiddam interdum mutare videntur*
> *Alterutram in partem filum, cum longius absint.*[30]

TEO. Certainly you are right when you say that the experts in perspective and geometry will vainly try to argue with the

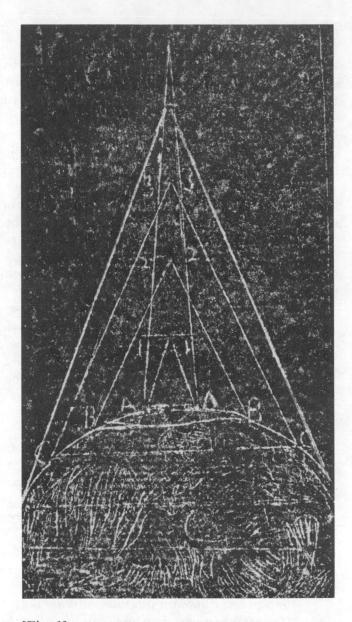

[Fig. 1]

Courtesy Bibliothèque Nationale, Paris

Epicureans using their own and ordinary principles; and I do not mean the fools, like the luminary [whose epistle graces] Copernicus' book, but also wiser men; and we will see how they can come to the conclusion that at such a distance as the diameter of the epicycle of Venus, it is possible to make rational inferences[31] from that diameter to the size of the planet, and other similar things.

I want, moreover, to tell you another thing. Do you see how large the earth is? Do you know that we can only see the portion within the artificial horizon?[32]

SMI. That is so.

TEO. Now, do you think that if you could place yourself outside the whole globe of the earth at any point whatever in the ethereal region, the earth would ever appear larger to you?

SMI. I think not: because there is no reason at all why the visual line of my sight should become stronger and extend its [the earth's] semi-diameter, which measures the diameter of the horizon.[33]

TEO. Well reasoned. We must believe, nevertheless, that the more distant the horizon becomes, the smaller it gets. But along with this decrease of the horizon, note that there is an increase in the confusion of the view of that which is beyond the already enclosed horizon,[34] as [Figure 1] shows, where the artificial horizon is 1-1, to which the arc of the globe A-A corresponds; the horizon of the first recession[35] is 2-2, to which the arc of the globe B-B corresponds; the horizon of the third recession[36] is 3-3, to which the arc C-C corresponds; the horizon of the fourth[37] recession is 4-4, to which the arc D-D corresponds. And so on, as the horizon decreases, the region subtended by the arc[38] will increase up to and beyond the line of the hemisphere.[39] At this distance, or thereabouts, we will see that the earth presents the same appearance[40] as the moon, with bright or dark parts, according to whether the surface is watery or earthy. In this way, as much as the visual angle narrows, the base of the hemispheric[41] arc likewise becomes bigger and the visible portion of the horizon appears smaller; this, nevertheless, is still called horizon even though, usually, it has only one proper meaning.[42] As we recede [from the earth], then, the region comprehended by the hemisphere, and the light, increase continually.[43] The more the diameter decreases, the more the light comes together, so that if we were farther away from the moon, its markings would be ever smaller until a small and entirely bright body would present itself to the sight.

SMI.   I think I have heard something uncommon and of no little import. But, if you please, let us consider the opinion of Heraclitus and Epicurus which, as you say, can stand firm against the laws[44] of perspective, because of the shortcomings of the principles set forth up to now in this field of knowledge.[45] Now, in order to discover these shortcomings and to see some of the fruits of your invention, I would like to hear an unraveling of the discourse by which it is very clearly proven that the sun is not only big but is even bigger than the earth. The beginning of this discourse is that a bigger luminous body which sheds its light on a smaller opaque body produces a cone of shadow whose base lies in the opaque body; the rest of the cone is produced beyond on the opposite side: As in the following figure [Figure 2], M, a bright body, projects a cone of shadow from the base C (bounded by H and I) to the point N.[46] The smaller luminous body, having formed a cone upon the larger opaque body, will not delineate a determined place where the line of its [the cone's] base can reasonably be drawn, and it appears instead that an infinite cone is formed: as in the same figure [Figure 2, where] A, the bright body, projects the two lines HD, IE from the cone of the shadow of the opaque body, C, which [lines,] since the conic shadow expands ever more and more, extend to infinity without having a limiting base. The conclusion of this discourse is that the sun is a body larger than the earth because it projects the cone of shadow of the earth near, but not beyond, the sphere of Mercury.[47] If the sun were a smaller bright body, we should decide differently; it would follow that, when that luminous body was situated in the

[Fig. 2]

Courtesy Bibliothèque Nationale, Paris

lower hemisphere[48] a greater part of our sky would be dark than bright,[49] it being assumed or conceded that all the stars derive luminosity from the sun.[50]

TEO. Now you will see how a smaller luminous body can illuminate more than half of a larger, opaque body.[51] You should reflect upon what we see through experience. Given two bodies [Figure 3], one of which is opaque and large, like A, and the other small and bright, like N;[52] if the luminous body is placed at the first, smallest distance, as you can see in the following figure [Figure 3], it will shed light along the length of the small arc CD, bounded by the line B1. If it is placed at a second, greater distance, it will be seen to illuminate [the area] within the bounds of the larger arc EF,[53] bounded by the line B2; if put at the third, even greater distance, it [the illumination] will end along the length of the bigger arc GH, delineated by the line B3. From this it follows that it is possible for the luminous body B, if it be placed at a very great distance, [and] if it have as much brightness as is required to penetrate so much space, to delineate an arc [on the surface of the sphere] which is greater than the semicircle. For there is no reason why that distance, which has so reduced the luminous body that it embraces the semicircle [i.e., the distance at which the luminous body illuminates the entire hemisphere] could not be extended further [so that it] embraces more.[54]

But I will tell you even more. Since the luminous body does not lose its diameter, [55] except very slowly and with great difficulty,[56] while the opaque body, however large it may be, loses it very easily and disproportionately, and, since with increasing distance the small chord[57] CD has become the bigger chord EF and then the largest GH[58] which is the diameter, so, as the distance increases, it will become other smaller chords beyond the diameter until the interposing body does not hinder the reciprocal view of two diametrically opposite bodies.[59] The reason for this is that the interference [with visibility] produced by the diam-

[Fig. 3]

By permission of the Houghton Library, Harvard University

147

eter decreases more and more with the diameter itself as the angle B becomes more acute. It is ultimately necessary that the angle become so acute (since they are fools who think that the physical division of a finite body can proceed infinitely and think that this actually does happen or can happen)[60] that it is no longer an angle but becomes a line along which two opposing visible bodies can be in view of each other without any intermediate point being an obstacle, since this opaque body has lost all proportion and difference in diameter, which the luminous bodies, on the contrary, retain.[61] But it is necessary only that the opaque interposing body maintain a sufficient distance from each of the other two so as to lose the said proportion and difference in its diameter. All this can be seen and observed with respect to the earth, the diameter of which does not prevent two diametrically opposed stars from viewing each other, in the same way that the eye, without any difference, can see both of them from the hemispheric center N [Figure 4] and from the points on the circumference ANO (you must think for this purpose that the earth is divided through the center into two equal parts so that any perspective line is on the locus). This is easily illustrated in the present figure [Figure 4]. Here, since the line AN is a diameter,[62] it makes a right angle with the circumference;[63] the second point[64] makes an acute angle; the third [point] a more acute [angle]; of necessity [the angle] must finally become extremely acute, and in the end [this process] will conclude so that it will no longer appear as an angle, but as a line. Consequently the relation and the difference[65] of the semi-diameter will be destroyed, and for the same reason the length[66] of the entire diameter AO will be destroyed. So it follows necessarily that two more luminous bodies, which do not lose their diameters so quickly, will not be impeded from seeing each other reciprocally, since their diameters do not disappear as does that of an opaque or less luminous interposing body.

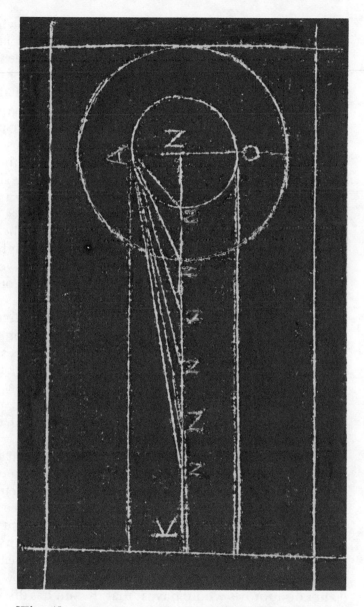

[Fig. 4]

By permission of the Houghton Library, Harvard University

We conclude the following of a larger body, which tends to lose its diameter more easily: even though placed exactly on a perfectly straight line, it will not hinder the perspective of any two bodies, however much smaller they may be, as long as they maintain the diameter of their visibility, which is lost in the larger body.[67] Now, in order to prepare a not too sophisticated mind to understand easily the argument and in order to ease as much as possible the difficulties of comprehension, you should make him do this experiment:[68] Let him put a stick near his eye; his sight will be entirely prevented from seeing the light of a candle placed at a certain distance. But, the more the stick approaches this light, being withdrawn from the eye, the less it will obstruct the view, until, being as close to the light as it originally was to the eye, it will perhaps not even obstruct the view of the light as much as the width of the stick.[69]

Now, after this, have him leave the stick in that position and put the candle at the same distance from the stick as the latter is from his eye. He will see that the stick obstructs even less. Thus, as the equal distances both of the eye and of the candle increase more and more, he will finally see only the light, without perceiving the stick. With this experiment, any fathead will be easily led to understand what has been said above.

SMI. I feel very satisfied with this argument, but I am still confused about what you said before: how we, rising from the earth and losing sight of the horizon (the diameter of which becomes narrower and narrower), come to see this body to be a star. I'd like you to add something to what you have already said since you think that there are many, or rather, innumerable earths similar to this one. I remember having seen that Cusanus,[70] of whose judgment I know you do not disapprove, would have it that the sun has dissimilar parts just as do the moon and the earth. In fact, he says that if we fixed our eyes carefully on the sun, we would see that it presents an evident opacity in the midst of its splendor, more in the circumferential zone than else-where.[71]

TEO. By him divinely said and understood, and by you quite laudably applied. If I remember rightly, I said not long ago that, since the opaque body easily loses its diameter while the luminous body loses it with difficulty, it happens that distance annuls and fades the appearance of the dark body, and [thus] the appearance of the diaphanous body which is illuminated, or bright for other reasons, becomes, so to speak, united, so that the scattered luminous parts form one visible, continuous light. For these reasons, if the moon were further distant from us, it would not eclipse the sun.[72] Everyone who knows how to think about these things will easily conclude that at a greater distance it [the moon] would be even more luminous; if we were [on the moon] it would not be more luminous to our eyes; just as we, being on the earth, do not see the light which the earth sends out to those who are on the moon, a light which is perhaps greater than that which [the moon] reflects from the rays of the sun, scattered on its liquid crystal. At present, I do not know if we should decide in the same way or otherwise, concerning the light peculiar to the sun. Now you see how far we have digressed from our subject; I think it's time to return to the other parts of our argument.

SMI. It will be useful to hear the other claims Nundinio was able to bring forth.

The Third Proposition of Doctor Nundinio

TEO. Nundinio then said that it cannot be possible that the earth moves, since it is the center and mid-point of the universe, in which it is inherent to be the fixed and constant basis of all motion. The Nolan answered that one who believes that the sun is in the middle of the universe can say the same thing and that for this reason the sun is immobile and fixed, as Copernicus and many others, who had imposed a circumferential limitation to the universe, maintained.[73] Consequently [Nundinio's] reason [for saying this] (if it is

151

a reason) is useless against them and it presupposes its own principles. It is also useless against the Nolan, who holds that the universe is infinite, whence it follows that no body can simply be in the middle of the universe or at its periphery or anywhere between these two limits except through certain relations to other nearby bodies and artificially imposed limits.[74]

SMI.   What do you think of that?

TEO.   It is most sublimely said, since of natural bodies not one is verified to be simply round and, consequently, to have a center. In the same way, of all the motions which we perceive sensibly and physically in natural bodies, there is not one which does not differ in great measure from simple circular and regular motion about some center. They can force themselves as much as they like, those who invent such stuffings and fillings as unequal orbs and diverse diameters and other plasters and recipes in order to doctor Nature, [vainly] making all kinds of efforts so that they can come to the conclusion, in the service of Master Aristotle or some other, that all motion is continuous and regular about the center. But we, who consider not fantastic shadows but the things themselves; we, who see an aerial, ethereal, spiritual, liquid body, having both motion and rest,[75] a bosom immense and infinite—which we must affirm if only because we cannot see any limit with our senses or our reason—, we know for sure that this [entity], which has been caused and initiated by an infinite cause and principle,[76] must be infinitely infinite, according to its own corporeal capacity and manner. And I am sure that neither Nundinio himself nor all those who profess to understand it could ever find a half-probable argument[77] by which [it is demonstrated] that this corporeal universe can be bounded, and consequently that the stars which are contained in its space are likewise of a finite number; and moreover that its middle and center is determined by nature.

SMI.   Now, did Nundinio add something to this? Did he bring forth some argument or possibility which implies that, first, the universe is finite; second, that it has the earth as its center; third, that this center is all in all immobile [and devoid] of local motion?

TEO. Being one of those who say what they say through faith or habit and deny what they deny because of unpopularity and novelty (as is common among those who think little and are not masters of their own rational as well as their natural actions), Nundinio stood speechless and astonished as one who had suddenly seen a new ghost. Being somewhat more discreet and less boastful and malevolent than his friend, he was silent and did not utter another word, since he could not advance any arguments.[78]

FRU. It is not so with Doctor Torquato, who always wants to fight whether [he is] wrong or right; whether for God's sake or for the Devil's; when he has lost the shield of defense and the sword of offense; when, I mean, he has neither further answer nor argument, he leaps with kicks of rage, whets the claws of slander, grits the teeth of insult, and throws open the throat of clamor, so that he prevents contrary reasons from being spoken and reaching the ears of those who are present, as I have been told.

SMI. So [Nundinio] did not say anything else?

TEO. Not about this subject, but he offered another proposition.

Fourth Proposition of Doctor Nundinio

As the Nolan had just mentioned that there are innumerable other earths similar to ours, Nundinio, who had nothing to say to this point, but wanted to argue, began to ask questions off the subject. They were discussing the mobility and immobility of this globe, and he digressed to ask about the nature of other globes, and wanted to know of what substance those bodies were made, which are believed to consist of quintessence, that is of an unalterable and incorruptible material, the most dense parts of which are the stars.

FRU. These questions seem to me beside the point, even though I don't understand much about logic.

TEO. The Nolan, being kindly, didn't reproach him for this, but, having told him that he would have liked Nundinio to continue to discuss the main subject or to ask questions about it, he answered that the other globes, which are earths, are not at all different from this one in kind; but [differ] only in being bigger and smaller, [just] as inequality occurs in any other species of animals through individual differences. At present he thought that those spheres which are fire, such as the sun, are different in kind, in the same way as heat and cold, intrinsic brightness and induced brightness.[79]

SMI. Why did he say that he thought so, instead of affirming it absolutely?

TEO. Because he feared that Nundinio would once more digress from the question which he himself had just seized, and would grasp and glue himself to [the digression]. I grant that, since the earth is an animal and consequently a heterogeneous body, it must be a cold body in those parts (mostly external) which are ventilated by air; in other parts (which are greater in number and size) it must be warm and hot. I grant also that, arguing in part on the basis of the principles of the adversary, who wishes to be considered and professes to be a Peripatetic, and in part on the basis of my own principles which are not [merely] granted but proved, the earth in some senses[80] would become as hot as the sun.

SMI. How is that?

TEO. Because, from what we have said before, due to the disappearance of the dark and opaque spots of the globe and from the union of the crystalline and bright parts, more and more light diffuses out to the farthest regions. Now, Aristotle and many others affirm that light is the cause of heat. They hold, moreover, that the moon and other stars are more or less hot depending on how bright they are, so that when some planets are called cold, they mean it to be understood only in a certain comparison and relation. [If, then, light is the cause of heat,] the earth, because of the rays it sends to the remote parts of the ethereal region, necessarily communicates the power of its heat as much as the power of its light. But we do not believe that a thing is hot just because it is bright, since we see around us many things which are bright but not hot.

Coming back to Nundinio, at this point he started to show his teeth, gape his jaws, squint his eyes, wrinkle his eyebrows, flare his nostrils and utter a capon's crow from his windpipe, in order to make the people present understand by that laughter that he understood well, that he was right while the other was saying ridiculous things.

FRU. Is not the truth of what the Nolan said proven by the fact that Nundinio laughed at it so much?

TEO. Thus it is with him who gives sweets to swine. Asked why he was laughing, [Nundinio] replied that the statement and fancy that there were other earths with the same properties and appearances[81] had been taken from the *True Tales* of Lucian.[82]

The Nolan said that if Lucian, stating that the moon was another planet just as inhabited and cultivated as this one, wished to mock those philosophers who say that there are many worlds (and particularly the moon, whose resemblance to this our globe is the most noticeable, since it is the nearest to us), he had no reason to do so, but showed that he shared in the common ignorance and blindness. For, if we reflect, we will find that the earth and many other bodies, which are called stars and are the principal members of the universe, inasmuch as they give life and nourishment to the things which derive their substance from them and likewise give it back to them, they [the stars] must all the more so have life in themselves. By means of this life, they move according to an intrinsic principle toward the things and through the spaces appropriate to them, with an ordered and natural will. And there are no other extrinsic movers which, by moving imaginary spheres, transport these bodies as if they were nailed to them. In fact, if this were the case, the motion would be violent[83] and outside the nature of the mover; the mover would be more imperfect [than the moved] and both the mover and the motion

THE ASH WEDNESDAY SUPPER

[would be] labored and toilsome; many other drawbacks, moreover, could be added. Consider, then, that as the male moves to the female and the female to the male, so every herb and animal moves, more or less purposefully, to its vital principle—that is, to the sun and other stars; the magnet moves to the iron, the straw to the amber,[84] and, in sum, everything seeks its like and flees its opposite. Everything is caused by the sufficient interior principle by which it is naturally stirred, and not by an external principle, as we observe occurring to those things which are moved contrary to or outside their own nature. Thus the earth and the other stars move according to the peculiar local differences of their intrinsic principle, which is their own soul. "Do you think," asked Nundinio, "that this soul is sensitive?" "Not only sensitive," answered the Nolan, "but also intellective, and not only intellective as our souls, but perhaps even more so."[85] At this point Nundinio kept quiet and did not laugh.

PRU. It seems to me that the earth, being animated, must be displeased when we dig caves and grottoes in its back, just as we feel pain and displeasure when our teeth are extracted or our flesh is pierced.

TEO. Nundinio did not have enough Prudence to think this argument worthy of being advanced, although it had occurred to him. In fact, he was not so ignorant a philosopher that he couldn't understand that, even if the earth has sensibility, it is not a sensibility similar to ours; if it has limbs, they are not similar to ours; if it has flesh, blood, bones and veins, they are not like ours; if it has a heart, it is not similar to ours; and so on for all the other parts which are equivalent to the parts of all others which we call animals and usually consider to be the only animals. Nundinio is not such a good Prudence and such a bad physician[86] that he does not know that to the great mass of the earth these are entirely imperceptible occurrences which are so easily felt by our feebleness. I take it as understood that not otherwise than in animals which we recognize as such, its parts are always in continuous altera-

156

tion and movement and have a certain ebb and flow, always absorbing something from the exterior and emanating something from the interior: just as the nails grow, the fur, wool and hair feed, skins mend and hides harden; so, in the same way, the earth receives the efflux and influx of the parts through which many living beings (manifest to us as such) show us their life in a different way. Thus it is more than plausible that, since everything participates in life, many and innumerable beings live not only within us but also in all composite things; and when we see something which is said to die, we must not believe that that thing dies but rather that it changes and terminates its accidental composition and unity, since the things which we see incurring death always remain immortal. This is even more true of the so-called spiritual entities than of the so-called material and corporeal ones, as we will show some other time.

Now, coming back to the Nolan, when he saw that Nundinio was quiet, he took timely revenge for the nundinial[87] derision with which Nundinio had compared his positions with the *True Tales* of Lucian. He expressed his rancor a little, telling him that, in an honest discussion, he ought not to have laughed at and mocked what he was not able to understand. "Because," said the Nolan, "as I do not laugh at your fantasies, you should not laugh at my wise sayings; and if I dispute with you politely and respectfully, you should do likewise at least as much to me, whom you know to be of such skill that, if I wanted to defend the stories of Lucian as true, you would not be able to destroy them." And in this way he responded with some anger to the other's laughter, after having replied reasonably to the question.

Fifth Proposition of Nundinio

Since the Nolan and all the others urged Nundinio to

157

formulate some proposition, instead of asking questions about why, how, and which . . .

PRU. *Per quomodo et quare quilibet asinus novit disputare.*[88]

TEO. . . . at the end, he asked something which every pamphlet is full of, that is: if it were true that the earth moves toward the part we call the Orient, it would be necessary that the clouds of the air appear always to rush toward the Occident on account of the very swift and speedy motion of the globe, which in the space of twenty-four hours must complete so great a circle. To this the Nolan replied that the air, through which the clouds and the winds fly, is part of the earth, because by "earth" he meant (as it must be) the whole complex,[89] the whole entire living creature[90] formed from its unlike parts. Hence the rivers, the stones, the seas, all the vaporous and turbulent air enclosed by the highest mountains, belong to the earth as its own limbs; moreover, they are like the air in the lungs and other cavities of living creatures, with which they breathe and dilate their arteries and perform all the other functions necessary to life. The clouds thus move according to the circumstances inside the body of the earth,[91] and belong, as do the waters, to its bowels. This was understood by Aristotle, who says, in the first book of the *Meteora*, "Above the air which encircles the earth, humid and warm because of the exhalations from it, there is another air, hot and dry, in which there are no clouds. This air lies outside the circumference of the earth and that surface which defines it, in order to render it perfectly round. The generation of the winds takes place only in the bowels and parts of the earth"; but above the high[est] mountains neither clouds nor winds appear, and there "the air moves in regular circles,"[92] as does the entire body [of the earth]. Probably Plato meant the same thing when he said that we live in the hollows and dark parts of the earth and that the same relation exists between us and the creatures who live above the earth, as between fish and us who live in a thicker humidity.[93] He means that this vaporous air is in some sense water, and the pure air, which contains happier living creatures, is above the earth, so that this air of ours appears water to them in the same way that Amphitrite [the Ocean] is water to us. So we can respond to the argument proposed by Nundinio in this way: the sea is not on the surface but in the bowels of the earth, just as the liver, source of the humors, is inside ourselves; the turbulent air is not outside but within, as in the lungs of living creatures.

SMI. But how can it be that we see the whole hemisphere [of the sky], if we live in the bowels of the earth?

TEO. Due to the mass of the globular earth—not only on the upper surface but also on the interior surfaces—it happens that if one views the horizon, one convexity gives place to another; so that there cannot be any obstacle of the sort that we see when a mountain interposes between our eyes and a stretch of sky, hindering the perfect sight of the circle of the horizon because of its nearness to us. The distance, then, of these mountains which follow the convexity of the earth, which [latter] is not flat but round, is such that we are not sensible of being in the bowels of the earth; as we can see in the present figure [Figure 5]: the true surface of the earth is ABC, within which surface there are many particular [ones] of the sea and others of continents, as for example M; from this point we see the whole hemisphere no less than from a point A or from other points on the uppermost surface. The explanation of this is twofold: because of the great size of the earth, and because of the convexity of its circumference. Thus from point M one is not so much hindered that he cannot see the [whole] hemisphere, because the highest mountains do not interpose at point M, as the line MB (as I believe would happen if the surface of the earth were flat). But the lines MC, MD do not cause any obstacle, as can be seen, because of the circumferential arc. We must note, moreover, that as M relates to C and to D, so also K relates to M. Consequently, we should not consider what Plato said about the very large hollows and gulfs of the earth to be a fable.[94]

[Fig. 5]

By permission of the Houghton Library, Harvard University

160

SMI. I would like to know whether those who are near the highest mountains suffer from this hindrance.

TEO. Only those who are near the lesser mountains; because the mountains are not very high unless they are at the same time very large in proportion, so that their size is not noticeable to our sight. In this manner these mountains come, together with the former, to comprehend more and many artificial horizons[95] within which the circumstances[96] present in some cannot alter the others.[97] However, by the "highest mountains" we do not mean such [mountains] as the Alps, the Pyrenees and similar mountain ranges, but the whole of France, which extends between two seas, the northern Ocean and the southern Mediterranean; from which it rises more and more toward the Auvergne as well as from the Alps and Pyrenees, which were once the tops of a very high mountain. This mountain, being entirely shattered by time (which produces others in other parts through the vicissitudes of the renewal of the parts of the earth), formed many individual so-called mountains.[98] But, as for a certain instance which Nundinio produced concerning the mountains of Scotland,[99] where he has perhaps been,[100] it showed that he could not understand what is meant by highest mountains. For truly, the whole of this island of Britain is a mountain raising its head above the waves of the Ocean Sea, and the most eminent point in this island should be taken as the summit of this mountain. If this summit reaches the tranquil zone of air, it proves that this is one of those highest mountains and is perhaps in the region of the happiest living creatures. Alexander of Aphrodisias[101] argues that Mount Olympus displays, in the ashes of the sacrifices, the condition both of a very high mountain and of the air lying above the extremes and limbs of the earth.[102]

SMI. You have satisfied me most ably and you have opened wide to me many secrets of nature which are hidden under this key. In replying to the argument derived from the winds and the clouds, you also answered that question raised by

161

Aristotle in the second book of *De caelo et mundo:*[103] There he says that it would be impossible that a stone, which has been thrown high into the sky, could fall down along the same perpendicular straight line. Instead, it would be necessary that the stone be left far behind, toward the West, because of the very rapid motion of the earth. But in fact, since this throwing of the stone occurs inside the earth, it necessarily follows that any relation of verticality and obliquity changes according to the motion of the earth. There is, in the same manner, a difference between the motion of a ship and that of the things inside the ship because, if this were not true, when the ship is moving across the sea, no one could carry anything along a straight line from one side of the ship to the other, and it would not be possible to jump and come down with one's feet in the same place as before.

[TEO.] [104] Thus, everything which is in the earth moves with it. If from a place outside the earth something were thrown at it, it would lose the verticality [of its motion] because of the motion of the earth. If someone standing at point C on the bank of a river throws a stone straight at a ship, AB[105] [Figure 6] passing by on the river, he will miss hitting it by as much as the space determined by the speed of the current.[106] But if someone stands on the mast of the said ship which is moving at whatever speed, he will not miss at all, throwing the stone or another heavy thing along a straight line from point E, which is at the masthead, or in the crow's nest, to point D which is at the foot of the mast or at another part of the hold and body of the said ship. So if someone, who is inside the ship, throws a stone perpendicularly from point D to point E, the stone will fall downwards along the same line, however the boat may move, as long as it does not pitch.

SMI. Considering this difference, we open the door to many very important secrets of Nature and of profound philosophy, since it is a matter more common and less inquired into

[Fig. 6]

By permission of the Houghton Library, Harvard University

than the difference between one who has doctored himself and one who has been doctored by someone else. It is evident that we take greater pleasure and enjoyment in eating with our own hands, than in being fed by the arms of others. When children are able to use their own spoons for picking up their food, they are not willingly fed by others, as if Nature in some way has made them learn that there is not so much pleasure and profit in it. But do you see how nursing babies hang with their hands from the breast? I have never found a robbery more frightening than when it has been committed by a domestic servant: I do not know why a familiar person bears in himself more shadow and portent than a stranger, as if he bore a kind of bad omen and dreadful presage.

TEO. Now, returning to our subject: If there are two persons, one inside the moving ship and the other outside it, and both of them, having raised their hands to nearly the same point in the air, let stones fall from the same place at the same time without applying any thrust,[107] the first person's stone will reach a predetermined point without any deviation from its line, while that of the second person will be left behind. This results from nothing other than that the stone which falls from the hand of the person in the ship and which, as a result, moves with the ship's motion, has such an impressed force[108] as is not possessed by the other, which proceeds from the hand of the person outside the ship; although the stones have the same weight, pass through the same air, and start (assuming it possible) from the same point and bear the same thrust. For this difference we can adduce no other reason than that things which are fixed to or in like manner belong to the ship move with it, and that one stone carries with it the motive force which moves it with the ship, while the other does not partake of it.[109] From this it can be clearly seen that it is not by the point from which the motion starts, nor by the point to which it is directed, nor by the medium through which it moves, but by the efficacy of the first impressed force that it acquires the virtue[110] of rectilinear motion, on which all differences depend. I think we have sufficiently considered the propositions of Nundinio.[111]

SMI. We will return tomorrow, in order to hear the arguments proposed by Torquato.

FRU. *Fiat.*[112]

END OF THE THIRD DIALOGUE

Notes to the Third Dialogue

1. Into these words, into these sentences he burst.

2. Do you understand, milord, what we have said?

3. It is curious that Frulla suggests that Bruno may have understood English since, in the Second Dialogue (p. 113), Bruno had to have the boatmen's words translated for him. It may be that Bruno intended Frulla's question as a device to introduce the commentary which follows.

4. Some are deaf from natural defect, some through accident, some by personal choice.

5. Bruno arrived in England in the spring of 1583, perhaps in April and certainly by June.

6. On the knowledge of Italian in England in the sixteenth century, see L. Einstein, *The Italian Renaissance in England* (New York, 1902), pp. 97-107 & passim.

7. The erroneous belief that Copernicus had proposed the motion of the earth only as a mathematical scheme, and not as a physical reality, was due to the spurious preface written by Andreas Osiander, a Protestant theologian. See n. 8 below.

8. The prefatory epistle to Copernicus' *De revolutionibus* is anonymous, but it was actually written by Andreas Osiander, to whom Copernicus had given the task of supervising the first edition (1543) of his book, and included in the book without Copernicus' knowledge. Osiander tried to disguise the true purpose of *De revolutionibus* by saying that all it purports to do is to "save the phenomena." Bruno appears to have been the first to point out that the preface did not reflect Copernicus' own beliefs. Kepler was probably the first to realize that it was Osiander who had written the *"Ad lectorem, De hypothesibus huius*

operis." Cf. Edward Rosen, *Three Copernican Treatises* (New York, 1959), pp. 23-25, where Osiander's preface is translated.

9. It., [*h*]*istoria*. Florio gives, *inter alia*, "a declaration of true things in order set downe."

10. Having, in fact, only the function of mathematical economy, the hypothesis need not correspond to the actuality of the movements, but only to their measurability.

11. The correct areal ratio is closer to 14.

12. This passage is almost literally translated by Bruno from Osiander's preface.

13. Pope Paul III.

14. It., *fisico*, meaning one who understands or teaches the causes of natural things, a physician. The modern word "physicist" has a connotation different enough to lead to misunderstanding of the enterprise of natural philosophy in the Renaissance. In particular the macrocosm of the external physical world (the domain of the modern physicist) and the microcosm man (the shared domain of the modern physician) were seen as indissolubly linked, in a manner which has found no place in modern natural science.

15. Niceta [Hicetas] Syracusus is mentioned by Copernicus (*De rev.* I, v); he may have been the teacher of Hecphantus. Those labelled "Pythagorean" belonged to the Pythagorean school, as did Philolaus. Heraclitus Ponticus was a pupil of Plato and Seusippus, and afterwards of Aristotle. (These others are also mentioned by Copernicus, *loc. cit.*)

16. *Timaeus* 40 B & C.

17. Nicolaus Cusanus, *De docta ignorantia*, 11 & 12.

18. It., *superliminario*.

19. Here Bruno has misinterpreted Osiander in a way which is about to get him into logical trouble. Osiander has argued that the Copernican system necessitates a variation in the distance between Venus and the Earth, and therefore a variation in the apparent diameter of Venus. This variation does indeed take place; however, the disk of Venus cannot be resolved by the naked eye and the variation cannot be perceived without a telescope. However, in what follows Bruno seems to have inferred that Osiander's remarks apply to the apparent brightness of Venus as well as to its apparent diameter. In any case, he consistently confuses the two things. In the lengthy (and totally erroneous) argument immediately following he "proves" that a variation in distance will *not* result in a significant variation in apparent brightness. What Bruno seems not to have known is that the variation in the apparent brightness of Venus *is* perceptible to the naked eye, and had been known to astronomers from antiquity.

To compound the irony of the whole matter, the Ptolemaic system also predicts a variation in the apparent brightness of Venus—a point which Osiander seems to have missed, and which surely never occurred to Bruno.

20. It., *raggione:* "reason" or "law of nature," or "effect" or "argument."

21. A port city on the Adriatic coast of present-day Albania.

22. Bruno here confuses total brightness, brightness per unit area, and apparent size. His calculation is in error, moreover, since the apparent brightness of a light depends not inversely on the distance, but inversely on the square

of the distance. He seems to imply, furthermore, that the precise law relating apparent brightness to distance depends on the intrinsic brightness itself, which is inconsistent with his arithmetic calculations.

23. A Greek road measure of about 600 feet.

24. This argument is based on a confusion kindred to that discussed in n. 22, above. By confusing actual diameter with apparent angular diameter, Bruno reaches an absurdity. In actuality, of course, it is the angle subtended by an object which increases as it approaches the observer, and not its size.

25. H. Diels, *Die Fragmente der Vorsokratiker, sub. nom.* Heraclitus, fragments 3-4.

26. The passage Bruno refers to is actually in the *Epistle to Pitocles.*

27. Diogenes Laertius is one of the most important sources for information about the lives and teachings of the ancient philosophers; their works would largely be unknown save for the fragments compiled by Diogenes Laertius (A.D. third century) in his *Lives, Opinions and Sayings of Famous Philosophers.* (Cf. for Bruno's discussion here, vol. X, 91.)

28. It., *color*; the meaning of this is unclear, unless by *color* Bruno means "brightness" or "intensity."

29. This is also asserted by Lucretius the Epicurean in the fifth book of *On the Nature of Things.*

30. Lucretius, *De rerum natura* V, 564-590: And the disc of the sun cannot be much larger and its brilliance much less than what appears to our senses. In fact, however wide be the spaces through which its fires send their splendor and breathe their heat to our limbs, the enormous distance does not at all diminish the amount of flame or the brightness of the light. And the moon is not larger than it appears, whether it shines through the sky with reflected light or with its own light. Finally, all the stars that we see from the earth sparkling clearly and distinctly in the sky, can be only a little larger or smaller than they appear since, as on the earth, fires diminish or grow very little according to the distance.

31. It., *inferir raggione.*

32. It., *orizonte artificiale.* Very likely Bruno means here what John Dee (*Propaedeumata Aphoristica,* 1568) calls the "sensible horizon." This is what we ordinarily mean by the horizon. Dee distinguishes this from a "true horizon," by which he means the plane containing the great circle normal to the radius vector of the observer. Dee imputes much astrological significance to the fact that the rising and setting times of stars across these two "horizons" are not precisely the same. See also p. 161. We are indebted to Professors Wayne Schumaker and John Heilbron for allowing one of us (L.S.L.) to read their annotated translation of the Dee work prior to its publication.

33. The meaning of this passage is unclear.

34. The meaning intended here is probably: "As the apparent size of the visible part of the earth decreases [with the recession of the observer], the newly visible zone of the earth is seen less distinctly [than what was seen at a lesser distance]."

35. It., *diminuzione,* lit., "diminution." We have used "recession" to clarify the argument.

36. Bruno has lost count. He means, of course, the second recession, corresponding to the third point.

37. Bruno is still confused. Here he means the third recession, corresponding to the fourth point. The points 4-4 and D-D are not labeled on the diagram, but it is clear where the labels should be. It is possible that in omitting them, Bruno is implying that they may lie at infinity. Cf. n. 56, Dial. 4, for a discussion of Bruno's use of diagrams.

38. It., *la comprehensione de l'arco.*

39. This argument is confused, and the conclusion is obviously wrong, geometrically speaking. The points 1-1, 2-2, etc., have no meaning at all, being the intersections of the plane projections of two arbitrarily drawn cones, neither of which is tangent to the sphere. From the point of view of a given observer, the horizon must of course be constructed by drawing from his eye those lines which are tangent to the circle representing the earth. It is true that the horizon recedes and encloses more area as the observer's height increases; it can never be true, however, that the horizon will comprehend more than a hemisphere, as Teofilo asserts.

It appears that Bruno may be trying to point out the fact that, from the point of view of an ascending observer, the earth initially fills the visual field completely, but ultimately, at a sufficient altitude, ceases to do so. The narrow unlabeled angle ending at A-A may be intended to delimit the field of vision which, however, is not independent of the observer's altitude.

40. It., *accidenti.*

41. What Bruno calls a hemisphere is in fact a sector.

42. See n. 32.

43. Bruno appears to be arguing that the visible area increases even though its apparent diameter (i.e., the visual angle it subtends) decreases. But since a distant observer sees more of the earth, and since its brightness is independent of distance, the earth appears brighter at a distance.

44. It., *raggioni perspettive.*

45. It., *scienza.*

46. The symbols in the text do not correspond correctly with those in the figure. In order to make sense of the argument, we must substitute the proper symbols and add two. Let X and Y be respectively the points of tangency of the lines HI and FI with the circle C. Assume also (as seems to have been intended in the figure) that the flames emanating from the luminous body A extend as far as the points H and F. The following essentially correct argument is then obtained: " . . . A, a bright body, projects a cone of shadow from the base C (bounded by X and Y) to the point I. The smaller luminous body, having formed a cone upon the larger opaque body, will not delineate a determined place where the line of its [the cone's] base can reasonably be drawn, and it appears instead that an infinite cone is formed: as in the same figure [where] B, the bright body, projects the two lines BD, BE from the cone of the shadow of the opaque body, C, which, ever more and more expanding the conic shadow, extends to infinity without having a limiting base. . . . "

This is not the only figure in which the symbols do not correspond to those in the text. It is possible that this inconsistency may have been due to the habit of sixteenth-century printers (in this case, John Charlewood) of employing the same woodblocks in different publications (cf. F. A. Yates, "The Emblematic

Conceit in Giordano Bruno's *De gli eroici furori* and in the Elizabethan Sonnet Sequences," *Journal of the Warburg and Courtauld Institutes*, VI [1943], p. 110). However, it is known that Bruno often did cut the diagrams in his works with his own hand (Yates, *GB&HT*, p. 320). This may be the case for the diagrams in the *Cena;* even the most sophisticated diagram (that of the ship, Figure 6) was probably cut by Bruno himself (we are indebted to Professor Yates for this information).

There is, moreover, good reason to believe that the lack of correspondence in the symbols was by no means accidental. For a discussion of Bruno's reasons for doing this, see the Introduction, pp. 44ff. and 51-2.

47. It is indeed true that the convergent point of the umbra of the earth is closer to the earth than the distance of closest approach of Mercury. If, however, Bruno wished to clinch his argument with the observation that the earth's shadow never eclipses Mercury, and that the earth's umbra must therefore converge, he would be in difficulty, since the earth can never be between Mercury and the sun. This fact is reflected in both the Copernican and Ptolemaic models. Thus, Bruno's argument is logically sound but fails for lack of experimental proof. It also shows a lack of attention to the details of astronomy, since the same objection does not apply to a similar argument using Mars instead of Mercury. But this would still not suffice to prove that the sun is larger than the earth, except with extended observation and detailed analysis. The orbital planes of the earth and Mars are sufficiently different that only very rarely do the sun, earth, and Mars lie on a straight line.

48. I.e., below the horizon.

49. That is, by the cone of DBE. Bruno argues that, if the sun were smaller than the earth, the umbral cone would diverge. If the stars are illuminated by the sun we would see many of them darken as a result.

50. We will see later that Bruno argues that the relation is reciprocal, with all the heavenly bodies interchanging light. For Bruno, this interchange is essential, for philosophical reasons, to the vitality of the universe.

51. Here again, the argument does not make sense if taken literally. See the discussion in the Introduction, pp. 43-4 and n. 63, of the metaphorical meaning intended by Bruno.

52. Here the symbols A and N do not seem to refer to anything in particular. In what follows the notational discrepancies between the text and the figure are not sufficiently great to make the argument obscure. Note that Bl, B2, etc., in the corresponding text refer to increasingly distant points b in the figure.

53. It., *verrà ad illuminare secondo la raggione de l'arco maggiore E F*, . . .

54. Bruno argues that, as the luminous point recedes beyond a certain distance from the opaque body it comes to illuminate not only the entire hemisphere facing the light, but some (and eventually all) of the opposite hemisphere. The meaning of this conclusion must be sought in metaphysical terms.

Bruno really means not "delineate an arc bigger than a semicircle," but "illuminate more than a hemisphere."

55. See n. 24, above.

56. See above, pp. 139 ff.

57. Actually, Bruno means an arc. He has apparently forgotten that the plane drawing of Figure 3 is intended to represent a three-dimensional figure.

58. IK is actually the diameter.

59. This remark, puzzling by itself, foreshadows a more complete argument which Bruno makes immediately. He is arguing here that the effective diameter of the opaque body, for purposes of casting shadow, is the chord connecting the tangents to the opaque body from the points b, which bound the illuminated portion of the opaque body. Since the length of this chord diminishes to zero as the opaque body comes to be completely illuminated (as Bruno has just argued must happen at sufficiently large distances), the effectiveness of the opaque body for casting shadow vanishes when the luminous body is infinitely distant, or perhaps very distant.

60. Bruno here (as elsewhere) makes a distinction between mathematical and physical operations. While he might or might not have been willing to grant that there is no smallest non-zero number, he is explicitly denying the analogous possibility for physical bodies.

61. Here again Bruno confuses diameter and angular diameter. The confusion is, however, no longer essential to his argument, since he has already used it to the extent necessary, in shrinking the opaque body to a point.

62. Actually, it is a radius.

63. Bruno apparently means that AN makes a right angle with the tangent extending to the left from A.

64. I.e., the next point N to the left in the diagram.

65. It., *la relazione e la differenza*; by these terms Bruno means angular magnitude, which (as we have seen) he consistently confuses with absolute magnitude.

66. It., *differenza*.

67. It is risky here as elsewhere to infer what Bruno "really means" or to impute specific motivations to Bruno in his setting forth of geometric or physical arguments, since his thinking is so confused in such matters. It is nevertheless possible that Bruno, besides arguing that every luminous body in the universe can exchange light with every other one without obstruction by intervening bodies, is here trying to make a virtue of a major objection to the Copernican theory: the absence of stellar parallax. Having reiterated that what follows must be taken with extreme caution, let us "reconstruct" Bruno's intentions.

In Figure 4, the two lines extending to the left from A and O, and the line NK, are parallel. If we assume that they represent lines of sight to a distant star from three points on the earth, it may be that Bruno attributes their parallelism to the fact that the earth has actually shrunk to a point (i.e., the three lines are actually one and the same) rather than considering the parallelism to be a limiting case for the convergence of the three lines, when the distance to the star is increased without limit. Given Bruno's evident lack of sophistication in geometry, he could not possibly have reasoned clearly along these lines. However, he was almost certainly familiar (at least in a casual way) with the works of persons—notably Thomas Digges—who were entirely capable of such reasoning. (Though the theory of limits was not made rigorous until the eighteenth century, its basic elements had been present in the works of Archimedes.) Thus Bruno may feel that he is not only paraphrasing but improving on the arguments of other Copernicans. Such an "improvement" is important to Bruno's essential, nonphysical discussion; if our "reconstruction" is correct, Bruno is using the observed absence of stellar parallax to substantiate his "geometrical" argument on the shrinking of opaque bodies. The latter, transformed into a theological metaphor, is central in what follows.

68. This statement expresses explicitly in the small a central issue in the *Ash Wednesday Supper*. For Bruno, the purpose of experiment is merely heuristic and at best supportive of the really sound arguments which can be made from first principles. In holding this view, Bruno was hardly unique. However, it is worth noting that the same point of view permeates the work in a much larger sense. For the "experiment" described here is intended to bear the same relation to the pseudo-geometric argument Bruno has just made, as Copernicus' entire work bears to Bruno's. That is, the Copernican system is a heuristic "key" to prepare the mind for the much more difficult, though more rewarding, task of reaching far deeper conclusions on the basis of much sounder *a priori* arguments. Once the mind has comprehended the latter, of course, the importance of the former is much diminished. (Bruno has obviously not performed the experiment, though at least one of his modern commentators states that his conclusion is essentially correct!)

69. According to Bruno's preceding argument, the stick should obstruct the view the least when it is halfway between the eye and the candle and not when it is near the candle where, by symmetry, it should obstruct the view as much as when it is near the eye. Bruno does not note the inconsistency of this argument with that which follows in the next paragraph.

70. Nicolaus of Cusa (Nicolaus Cusanus).

71. In *De docta ignorantia* (in *Opera* I, 39), Cusanus says that the sun is not a homogeneous mass of fire but, rather, that it has a central solid terrestrial nucleus, then a medial bark of aqueous nature, and a shining crust of fire. In the same way, the heterogeneous masses of celestial bodies, such as the earth, can have the appearance of suns, since, as he explains later on, the brightness of the surface overcomes and annuls the central darkness.

If one glances at the sun (a risky procedure), the illusion is sometimes present that the rim is brighter than the inner part. If, however, the sun rotates on its axis, as Bruno later maintains, the bright part could not always be at the rim.

72. Bruno is confused again. This statement follows from his preceding argument but not from the present one.

73. The heliocentric system of Copernicus does not necessarily imply the doctrine of the infinite universe. Copernicus certainly did not assert that the universe is infinite; before Bruno, we know of only one man who proclaimed the reality of the infinite universe: Thomas Digges (see Introduction, pp. 25, 26).

74. Since the universe is infinite, any point can be chosen as the center. This theory is explained in Bruno's *De immenso* III, 2. This teaching was also found in the works of Nicolaus Cusanus; cf. Ernst Cassirer, *The Individual and the Cosmos in Renaissance Philosophy* (Philadelphia, 1972), passim; and

Alexandre Koyré, *From the Closed World to the Infinite Universe* (Baltimore, 1968).

75. It., *capace loco di moto e di quiete*.

76. A subtle play on words is lost in translation. In Italian, *principiate* = initiated (or begun); *principio* = principle.

77. It., *raggione*.

78. It., *raggioni*.

79. It., *lucido per sè e lucido per altro*.

80. It., *comparazione*.

81. It., *accidenti*.

82. I.e., the *Vera historia* of Lucian. Bruno's reference is to Book I. Contrary to the title *(True History)*, Lucian himself says that his book contains many idle stories. Lucian (125-192 A.D.) was a Greek wit and satirist whose works, usually in dialogue form, mocked and railed against traditions and prejudices; he was widely admired and imitated during the Renaissance by the Humanists (especially by Erasmus).

83. Aristotle and his followers divided motion into natural motion, which bodies possess by their nature, and violent motion, which is imposed externally, as when a horse pulls a cart. See the Introduction, pp. 29 ff., for a discussion of Aristotle's physics.

84. This effect is an example of electrostatic attraction.

85. St. Thomas Aquinas defined three kinds of soul: vegetative, sensitive, and intellective. The first inheres in all living things; the first and second in animals; and all three in man.

86. It., *medico*.

87. I.e., noisy, chattering.

88. With "how" and "why" any ass can dispute.

89. It., *machina*.

90. Here and elsewhere, we have followed Florio in translating *animale* as "living creature" rather than "animal." The latter has special connotations in modern English not intended by Bruno.

91. It., *Le nuvole dunque da gli accidenti, che son nel corpo de la terra, si muoveno. . . .*

92. A somewhat free version of Aristotle, *Meteorologicorum* I, 3, 15-17.

93. I.e., thicker than that of the creatures who live above the earth. Plato, *Phaedo* 109 B-E.

94. No attempt should be made to interpret this pseudogeometric argument literally.

95. See above, n. 32.

96. It., *accidenti;* it is not clear what Bruno precisely means by this word here.

97. The meaning of this passage is obscure. What follows, however, has an important meaning for Bruno (see Introduction, pp. 46-8).

98. Bruno uses the words *montagna* and *monte*, apparently interchangeably: *forma tante montagne particolari le quale noi chiamiamo monti*.

99. No such mention is made. Perhaps Bruno is referring to a passage which he later edited out. Cf. F. A. Yates, "The Religious Policy of G. B.,"

Journal of the Warburg and Courtauld Institutes, III, 3-4 (1940), p. 203: referring to this allusion, she says, "In the year in which the *Cena* was written the Puritans at Oxford were encouraged to go forward in their designs by certain 'Scotch ministers.'"

100. Bruno seems to indicate that Nundinio may have been one of those Oxford professors who had close contacts with Scottish Calvinists (see n. 99, above).

101. Alexander of Aphrodisias was the greatest of the ancient Aristotelian commentators. He lived about A.D. 200, and he influenced the ancient Neoplatonist Plotinus, thus introducing a sizeable Aristotelian element into the Platonist tradition.

102. This legend derives from the pseudo-Aristotelian *Problemata* (XXVI, 39); Bruno wrongly attributes it to Alexander of Aphrodisias. According to the legend, someone, having written in the ashes of the sacrifices offered on the summit of Mount Olympus, returned there the next year and found that the inscription in the ashes was intact, a sign of the perpetual calm appropriate to that high region.

Bruno contradicts himself, as he has previously argued that what we perceive as high mountains are not in fact high enough to reach the upper air. (Mount Olympus, of course, is by no means the highest of even the "ordinary" mountains in Europe, let alone the world.)

103. Aristotle, *De caelo et mundo* II, 14, 296 B 23.

104. The Gentile edition of the *Cena* does not change speakers here; Smith continues. However, the editions by Aquilecchia (Turin, 1955 and Florence, 1972) have Teofilo speak at this point. We have followed the later editions, as we agree that this best follows the dialectic of the discussion.

105. There are no letters in the figure. See n. 46, above, and the Introduction, pp. 44-6.

106. It., *corso.* Bruno here implies, contrary to what is shown in Fig. 6, that the ship is drifting with the current.

107. It., *spinta.*

108. It., *virtù impressa.*

109. An equally acceptable translation of this passage, with slightly different meaning, is as follows: " . . . and that one stone carries with it the force of the mover [i.e., the first person] who is moving with the ship, the other [stone] that [the force] of the person who is not." It., . . . *e la una pietra porta seco la virtù del motore il quale si muove con la nave, l'altra di quello che non ha detta participazione.*

110. It., *virtù.*

111. This discussion is full of errors due to a general sloppiness in defining the condition of the experiment, and a confusion between vertical and rectilinear motion. Nevertheless, the conclusion is correct. A clear and completely correct exposition is given by Christian Huygens (1629-1695) in his *On the Movement of Bodies Through Impact,* a selection from which can be found in *Selected Studies in the Physical Sciences for Physical Sciences 105-108,* sixth edition (University of Chicago Press, 1960), pp. 138-149, translated from the German edition (Ostwald's *Klassiker* No. 138, Leipzig, 1903) by B. F. Hoselitz. (The original is in Latin.)

Oddly enough, Bruno's argument, if pursued, would contradict his main thesis. He has argued that the upper atmosphere, above the highest mountains, serves as a cap to insure that the lower atmosphere and all other things beneath it are so confined as not to fly away on account of the rotation of the earth. In the case of the ship, there is no such cap, and the experiment of falling bodies works nonetheless. Bruno thus demonstrates that no cap of upper atmosphere is necessary and that, therefore, we need not consider ourselves to be living inside, rather than on, the earth. This physical argument tends to vitiate the metaphysical discourse concerning the vital organs of a living earth.

The ship experiment had a long history before Bruno (and, as in the case of Bruno, as a thought experiment). Cf. Richard C. Dales, *The Scientific Achievement of the Middle Ages* (Philadelphia, 1973), Ch. 7 (especially p. 138). Copernicus may have picked up the idea of using the example of a man on a moving boat from Buridan and Oresme (who had discussed the motion of the earth as a hypothesis); Bruno could have gotten the idea from any one or all of these writers. Although Galileo included the ship experiment in his *Dialogue on the Two Great World Systems,* it was presented only as a thought experiment. The ship experiment was not actually performed until 1641, by Gassendi, who described it in his *De motu impresso* (Paris, 1641). Cf. Alexandre Koyré, *Newtonian Studies* (Cambridge, Mass., 1965), p. 176. (But cf. Alexandre Koyré, *Metaphysics and Measurement* [Cambridge, MA, 1968], pp. 124-125, where it is suggested that Thomas Digges may actually have performed the experiment in 1576; in any case, he described it correctly.)

112. So be it.

FOURTH DIALOGUE

FOURTH DIALOGUE

SMI. Do you want me to tell you the reason?[1]

TEO. Go ahead.

SMI. Because the Holy Scriptures (whose venerable meaning proceeds from superior inerrant intelligences) indicate and presume the contrary in many places.

TEO. Now, as for this, believe me, if the gods had deigned to teach us the theory of natural things as they favored us in propounding the practice of morality, I would rather embrace their revelations on faith than to be moved in the slightest by the certainty of my judgments and my own opinions. But as anyone can see as clear as day, those divine books which serve our intellect do not deal with demonstrations and speculations about natural matters, as if with philosophy. Rather, with a view to our understanding and feelings, the scriptures direct the practice of moral actions through laws. Having then this object before his eyes, the Divine Legislator did not bother, in addition, to discuss that truth which would not have helped the common people in turning away from evil and following good. Rather, he leaves this meditation to contemplative men, and speaks to the common people according to their way of understanding and speaking, so that they can understand what is most important.[2]

See page 194 for Notes to the Fourth Dialogue.

SMI.   It is certainly appropriate, when one seeks to direct history[3]
and to give laws, to speak according to the common
understanding, and not to be concerned with indifferent
matters. Mad would be the historian who, in treating his
subject, wished to introduce new words to improve old
ones, since the reader would be constrained to observe and
interpret him as a grammarian rather than to understand
him as a historian. This applies even more to one who
wishes to give the law and model of living to all men; were
he to use words comprehensible only to himself and a few
others, and to consider and make much of subjects irrele-
vant to the purpose of the laws, it would surely appear that
he was addressing his teaching not to the public and to the
multitude of men, for whom the laws have been ordained,
but to the wise and noble spirits and those who are truly
men, who can do what is proper without laws. For this
reason Al-Gazali,[4] a philosopher, high priest, and Moham-
medan theologian, said that the purpose of the laws is not
so much to seek the truth of things and speculations as to
achieve benign usages, the advantage of civilization, the
concord[5] of peoples and practices for the convenience of
human intercourse, the maintenance of peace, and the
growth of commonwealths. Oftentimes, then, and for
many purposes, it is more foolish and unthinking to talk
about things with regard to their truth than in terms of the
occasion and their convenience. So if the Sage, instead of
saying, "The sun riseth and goeth down, turneth toward
the south and boweth to the north wind,"[6] had said: "The
earth turns round to the east, leaving behind the sun which
sets, bows to the two tropics, that of Cancer to the south and
Capricorn to the north wind," his listeners would have
stopped to think: "What, does he say that the earth moves?
What kind of fables are these?" In the end, they would have
accounted him a madman and he really would have been a
madman. Still, in order to satisfy the importunity of some
impatient and rigorous rabbi, I would like to know if, with
the aid of the very same scriptures, it is quite easily possible
to confirm what we are saying.

TEO. Do these reverend fathers perhaps expect us to interpret literally Moses' statement that God made, among all the other luminous bodies, two great ones, the sun and the moon,[7] because all the others are smaller than the moon, according to the vulgar meaning and ordinary way of understanding and speaking? Are there not a great many stars bigger than the moon? Can they not be bigger than the sun? In what way does the earth fail to be a more beautiful and larger star than the moon? The earth, too, reflecting the great splendor of the sun on the surface of the Ocean and other, inland, seas, can appear to the other worlds, called stars, as a very bright body no less than they appear to us as so many shining faces. Certainly, when [Moses] referred to the moon and the sun, and not to the earth, as a small or large light, he spoke well and truly according to his purpose,[8] since he had to make himself understood through common words and opinions, and not write as one who uses knowledge and wisdom like a madman and a fool. To speak with words of truth when there is no need is to require special understanding from the mob and the stupid multitude of whom [practical] training is required—that would be like requiring the hand to have an eye, when it has been made by Nature not for seeing, but for working under and supporting the sight. So, even though the writer understood the nature of spiritual substances,[9] why should he have spoken about them except insofar as some of them have a beneficent applicability to men, when they are messengers?[10] Even though he knew that the moon and other terrestrial bodies, visible or invisible to us, experience everything that our world experiences or, at least, similar things, do you think it would have been the duty of a lawgiver to bother himself and mankind with all these cares? What have the observance of our laws and the exercise of our virtues to do with all these other things?

Thus, when divine men speak, presupposing the commonly accepted meaning of natural things, I would not have them serve as authorities; rather, I would have everyone respect the words of divine men when they speak indifferently and when the common people need make no distinction. [I would have everyone] respect the inspiration of poets who have spoken of such things with superior vision; and [we should] not take as metaphor what has not been said metaphorically or on the contrary take to be true what has been said as a simile. But not everybody, to be sure, has the desire to understand this distinction between truth and metaphor, just as it is not given to everyone to be able to understand it.

Now, if we want to consider a contemplative, natural, moral and divine book, we will find that this point of view is very favored and propitious. I speak of the Book of Job, which is one of the most peerless books we can read; rich in excellent theology, natural and moral knowledge, the height of most wise discourse; so that Moses added this book as a sacred thing to the books of his laws. One of the characters in this book, wishing to describe God's provident power, said that he fashioned tranquility among his eminent, sublime children[11] who are the stars, the gods; of whom some are fire and others water (as we say: other suns and other earths); and these are in harmony because, no matter how different they are, they all live, feed, and grow through each other; whereas they do not mingle, but move at a certain distance one around the other. Thus, the universe is divided into fire and water, which are subject to the two formative and active first principles, cold and hot. Those bodies which shed heat are the suns, which are bright and hot in themselves; those which give off cold are the earths which, being in like manner heterogeneous bodies, are rather called waters, since such bodies are made visible by the waters, whence we justly name them after those regions which make them perceptible; perceptible, I mean, not by themselves but by the light of the suns shed on their surfaces. Moses also follows this doctrine; he uses the word *firmament* for the air in which all these bodies exist and are situated, and by whose extent the inferior waters, that is, those on our globe, are divided and distinguished from the superior waters of the other globes; that is why it is said that waters are divided by waters.[12] And if you consider well many passages of Holy Scripture, you will see that the gods and ministers of the Highest are called waters, abysses, lands, and ardent flames. Who prevented the writer from calling these bodies neutral, unalterable, immutable, quintessences, denser parts of spheres, beryls, carbuncles, and other fantasies on which, although [they are] meaningless, the common herd could nonetheless have grazed?

SMI.   I am certainly much impressed by the authority of the Book of Job and of Moses, and I more easily accept real than metaphorical and abstract opinions; but some parrots of Aristotle, Plato, and Averroës, by means of whose philosophy they have promoted themselves to theologians, say that these statements have metaphorical meaning so that by virtue of their metaphors they extract any meaning they please, through jealous preference for the philosophy on which they were raised.

TEO.   You can judge how stable these metaphors are, by the fact that the same scriptures are in the hands of the Jews, Christians, and Mohammedans, all very contrary and different sects, which engender innumerable other still more contrary and different ones; all of them can find in the scriptures those statements they like and consider appropriate to themselves, which are not only diverse and different from those of the others, but even completely opposite, making of a "yes" a "no" and of a "no" a "yes"; as, for example, in certain passages where they say that God speaks ironically.

SMI.   Let us leave off condemning them. I am sure they do not care whether or not this is metaphorical; thus we can easily appease them with our philosophy.

TEO.   We need not fear the censure of honored minds, truly religious and well-born men, friends of polite conversation and good doctrines. For, having considered well, they will discover not only that this philosophy contains the truth, but also that it supports religion better than all other kinds of philosophies, such as those which suppose the world to be finite, the effect and efficacy of divine power limited, the intelligences and intellective natures only eight or ten, the substances of things corruptible, the soul mortal (when it rather consists of an accidental disposition and effect of constitution and dissoluble union and harmony);[13] [and] the execution of divine justice over human actions consequently void. [In these other philosophies,] the knowledge of particular things is made remote from the prime and universal cause,[14] and there are enough other drawbacks. These philosophies not only blind the light of the intellect through being false but, being also impious and lazy, they quench the fervor of good actions.

SMI. I am very pleased to have this information on the philosophy of the Nolan. But let us come now to the discourses between him and Doctor Torquato who, I am sure, cannot be as much more ignorant than Nundinio as he is more presumptuous, rash, and arrogant.

FRU. Ignorance and arrogance are two inseparable sisters in one body and soul.

TEO. With the same emphatic attitude in which the *divum Pater* appears in the *Metamorphoses*,[15] seated in the midst of the council of the gods on the point of thundering that tremendous sentence against the profane Lycaon,[16] did Torquato, having admired his own golden necklace . . .

PRU. *Torquem auream, aureum monile.*[17]

TEO. . . . and having looked at the Nolan's breast to see if any buttons were missing, rose, withdrew his arms from the table, shook his back a little, puffed and sprayed somewhat with his mouth, arranged the velvet *beretta*[18] on his head, twisted his moustache, put his perfumed face in order,[19] arched his brows, expanded his nostrils, settled himself with an oblique look, put his left hand to his left side in order to start the duel, pointed the first three fingers of his right hand and began to wag his hand back and forth,[20] saying: "*Tunc ille philosophorum protoplastes?*"[21] Immediately the Nolan, suspecting that the discussion was becoming something else, stopped him, saying: "*Quo vadis, domine, quo vadis? Quid, si ego philosophorum protoplastes? Quid, si nec Aristoteli, nec cuiquam magis concedam, quam mihi ipsi concesserint? Ideone terra est centrum mundi immobile?*"[22] With these and similar proddings and with that great patience which he possessed, he exhorted him to advance propositions through which he [Torquato] could argue positively or probably in favor of the other protoplasts and against this new protoplast. And turning to the others, smiling a half-smile, the Nolan said: "This man came here provided not with reasons, but with words and jokes which perish of cold and hunger." And, since everybody asked him to come to the subject, Torquato uttered these words: "*Unde igitur stella Martis nunc major, nunc vero minor apparet, si terra movetur?*"[23]

SMI. O Arcadia! Is it possible that there be *in rerum natura*[24] a person with the title of philosopher and physician[25] . . .

FRU. . . . and doctor and *torquato*.[26]

SMI. . . . who could come to this conclusion? What did the Nolan answer?

TEO. He was not bemused by that, but answered that one of the main reasons why Mars sometimes appears larger, sometimes smaller, is the motion of the earth and of Mars, each in its own circle, so that it happens that sometimes they are closer and sometimes farther apart.[27]

SMI. What did Torquato reply?

TEO. He suddenly asked about the relationships of the motions of the planets and the earth.

SMI. And the Nolan had such patience that, seeing this presumptuous and gross-witted man, he did not turn his back and go home, saying to the person who had invited him, that . . .

TEO. He replied, instead, that he had come there neither to lecture nor to teach, but to answer; that the symmetry, order, and measure of the celestial motions are assumed as they are and had been understood both by the ancients and modern men; that he did not dispute them on this, and had no case against the mathematicians, with which to deprive them of their measurements and theories, which he endorsed and believed; but that his interest was directed toward the nature and verification of the cause of these motions. "Besides," said the Nolan, "If I took the time to answer this question, we should stay here the whole night, without ever discussing, and pitting the bases of our ideas against, the common philosophy. In fact, both we and they admit any supposition in order to establish the true measure of the quantity and quality of the motions, about which we both agree. Why, then, should we rack our brains over something which is beside the point? Instead you should see if from the observations made and the verifications granted you can deduce anything contrary to our conclusions; then you would have the liberty of expressing your condemnation."

SMI. It would have been enough to tell him to speak to the point.

TEO. Now, none of those present was ignorant enough not to show by facial expression and gesture that he understood that this man was a black sheep[28] *aurati ordinis.*[29]

FRU. *Id est,* the [ram with the golden] fleece.[30]

TEO. So, in order to churn things up, those present asked the Nolan to explain what he wanted to defend, so that the aforesaid Doctor Torquato could bring forth some arguments. The Nolan answered that he had already explained too much and that if the arguments of his adversaries were scanty, that was not due to lack of material, as must be obvious even to the blind. Nevertheless he confirmed again that the universe is infinite and consists of an immense ethereal region; that it is really a heaven, called also space and gulf, in which many stars are situated[31] no differently from the earth: and thus the moon, the sun and innumerable other bodies are in this ethereal region as we see the earth to be; that one should not think that there is another firmament, another basis, another foundation supporting these great living creatures which together constitute the world[32] and which are the true means and infinite material of the infinite, active divine power; we can come to understand this as well with the faculty of orderly thought and discourse, as by divine revelations which say that the ministers of the Most High cannot be numbered; Whom thousands upon thousands serve and to Whom tens of hundreds of thousands minister.[33] These are the great living creatures, many of whom are visible to us in their entirety,[34] because of the bright light diffusing from their bodies. Of the others, some are actually warm like the sun and innumerable other fires, and some are cold, like the earth, the moon, Venus and innumerable other earths. In order to communicate with one another and to share the vital principle with one another, some of them describe orbits around the others in certain spaces and with certain distances, as is manifest in those seven which circle the sun; one of them is the earth which, moving in twenty-four hours from the side called West toward the East, causes the universe to appear to turn round it with a motion which is called mundane and diurnal. This fancy is completely false, against nature, and impossible, while it is possible, fitting, true, and necessary that the earth turn around its own center, in order to share light and darkness, day and night, heat and cold. At the same time, it turns around the sun in order to partake of spring, summer, autumn, and winter; around the so-called poles and antipodes,[35] in order to renew the centuries[36] and to change its surface so that where there was sea, there is dry land, where it was torrid, it is cold, where were the tropics, the equinoxes; and finally there is in all things a change—as on this, so also on the other stars, which, not without reason, the ancient true philosophers called *worlds*.

While the Nolan was saying all this, Doctor Torquato shouted: *"Ad rem, ad rem, ad rem!"*[37] At the end, the Nolan laughed and said that he was not arguing against him, or answering him, but simply proposing his ideas, and so he replied: *"Ista sunt res, res, res."*[38] At that point, it was the turn of Torquato to propose something *ad rem.*

SMI. Probably the ass thought he was among oafs and fools, and believed that they would take his *ad rem* as an argument or statement, and that a simple cry, together with his golden chain, would satisfy the assembled group.

TEO. Listen to me again. While everybody was waiting for that longed-for argument, behold, Doctor Torquato, turning to his table-mates, brought forth from the profundity of the scabbard of his conceit, and mounted on the edge of his moustache, an Erasmian adage: *"Anticyram navigat."*[39]

SMI. An ass could not have spoken better, and one who deals with asses should not expect to hear different words.

TEO. I think he was foretelling (even if he did not understand his own prophecy) that the Nolan was going to provide hellebore, in order to glue together the brains[40] of these mad barbarians.

SMI. If those present, who were polite, had instead been supremely polite, they would have hung a rope on Torquato's neck in place of the chain, and would have counted him out forty blows in commemoration of the first day of Lent.

TEO. The Nolan told them that Doctor Torquato, not he himself, was mad, since the former wore the collar; certainly, if Doctor Torquato had not worn it he would not have been worth more than his clothing which, moreover, would have been worth very little until the dust had been beaten off it with a stick. And with these words, he got up from the table, lamenting that Sir Fulke had not provided better guests.

FRU. Such are the fruits of England; you can search far and wide, but you will find these days that all of them are professors of grammar, among whom, in this happy country, there reigns a constellation of the most obstinate pedantry, ignorance, and conceit, mingled with rustic rudeness that would try the patience of Job. And if you don't believe it, go to Oxford and have someone tell you what befell the Nolan when he disputed publicly with the doctors of theology in the presence of Prince Albert Laski[41] the Pole and representatives of the English nobility. Have them tell you how learnedly he answered their arguments and how fifteen times, for fifteen syllogisms, the poor doctor, whom they put before the Nolan on this grave occasion as the Coryphaeus of the Academy, felt like a fish out of water.[42] Have them tell you with what uncouthness and discourtesy that pig acted, and about the extraordinary patience and humanity of the Nolan, who showed himself to be a Neapolitan indeed, born and raised under a more benign sky. Have them inform you how they put an end to his public lectures and those *de immortalitate animae* and *de quintuplici sphaera*.[43]

SMI. He who casts pearls before swine should not lament if they are crushed under foot. Now go on and tell us about Torquato.

TEO. Everyone rose from the table, some accusing the Nolan, in their own language, of impatience, instead of reflecting as they should have upon the barbaric, savage rudeness of Torquato and themselves. Anyway, the Nolan, who makes a practice of vanquishing in courtesy those who could easily surpass him in other things, changed his mind and, as if he had forgotten the incident, said amicably to Torquato: "Do not think, brother, that because of your opinions I wish to be, or can be, your enemy; I am, instead, as much of a friend to you as I am to myself. For I want you to know that some years ago, before becoming certain of my position, I considered it as simply true; when I was still younger and less wise, I thought it was probable; when I was a novice in speculation, I thought it so obviously false I marvelled that not only did Aristotle not disdain to take it [the mobility of the earth] into consideration, but he spent more than half of the second book of *De caelo et mundo* attempting to demonstrate the immobility of the earth. When I was a stripling, without any speculative intelligence at all, I thought that to believe it was folly, and I thought it had all been proposed by someone as a sophistic and captious matter for the exercise of those hateful minds who want to dispute for the fun of it, and who make a profession of proving and advocating that white is black. Thus, I could hate you on these grounds no more than I could hate myself when I was younger, more childish, less wise and less discreet. This is the reason why, instead of getting angry with you, I pity you and pray God that, as He gave me this knowledge, so (if it does not please Him to make you capable of seeing) at least He make you aware that you are blind. This would do much to make you more civil and kind, less ignorant and rash. Moreover, you should love me, if not for what I am now—that is, wiser and older—at least for what I was in my younger and more ignorant days when I was, in my tender years, as you are now in your old age. I mean that, even though I have never been so barbarous, uncouth, and boorish in discussion and disputation, I was once as ignorant as you. In this way, while I consider your present my past, and you consider my past as your present, I shall love you and you will not hate me."

SMI. Now that they entered into another kind of disputation, what did they say?

TEO. Briefly, that they were followers of Aristotle, of Ptolemy, and of many other most learned philosophers. The Nolan added that there are innumerable silly, foolish, stupid, and most ignorant men who in this wise are not only followers of Aristotle and Ptolemy, but millstones around their necks[44] as well; they could not understand what the Nolan meant and were not and could not be in accord with him, since only divine and most wise men such as Pythagoras, Plato, and others [could be of his opinion]. [He said,] "As for the multitude, who boast of having philosophers on their side, I would like them to consider that insofar as these philosophers conform to the vulgar crowd, they have produced a vulgar philosophy. As for those of you who place yourselves under the banner of Aristotle, I advise you

not to boast, as if you understood what Aristotle understands and have penetrated what he penetrates. There is, in
fact, the greatest difference between not knowing what he
did not know and knowing what he knew, because where
that philosopher was ignorant he has for followers not
only you but all your ilk, together with the London boatmen and dockers; while where that good man was learned
and judicious, I believe most surely that all men are left far
behind him. I really marvel at one thing; that is, that
having been invited and having come here to dispute, you
never once set forth any fundamentals or proposed any
reasons from which, in any way, you could draw conclusions against me or against Copernicus; in spite of the fact
that there are many really solid arguments and persuasions
at hand."

    Torquato, as if he now wanted to bring forth a very
noble demonstration, asked with august majesty: *"Ubi est
aux solis?"*[45,46] The Nolan replied that he could imagine it
wherever he liked and that he could conclude anything at
all, since the apogee changes, and is not always at the same
angle of the ecliptic; he added that he could not see the
purpose of that question. Torquato repeated the same
question, as if to show that the Nolan could not answer it.
The Nolan replied: *"Quot sunt sacramenta Ecclesiae? Est
circa vigesimum Cancri, et oppositum circa decimum vel
centesimum Capricorni,* or above the bell-tower of St.
Paul's."[47]

SMI. Do you know why he asked that?
TEO. In order to show those who did not know anything that he
was disputing and saying something; Torquato, moreover,
tried many *quomodo, quare, ubi,*[48] looking for one to
which the Nolan would respond that he did not know the
answer; he even asked how many stars are of the fourth
magnitude. But the Nolan said that he knew only what was
pertinent to the subject. The question about the apogee of
the sun proves once and for all how totally ignorant that
man was of the art of disputation. For to ask someone who

affirms that the earth moves around the sun, the latter being located in the middle of the errant planets, where the apogee of the sun is, is exactly like asking a person of the common opinion where the apogee of the earth is.[49] It is well known that the first thing taught to one who wants to learn how to argue is to inquire and ask not according to his own principles, but those held by his adversary. But for this clumsy oaf it was all the same, because he would have known how to draw arguments as well from those suppositions which were apropos as from those which were beside the point.

After that, they began talking among themselves in English for a while; then they put some paper and an inkpot on the table. Doctor Torquato laid out a sheet of paper which was both wide and long, took pen in hand, and drew a straight line through the middle of it, from one side to the other. In the center he drew a circle, of which the aforementioned line, passing through the center, was the diameter. Inside one semicircle he wrote *Terra* and within the other *Sol*. On the earth side he drew eight semicircles, where the signs of the seven planets were placed in order, and around the last semicircle he wrote: *Octava Sphaera Mobilis*,[50] and at the top: *Ptolemaeus*. Meanwhile the Nolan asked him what he meant to do with something known even to children. Torquato answered: *"Vide, tace et disce: ego docebo te Ptolemaeum et Copernicum."*[51]

SMI. *Sus quandoque Minervam.*[52]

TEO. The Nolan answered that when one is learning to write the alphabet he shows bad judgment in wanting to teach grammar to someone who knows more than himself. Torquato went on with his description and drew seven semicircles with similar symbols around the sun, which was in the center. And along the last one he wrote: *Sphaera Immobilis Fixarum*,[53] and at the bottom, *Copernicus*. Then he turned to the third circle, and at one point on its circumference he drew the center of an epicycle where, having first drawn the

[Fig. 7] (See notes 56-58.)

By permission of the Houghton Library, Harvard University

THE ASH WEDNESDAY SUPPER

circumference, he depicted the globe of the earth and then, in order that no one would deceive himself into thinking that the latter was not the earth, he wrote, in a beautiful hand: *Terra;* and at the point on the circumference of the epicycle, most distant from the center, he represented the symbol of the moon.

When the Nolan saw this, he said: "You see, this man wanted to teach me as Copernican doctrine a thing Copernicus himself did not intend; and he would have preferred having his throat slit rather than to say or write it. For even the greatest ass in the world knows that from that place the diameter of the sun would always appear the same; and many other conclusions would follow which would be impossible to verify."[54]

"*Tace, tace,*" said Torquato: "*tu vis me docere Copernicum?*"[55]

"I care little about Copernicus," said the Nolan, "and little care I whether you or others understand him. I just want to tell you one thing: before you come to teach me some other time, study harder."

The gentlemen present were so interested that they had Copernicus' book brought in; they looked at the figure[56] and saw that the earth was not drawn on the circumference of the epicycle, as was the moon. For Torquato wished the point which was in the center of the epicycle, on the circumference of the third sphere, to stand for the earth.

SMI. The reason for the error was that Torquato had looked at the pictures in the book without reading the chapters, or, even if he had read them, he did not understand them.

TEO. The Nolan burst into laughter and told them that that point was only the mark of the compass left when drawing the epicycle of the earth and the moon, which is one and the same.[57] Now, he said, if you really want to know where the earth is according to Copernicus' theory, read his own words. They read, and saw that he said that the earth and the moon were as if contained in the same epicycle, etc.[58] At this point, they went back to mumbling in their own language until Nundinio and Torquato departed, having taken leave of everyone with the exception of the Nolan, who sent someone after them to give them his regards. The gentlemen besought the Nolan not to be upset by the unkind incivility and rash ignorance of their doctors, but to pity the poverty of the country, which had been bereft of good scholarship, so far as members of the profession of philosophy and real mathematicians were concerned (and everyone being blind in these subjects, a pack of asses sell themselves as seers, and offer bladders as lanterns); and after the most courteous salutations, they left him to go their ways. We and the Nolan took another route, arriving home late, but without encountering any of the usual obstacles since it was far into the night; the horned and hooved beasts did not trouble us returning as they had in going because, taking their rest, they had retired to their folds and stables.

PRU. *Nox erat, et placidum carpebant fessa soporem corpora per terras, sylvaeque et saeva quierant aequora, cum medio volvuntur sidera lapsu, cum tacet omnis ager, pecudes etc.*[59]

SMI. Well, we have talked enough today. Please come back tomorrow, Teofilo, because I would like to hear more propositions concerning the teaching of the Nolan, seeing that the doctrine of Copernicus, though it is useful for calculations, is not always sure and specific as to the natural causes which are the most important.

TEO. I will be happy to come again.

FRU. I as well.

PRU. *Ego quoque. Valete.*[60]

END OF THE FOURTH DIALOGUE

Notes to the Fourth Dialogue

1. I.e., why I reject the system of Copernicus.

2. The view espoused by Bruno in this passage was that of the Church Fathers, but it was lost in Scholasticism, whose strong systematic methodology sought to give natural propositions the certitude of theological ones, making the Bible the common source of both. The separation of scientific knowledge from theological was attained by some Renaissance minds. In Bruno this tendency was heterodox, while in Campanella, Galileo, and Cardinal Baronio it appears as a clarification of the scope of the various branches of knowledge, and in particular as a reduction of theology to its own theological domain. One should note, to this point, Galileo's *Letter to the Grand Duchess* (1615), Campanella's *Apology for Galileo the Florentine Mathematician* (1616), and Cardinal Baronio's adage that the Bible "teaches how to go to heaven, but not how the heavens go." Serious challenges to this view were current less than a century ago, and there are still many who regard the Bible as a science textbook.

3. It., *quando uno cerca di far istoria.* . . .

4. Al-Gazali lived from 1058 to 1111.

5. It., *convitto.*

6. Ecclesiastes I:5-6: *Oritur sol, et occidit, et ad locum suum revertitur, ibique renascens, gyrat per meridiem, et flectitur ad aquilonem.* . . .

7. Cf. Genesis I:16: "And God made two great lights; the greater light to rule the day, and the lesser light to rule the night: he made the stars also."

8. It., *in suo grado.*

9. I.e., the stars, which are endowed with souls.

10. It., *se non quanto che alcune di quello hanno affabilità e ministerio con gli uomini, quando se fanno ambasciatori?*

11. Cf. Job XXV:2: " . . . he maketh peace in his high places"; the Latin Vulgate has: " . . . *qui facit concordiam in sublimibus suis.*"

12. Cf. Genesis I:7: "And God made the firmament, and divided the waters which were under the firmament from the waters which were above the firmament; and it was so."

13. Bruno here criticizes an important faction of the Aristotelian school which denied that the immortality of the soul could be rationally proven (while, at the same time, accepting the immortality of the soul as a teaching of the Faith). Writers like Pietro Pomponazzi (1462-1525) held that according to reason, the soul is absolutely mortal (and only relatively immortal), that the soul draws cognition, and indeed life, only from its necessary union with the senses. This connection being indissoluble, when the body dies so does the soul. It might be added that this opinion was opposed to the position of Thomas Aquinas (d. 1274), who held the soul to have an accidental, not necessary, connection and union with the body. The soul is thus absolutely immortal (and only relatively mortal, for, while in the body, perception derives from the senses) and when the body dies, the soul separates from its mortal garb, its capacity for cognition and existence in no way impaired by the extinction of the senses. It is to this latter opinion that Bruno seems to adhere; this is not surprising, as he maintained a deep respect for Aquinas. Cf. Yates, *GB&HT*, pp. 251 and 272.

Because of the danger of heresy implicit in some tenets of Aristotelian doctrine, Bishop Stephen Tempier issued a condemnation of 219 dangerous propositions in 1227 in Paris. Although this condemnation antedates Pomponazzi by almost three hundred years, it does indicate that the Church did not always feel at ease with a philosophical system of pagan origins.

A translation of Pomponazzi's *De immortalitate animae (On the Immortality of the Soul)* can be found in E. Cassirer, P. O. Kristeller, and J. H. Randall, Jr., eds., *The Renaissance Philosophy of Man* (Chicago, 1948), pp. 280-381; full discussions of his thought are included in: P. O. Kristeller, *Eight Philosophers of the Italian Renaissance* (Stanford, Cal., 1966), pp. 72-90; and the chapter on Pomponazzi in J. H. Randall, Jr., *The School of Padua and the Emergence of Modern Science* (Padua, 1961).

14. the knowledge . . . universal causes: this refers to the doctrines of Nominalism, the late Scholastic philosophical school, still popular in the Renaissance, which argued that terms such as Horse, Man, Virtue, etc., are merely terminological abstractions, with no inherent ontological significance. Thus the human mind cannot proceed from, say (to use the example found in Plato's *Symposium*), a knowledge of external human beauty to the beauty of the human soul; to the beauty of laws and institutions; to Beauty itself. In other words, according to Nominalism, there is no connection between a person's beauty and the Ideal Form, Beauty, which is seen merely as an abstraction for discursive purposes. Nominalists are also known as Occamists, after the founder of the school, William of Occam (*ca.* 1290-1349/50). An excellent discussion of this school is found in Augustin Renaudet, *Préréforme et humanisme à Paris pendant les premières guerres d'Italie (1494-1517)* (Paris, 1953) pp. 61 ff.

15. Ovid, *Metamorphoses* I, 178-179. Jove struck Lycaon with a lightning bolt and turned him into a wolf because Lycaon tried to kill the king of the gods. Ovid's explanation of the punishment differs from other accounts given by ancient writers; see n. 5, Pref. Epist.

16. It appears to us that Bruno has confused Ovid's version of the Lycaon myth with more ancient accounts (see n. 15, above) since he seems to refer to Lycaon's profanation of the altar of Jove with human sacrifices rather than to his attempted slaying of Jove, which is germane since he cites the *Metamorphoses.*

17. "Gold necklace, gold jewel." This is a pun on the name Torquato. See n. 23, Dial 1.

18. This was the badge of Oxford professors.

19. Lit., "in harness."

20. Cf. Rabelais' hilarious description of the debate between Thaumast and Panurge (*Pantagruel*, ch. 19).

21. Do you claim to be the father and chief of philosophers?

22. Where are you going, my lord, where are you going? What would you say if I was the founder and prince of philosophers? What would you say if I yielded neither to Aristotle nor to anyone greater [perhaps he means Plato] since they yield to me? Is, therefore, the earth the immobile center of the world?

23. Why, then, if the earth moves, does Mars appear now bigger, now smaller?

24. In the nature of things.

25. It., *medico*.

26. See n. 17 above, and n. 23, Dial 1.

27. This is a surprising statement from the Nolan (cf. Dial. 3, pp. 139 ff.). It would seem to signal Bruno's impatience with the reader who does not yet see that he is using the Copernican system only as a metaphor. This change of perspective continues to be evident in what immediately follows.

28. It., *pecoraccia*, literally, "big ugly sheep."

29. The Order of the Golden Fleece, founded in 1429 by Philip the Good, Duke of Burgundy. It was a highly prestigious order, founded to honor the House of Burgundy (and later Hapsburg Spain) as well as the most noble knights who were accepted into the order. As the poet Michault said, the Order of the Golden Fleece was instituted "Not for amusement, nor for recreation, But for the purpose that praise shall be given To God, in the first place, And glory and high renown to the good." (J. Huizinga, *The Waning of the Middle Ages* [Garden City, N.Y., 1954], pp. 86-87.)

30. This ram, the object of the quest of Jason and the Argonauts, became the heraldic emblem of the Order of the Golden Fleece.

31. As is clear elsewhere, *aver fissione* implies "located" and not "fastened."

32. world: used in the sense of "universe."

33. Cf. Daniel VII:10, to which this passage alludes: "A fiery stream issued and came forth from before Him; thousand thousands ministered unto Him; and ten thousand times ten thousand stood before Him. . . . "

34. Cf. the argument in the Third Dialogue concerning the illumination of the entire surface of a sphere sufficiently distant from a sufficiently bright body.

35. It., *oppositi punti emisferici*.

36. The reference is to the precession of the equinoxes; what follows in the rest of the passage is discussed in much greater detail in the Fifth Dialogue.

37. To the point, to the point, to the point!

38. These are the points, points, points.

39. *"Anticyram navigat."*: he is crazy! See n. 67, Dial. 1. Here Bruno writes *Anticyram*.

40. glue together the brains: Bruno may have intended a pun; he uses the verb *risaldare*, which means "to resolder" or "to fasten again." Since he has already mentioned insanity and hellebore (see n. 67, Dial. 1), it is clear that he means to restore Torquato's sanity—to glue his brains together.

41. Prince Albert Alasco, or Laski, visited Oxford University in June, 1583 in the company of Sir Philip Sidney. He was entertained with discussions on theological and philosophical matters, in which Bruno claims to have participated. See Yates, *GB&HT*, pp. 206-210. See also n. 40, Dial. 1.

42. Literally, a chick on a leash.

43. Bruno was forced by his audience to cut short his lectures on the immortality of the soul and the quintuple sphere.

44. It., *di essi loro ancora;* literally, "their anchor."

45. Where is the apogee of the sun?

46. The question is indeed relevant, if one is to concern oneself with the mechanics of the solar system. The fact that the earth's orbit around the sun is

elliptical has the consequence that neither the distance between the sun and the earth nor the angular rate of one about the other is constant. These observations are taken into account, in the Ptolemaic system, by means of the eccentric point, which is the center of the sun's circular orbit about the earth, and which is displaced from the center of the earth; and the equant point, a point located an equal distance on the other side of the eccentric from the earth, and around which the angular rate of the sun is constant. Copernicus, in dispensing with equants, devised a system which actually accounted less well than Ptolemy's for the apparent motion of the sun; he found it necessary to patch it up with still more epicycles.

47. How many are the sacraments of the Church? It [the sun] is about the twentieth degree of Cancer, and the opposition is about the one-hundred-tenth degree of Capricorn, or above the bell-tower of St. Paul's. See the Introduction, p. 49 for an explanation of this response.

48. hows, whys, wheres.

49. This is not true, though the question is couched oddly from the Copernican point of view. It would be more consistent with Copernican theory, though no more logical, to ask for the aphelion of the earth. "Apogee of the earth" is, of course, nonsense.

50. The eighth mobile sphere.

51. Watch, keep quiet, and listen: I will teach you Ptolemy and Copernicus. Even though Bruno has previously registered his contempt for Humanists and their grammatical niceties, he has perhaps here, as the Humanists so often did, sought to show Torquato's ignorance by placing the prenomial object *te* after the verb *docebo* rather than before it, as would be dictated by classical Latin prose; as well as by placing the verb in the middle of the sentence rather than at the end.

52. Sometimes the swine want to teach Minerva.

53. Immobile sphere of the fixed stars.

54. That the apparent diameter of the sun varies in the course of the year was known to astronomers of the time. According to Copernicus, however, this is due to the fact that the sun does not lie at the center of the earth's orbit. Bruno is mistaken in putting the earth on the moon's epicycle; see nn. 57 & 58, below.

Curiously, Bruno seems not to have realized that his remark about the apparent diameter of the sun contradicts his elaborate demonstration concerning what he maintains is the absence of variation in the apparent size of Venus, and of luminous bodies in general—or rather, the impossibility of connecting any such variation with their distance. Cf. pp. 139-143, p. 183, n. 27.

55. Silence, silence: do you want me to teach you Copernicus?

56. This refers to the diagram in Copernicus' *De revolutionibus* (1543 edition), p. 102. But in the actual Oxford debate Bruno used Marsilio Ficino's *De vita coelitus comparanda* rather than *De rev.* (cf. Robert McNulty, "Bruno at Oxford," *Renaissance News*, 13 (1960), pp. 300-5; Yates, *GB&HT*, pp. 208-9.) In this reconstructed version of the Oxford debate, Bruno portrays himself as familiar with Copernicus' diagram, and the Nolan is vindicated when the guests refer to it. In actuality, however, the Nolan seems to rely—as Torquato does not—on Bruno's own Figure 7, which represents not Torquato's drawing, but Bruno's "corrected" version of it, intended for the reader's benefit. It is easy to

jump to the conclusion, on a cursory reading of the text, that Figure 7 is intended to represent Torquato's "erroneous" drawing, since it reproduces the description of Torquato's actions in every other particular. If one does this, however, there is no possible way to make sense out of the text. Evidently, Bruno was not willing to have the only graphical representation of the Copernican system an "incorrect" one. In any case, Bruno's lack of concern for close correspondence between the text and the figures is not a matter of mere carelessness; the figures are not intended simply as a visual aid to the reader in following the text, but rather as an iconographic device to lead the reader toward deeper insights. Cf. the Introduction, pp. 44-6, and n. 46, Dial. 3. See also nn. 57 & 58, below, and n. 100, Dial. 5.

57. Actually, Bruno (and the Nolan) is in error and Torquato is correct, for the point in question in Copernicus' diagram was *not* the mark left by the foot of the compass in drawing the epicycle of the earth and the moon; it indeed indicated the earth, which does not have an epicycle. Had Bruno read the wording which labels the orbit of the earth on Copernicus' diagram, he would have found it quite clear: *"Telluris cum orbe lunari annua revolutio"* (Copernicus, ed. cit., p. 102). However, as we shall see (cf. n. 58, below), Bruno depends on Pontus de Tyard for his understanding of Copernicus.

58. Here again it is doubtful whether Bruno had ever read Copernicus, for he seems to be relying on Tyard's somewhat muddled translation of Copernicus. Cf. Yates, *The French Academies of the Sixteenth Century*, pp. 102-3 and Plate 6, which reproduces both Copernicus' and Bruno's figures.

What is either the same misunderstanding as Bruno's, or an ambiguous turn of phrase which can easily be interpreted in that way, was made by Pontus de Tyard (1521-1605), a member of Henri III's Palace Academy (with which Bruno had connections). The crucial phrase occurs in Tyard's *Discours philosophiques* (cf. the editions of it published prior to 1584: *L'Univers, ou discours des parties de la nature du monde*, 1552, p. 99; and *Deux discours de la nature du monde et de ses parties*, 1578, p. 70). Whereas Copernicus had written, *"Quartum in ordine annua revolutio locum obtinet,* **in quo terram cum orbe lunari tanquam epicyclo** *contineri diximus"* (De rev., ed. cit., p. 9), Tyard had translated these words as, *"Au quatrieme lieu est logee la sphere qui se tourne en un an:* **en laquelle comme dans un Epicycle, la Terre** & *toute la region Elementaire,* **avec la globe de la Lune est contenue."** (Emphases ours.) The words *"en laquelle . . . est contenue"* would appear to have been the source of Bruno's error; Bruno's corresponding words are: **"dicea la terra e la luna essere contenuto come da medesmo epiciclo."** (Emphasis ours.)

The progression is thus from Copernicus' unambiguous statement that the moon lies as if on an epicycle about the earth, to Tyard's ambiguous statement that the earth and the entire elemental region (i.e., the Aristotelian sublunar region), with the globe of the moon, are contained as if *within* an epicycle (which is correct if one thinks of the orbit of the moon as an envelope or outer bound of the earth-moon system), to Bruno's statement that the earth and the moon are as if contained in the *same* epicycle, by which Bruno unambiguously (and incorrectly) means that they are located *on* the epicycle.

59. Vergil, *Aeneid* IV, 522-5: It was night and on the earth the living beings, overwhelmed by labor, quietly fell asleep; the forests and the sea were

silent. It was the moment when the stars are in the midst of their course, and all the countryside, animals, etc., are quiet.

60. Me too. Keep well.

FIFTH DIALOGUE

FIFTH DIALOGUE

TEO. The other stars are neither more nor differently fixed to the heavens, than this star, which is the earth, is fixed in the same firmament which is the air. And the region of the Bear's tail no more deserves to be called the Eighth Sphere than does that of the earth (on which we live). For these bodies are distinct, with certain suitable intervals separating one from the other, in one and the same ethereal region, as in one and the same great space and field. Consider, then, the reason why seven of the heavens have been assigned to the planets, and only one to all the other stars. The varied motion which is seen in seven of them, and the one orderly one in all the other stars, which keep perpetually to the same equal distance and rule, make it seem that there is necessarily one motion, one place and one orbit for all of them; and that there are not more than eight sensible spheres for the luminaries, which are as if embedded in them. Now, if we come to an understanding which is sufficiently wise and enlightened, so that we recognize that this apparent motion of the universe[1] derives from the rotation of the earth, and if we consider, moreover, that the constitution of all the other bodies in the firmament[2] is similar to that of this body, we will be able first to believe, and then to conclude rigorously, the contrary of that dream, that fantasy, that basic mistake which has given and will give rise to innumerable others. This error arises thus: From the center of [our] horizon, turning our eyes to all

---

See page 226 for Notes to the Fifth Dialogue

203

sides, we can reckon the magnitude of the[3] distance from, between, and within those things which are fairly close to us; but, beyond a certain limit, all things appear to be equally distant. In the same way, if we look at the stars in the firmament, we will be able to distinguish the differences in motions and distances of some of the closer stars, but those which are farther or very far away will appear immobile and equally distant and far away as to distance. Sometimes one tree will appear close to another simply because it lies approximately along the same semi-diameter[4] and they may thus become indistinguishable; but nevertheless, for all of this, there may be much more distance between these trees than between those which seem much more separated, because of the difference of the semi-diameters. Thus it happens that that star is thought to be much bigger, which is much smaller; this one much farther, which is much nearer. See the following figure [Figure 8], where to O, the eye, the star A appears to be one with the star B; and even if they appear distant [from each other], they will seem very close; while the star C, being on a very different semi-diameter, will seem much more distant, while in fact it is much closer.[5] Thus, the fact that we do not see much motion in the former stars, and that they do not appear to separate from, or to approach one another, is not because they do not make their revolutions just like the latter. For there is no reason at all why the former should not have the same properties[6] as the latter; it is equally true for all of them that a body, in order to draw virtue[7] from another, must move itself around the other. Thus they must not be called fixed because they actually maintain the same distance from us and from each other, but [rather] because their motion is not perceptible to us.

This may be seen in the example of a very distant ship which, having covered a distance of thirty or forty yards, nonetheless appears to be stationary, as if it had not moved at all. Thus it is in proportion, considering greater distances, and the largest and most luminous bodies (of which

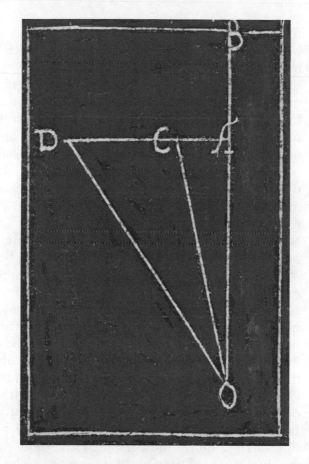

O, la uiſta, l' occhio.
O A B, O C, O D, lunghezze, longi
tudini et linee uiſuali .
A C, AD, CD, larghezze, latitudini.*

[Fig. 8]

By permission of the Houghton Library, Harvard University

*O, the viewpoint, the eye.
 OAB, OC, OD, lengths, longitudes and lines of sight.
 AC, AD, CD, breadths, latitudes.

it is possible that innumerable others are as large and as luminous as the sun, and even more so). Their circles and motions, though very great, are not visible. Thus, even if it happens that some of these stars make some sort of approach [to the earth], we do not see it, except through the lengthiest observations; these have not been undertaken, nor pursued, because no one has believed in, or looked for, or presupposed such motions; and we know that the beginning of inquiry is the knowledge and the understanding that the thing exists, or is possible and fitting, and that one may draw profit from [the inquiry].

PRU. *Rem acu tangis.*[8]

TEO. Now, Heraclitus, Epicurus, Pythagoras, Parmenides and Melissus[9] understood this point concerning bodies in the ethereal region, as the fragments we possess make manifest to us. In [these fragments] one can see that they recognized an infinite space, an infinite region, infinite matter,[10] an infinite capacity for innumerable worlds similar to this one, rounding their circles as the earth rounds its own. And this is the reason why they were formerly called *ethera*,[11] that is runners, messengers, ambassadors, nuncios of the One Highest, who, with musical harmony, tune the order of the constitution of nature, the living mirror[12] of the Infinite Deity. The name *ethera* has been stolen from them by blind ignorance, and attributed to certain quintessences in which these fireflies and lanterns are embedded like so many nails. These mobile bodies[13] possess the principle of intrinsic motion [through] their own natures, their own souls, their own intelligence. For the fluid and thin air would not suffice to move such dense, huge structures.[14] For to do so would require a tractive or impulsive force[15] or something similar, which cannot be done without the contact of at least two bodies, one of which pushes with its extremity and the other of which is pushed. It is certain that all things which are moved in this way acknowledge a principle of motion either outside or against their own natures; we say that it is violent or at least unnatural. It is, then, appropriate to the commodity of the things which are and to the effect of the most perfect cause, that this movement be natural, [coming] from an internal principle and a self-impulse without resistance. This is appropriate to all bodies which move without a tangible[16] contact with some other pulling or pushing body. Those who affirm that the magnet draws the iron, the amber the straw, the jet[17] the feather, the sun the heliotrope, think the contrary. But [the fact is that] in the iron there is a kind of sensible faculty[18] which is aroused by a spiritual force which diffuses from the magnet, by which it is moved to the magnet, [as] the straw to the amber and, generally, [as] everything which has desire and need moves toward the desired thing and transforms itself into it as much as possible, beginning with the desire to be in the same place.[19] Upon the consideration that nothing moves in space on account of an extrinsic principle, without a contact more forceful[20] than the resistance of the medium,[21] depends the further consideration that it is solemn foolishness and an impossible thing to persuade an orderly mind that the moon moves the waters of the sea (causing the tides), makes humors flow, fecundates fish, replenishes oysters and produces other effects, since for all these things it is properly a sign and not a cause. It is a sign and indication, I say, because the observation of these things [together] with certain dispositions of the moon, and other opposite and different things with opposite and contrary dispositions, proceeds from the order and correspondence of things, and from the laws of one mutation which are in conformity and correspondence with the laws of another.

SMI. From ignorance of this arises a multitude of scribblings, full of similar errors, which teach us so many strange philosophies. In them, signs, circumstances and accidents are called causes; among such follies is one concerning radiation,[22] according to which perpendicular and vertical rays are the cause of more heat, and acute and oblique ones of more cold; which, however, is an accident of the sun, which is the true cause, when it prevails more or less on the earth. Reflected and straight rays, acute and obtuse angles, perpendicular, incident, and plane lines, larger or smaller arcs: aspects such as these are mathematical circumstances and not natural causes. It is one thing to play with geometry and another to verify with nature.[23] It is not lines and angles which make fire heat more or less, but distance and nearness, long and short duration.

Teo. You understand that very well: see how one truth clarifies the other. Now, to conclude the matter, if these great bodies were moved extrinsically instead of by their desired end and good, they would be moved violently and accidentally, even if they were to have that power[24] which is called consistent,[25] since that which is truly consistent is natural; and the natural, whether willed or not, is an intrinsic principle which by itself leads the thing to its appropriate place. Otherwise, the extrinsic mover would not move without effort, or else would not be adequate[26] but excessive. And if you would have it adequate, accuse the efficient cause of insufficiency in its effect and of applying the most noble movers to moving rather less worthy things. This is like saying that the actions of spiders and ants are not determined by their own prudence and artifice but by inerrant divine intelligences which give them, for instance, impulses which we call natural instincts, or other things signified by meaningless words. And if you ask these savants what this instinct is, they will not be able to say anything else than *instinct,* or some other equally indeterminate and stupid word like instinct which, meaning instigating principle, is a very general term like "sixth sense," or "reason," or even "intellect."

Pru. *Nimis arduae quaestiones!*[27]

Smi. [Yes,] to those who do not wish to understand them, but obstinately wish to believe what is false. But let us return to ourselves. To those who believe with difficulty that the earth moves, saying that it is such a big, dense and heavy body, I would know very well what to answer. But I would like to hear your way of answering, because I see that you are so resolute about your reasons.

Pru. *Non talis mihi.*[28]

Smi. Because you are a mole.

Teo. The way to answer is as follows: The same thing can be said of the moon, the sun and of other huge and innumerable bodies which your adversaries would have so speedily circling the earth in such immense orbits. And yet they think it a great thing, that the earth turns around its own center in twenty-four hours and around the sun in one year. Note that neither the earth nor any other body is heavy or light in an absolute way. In its proper place, no body is heavy or light;[29] these differences and qualities do not apply to the principal bodies and particular perfect individuals of the universe, but have to do with the parts which are divided from the whole and are outside their proper bounds[30] like pilgrims;[31] they tend no less naturally toward their place of permanence than iron toward the magnet. The iron does not follow any determinate direction downward or upward or to the right, but goes to find the magnet in whatever place it may be.

The parts of the earth come from the air toward us because here is the sphere to which they belong; but if the latter were in the opposite direction they would go away from us, directing their course toward it. This is [also] the way it is with water and fire. Water in its place is not heavy and does not weigh on those who are in the depths of the sea. The arms, head and other limbs are not heavy to their own trunk, and no naturally constituted thing causes violent motion[32] in its own place.

Gravity and levity[33] are not observed in a thing which possesses its natural place and disposition, but in those things having a certain impetus[34] by which they force themselves to a place appropriate to themselves. For it is an absurd thing to call any body naturally heavy or light, since these qualities do not apply to a thing which is

209

within its natural constitution, but outside it. This never happens to a sphere, but sometimes to its parts. According to our viewpoint, however, these qualities [gravity and levity] are not determined by local differences but are always determined by the location of the sphere to which they belong and the center of their conservation. So, if there were another kind of body inside the earth, the parts of the earth would naturally rise out of that place, and if there were any spark of fire, to speak in the common fashion, upon the concavity of the moon,[35] it would come down at the same speed with which it ascends upward from the convexity of the earth. Thus, water would descend no less to the very center of the earth, if there were space, than it ascends to the surface from that center. Similarly, the air moves to any place whatsoever with equal facility.[36]

What then do gravity and levity mean? Do we not sometimes see the flame go downward and in other directions, to kindle a body disposed to its nourishment and conservation? Thus, everything which is natural is very easy; every natural place and movement is highly appropriate. With the same facility with which things stable by nature remain fixed in their place, those which are mobile by nature travel through their spaces. And in the same way that the former would only move violently and against their nature, the latter would remain fixed only violently and against their nature. It is thus certain that, if it were naturally appropriate to the earth to remain fixed, its motion would be violent, against nature, and difficult. But who has discovered this? Who has proved it? Common ignorance, and lack of good sense and reason.

SMI. I understand very well that the earth in its own place is no heavier than the sun in its own place, or than the members of the principal bodies, like the waters, in their own spheres; so that, if the waters were separated from their spheres, they would move toward them, from any place and situation and in whatever direction. For this reason we could say that from our perspective they are no more heavy than light, heavy and light being the same, as we see in the comets and other igneous beings which send flames from within their fiery bodies in every direction, whence they are called *hairy*, [or] at other times [they send flames] toward us, whence they are called *bearded*, [or] at other times in other directions, whence they are called *tailed*. The air, which is the most universal container and is the firmament of spherical bodies, issues from everywhere, enters everywhere, penetrates everything and diffuses to everything; for this reason, the argument, advanced by those who say that the earth is fixed because it is heavy, dense and cold, is an empty one.

Teo. Praise God that I find you so intelligent, and that you save me so much effort! You have well understood that principle with which you can answer the most vigorous persuasions of vulgar philosophers, and [you] have addressed yourself to many profound contemplations of nature.

Smi. Before coming to other questions, I would now like to know how we can say that the sun is the true element of fire, and first heat, and that it is fixed in the midst of those errant bodies among which we understand the earth to be. It seems to me, in fact, more likely that this body [the sun] moves, than those others which we can see through the experience of our senses.

Teo. Tell me the reason.

Smi. The parts of the earth do not move, whether because they are stable by nature or because they are restrained by violence. Thus the waters outside the sea, the rivers and other natural containers[37] are also stable. But the parts of a fire, when they are unable to rise, as when they are held in the cavities of furnaces, unfold and circle around, and there is no way of stopping them. If, then, we want to consider and to trust one argument of the other side,[38] motion is more appropriate to the sun and to the element of fire than to the earth.

Teo. First of all, I answer that it would be enough to grant that the sun turns around its own center, not around some other

211

center, since it is enough that all the surrounding bodies move around it, not only because they need it, but also because it perhaps might desire them. Secondly, we must consider that the element of fire is the basis of primary heat and is as dense and dissimilar a body in its parts and members as is the earth. For what we see moving in that particular way is ignited air, called flame, just as the same air, altered by the cold of the earth, is called steam.

SMI. I think I have a way of confirming what I said, because steam moves slowly and lazily, while flame and vapor[39] move very quickly; the latter, which is more like fire, appears much more mobile than air, which is more like earth.

TEO. The reason is that fire tries harder to escape from this region, which is more appropriate to a body of opposite nature. If water or steam were to find itself in the region of fire or in a similar region, it would escape at a greater speed than vapor[40] which has a certain similarity and participation [of nature] with it more than contrariety or difference. Be satisfied with this, because I am not very sure about the Nolan's opinion on the movement or stability of the sun.[41] That motion, then, which we see in flames held and contained in the concavities of furnaces, derives from the fact that the virtue of fire follows, ignites, alters and transmutes the vaporous air, from which it wishes to augment and nourish itself, while the air withdraws and flees the enemy of its being and good order.

SMI. You have spoken of the vaporous air; what would you say of the pure and simple air?

TEO. That is no more subject to heat than to cold; it has no more room and refuge for humors, when it has been thickened by cold, than for steam and vapors, when it has been deprived of water by heat.

SMI. Since in nature there is nothing which is without providence and without a final cause, I would like to know again from you (since it is possible to understand it perfectly from what you have said): What is the cause of the local motion of the earth?

TEO. The cause of such motion is the renewal and the rebirth of this body, which cannot last forever under the same disposition. Just as things which cannot last forever through the individual (speaking in common terms) endure through the species, [in the same way,] substances which cannot perpetuate themselves under the same countenance, do so by changing their configuration.[42] For the matter and substance of things is incorruptible and every part of it must be the subject of every form, so that every part can become every thing (insofar as it is able), and be every thing (if not in the same time and instant of eternity, at least at different times, at various instants of eternity, successively and alternately). For even though the matter as a whole is capable of all the forms at once, each part of the matter, nevertheless, is not capable of all the forms at once. However, since death and dissolution are not appropriate to the entire mass of which this globe—this star—consists, and since annihilation is impossible to Nature itself, therefore it renews itself with the passage of time in some order, altering, changing, and transforming all of its parts. This takes place in succession, each part taking the place of all the others; for otherwise these bodies, which are dissoluble, would actually dissolve at some time, as occurs to us as individuals and to lesser animals. But as Plato in the *Timaeus*[43] believed, and we still believe, the first [thing] said to these [bodies] was, "you are dissoluble, but you will not dissolve." It happens, then, that there is no part in the center and the midst of the star which does not come to the outside and circumference of it; there is no external or outside portion of it which at some time does not of necessity come inside or become internal. Everyday experience proves this: many things descend into the womb and the bowels of the earth, while many others emerge from them. And we ourselves and our possessions come and go, pass and return, and there is nothing of ours which does not become estranged from us, and there is nothing foreign to us which does not become ours. And there is nothing of which we are a part which does not of necessity become part of us at some time, and there is nothing which is a part of us of which we do not of necessity become a part at some time. [This is the case] whether things are of one substance in one kind, or of two substances in two kinds. (For I have not yet determined whether or not the substance or matter we call spiritual changes into that we call corporeal and *vice versa*.)

So, everything within its own kind has every [possible] alternation of dominion and servitude, of happiness and unhappiness, of that state we call life and that we call death, of light and dark, of good and evil. And there is nothing to which it is naturally appropriate to be eternal, except for the substance which is matter, to which it is no less appropriate to be in continuous mutation. I do not speak now of supersubstantial substance,[44] but I return to the discussion in particular of this great individual which is our perpetual nurse and mother, about the cause of whose local motion[45] you asked. And I say that the cause of the local motion of the whole, as well as of each of its parts, is the purpose of change. [This is] not only because every thing can be found everywhere, but also because by such means every thing can have all dispositions and forms. For this reason, local motion has most properly been considered the source of all other mutations and forms, and without it there could be nothing else.[46] Aristotle was able to recognize transformations according to dispositions and qualities, which are present in every part of the earth, but he did not understand that local motion which is their source. However, at the end of the first book of his *Meteora* he spoke as one who prophesies and divines. Even if sometimes he did not understand himself, nevertheless, limping along (so to speak) and ever mingling something of his own error with divine furor, for the most part and in the main he spoke the truth.

Now let us consider the true and worthy things [Aristotle] said, and then we will add the causes which he was unable to understand. "Not always," he says,[47] "are the same parts of the earth moist or dry, but they change according to the generation or drying up of rivers. Thus, what was and now is the sea, has not always been and will not always be the sea; what will be and was land, is not nor was always land; but we must believe that, with a certain alternation and according to a certain cycle and order, where there is one, there will be the other, and *vice versa*." If you ask Aristotle the principle and cause of all this, he answers that "the interior [parts] of the earth, like the bodies of plants and animals, are perfect [at first], and then grow old. But there is a difference between the earth and the said other bodies: For in all their parts at the same time there is progress, perfection and waning, as he says, being and old age. But for the earth all this happens successively to each of its parts. The succession of cold and heat causes growth and diminution, which follows the sun and its course,[48] [and] by means of which the parts of the earth acquire diverse forms and properties.[49] So some watery places persist for a certain period and then dry up and grow old, while others spring to life again and some parts accordingly become watery. So we see springs vanish; rivers now small become large, those now large become small and finally dry up. And from the disappearance of the rivers, it follows of necessity that ponds disappear and the seas change. But, since all this occurs successively all around the earth and at long and slow intervals, we can hardly notice these transformations in our lifetimes or in those of our fathers. Thus it happens that the age and the memory of all peoples fades, and great corruptions and transformations come by desolation and abandonment, by wars, by plagues and by deluges, by changes in languages and writing, by migrations, and by places becoming barren; so that we do not remember these transformations, which have been happening from the beginning through the long, changeable and turbulent centuries." Sufficient evidence of these great transformations is given by the remains of ancient Egypt, at the mouths of the Nile, all of which, with the exception of the mouth of Canopus,[50] were made by hand; by the houses of the city of Memphis, where the lower parts were inhabited after the upper; "and by Argos and Mycenae,[51] of which the first was marshy and very sparsely inhabited at the time of the Trojans; Mycenae, being much more fertile, was much superior. Nowadays it is just the opposite, Mycenae being completely dry and Argos temperate and quite fertile."[52]

"Now, the same thing that happens to such small places, happens also to larger places and to entire regions."[53] So we see that many places, once watery, are now continents, while the sea has covered many others. We see that these transformations take place little by little, like those of which we have already spoken, and as is shown to us by the corrosion of very high mountains, very far from the sea, on which the marks of violent waves seem almost fresh. The histories of Felix the Martyr of Nola,[54] say that at that time, one thousand years ago more or less, the sea was at the walls of [Nola], near a temple which is still called Porto, and which is now twelve thousand yards[55] from the sea.

Do we not see the same thing all over Provence? Do not the stones scattered in the fields show that they were once tossed by the waves? Do you think that the climate of France has changed no more than a little from the time of Caesar? At that time it was not fit for vines, while now it exports wines as delicious as those from other parts of the world, and even in the northernmost areas the fruits of the vine are harvested. And this year I have eaten grapes from the gardens of London; they are not as good as the worst of France, but I was assured that their like had never [before] been produced in England.

Consider France and the parts of Italy which I have seen with my own eyes; the Mediterranean Sea, leaving them drier and warmer, inclines toward Libya;[56] and from the fact that France and Italy are gradually becoming warmer and warmer, while England is becoming more temperate, we must conclude that in general the characteristics[57] of regions are changing and that the disposition to cold is diminishing toward the Arctic pole. Ask Aristotle: Why does this happen? He answers: Because of the sun and circular motion.[58] This statement is not so much confusing and obscure as most divinely and loftily and truly said by him. What? Can it be that he was speaking as a philosopher? No, rather as a seer or else as one who understood but did not dare to speak, [or] perhaps as one who sees but does not believe what he sees and, even if he believed it, would be afraid of affirming it, fearing that someone might come and constrain him to bring forth that reason[59] which he does not possess. He speaks, but in a way that silences those who wish to know more, or perhaps it is a way of speaking derived from the ancient philosophers.

[Aristotle] says, then, that heat, cold, dryness and moisture wax and wane in every part of the earth, in which everything has renewal, durability, old age and diminution; and wishing to explain the cause of this, he says: *propter solem et circumlationem.*[60] Why did he not say: *propter solis circulationem?*[61] Because, like all the philosophers of his time and inclination, he was convinced that the sun could not cause this diversity with its motion since, given the amount by which the ecliptic declines from the Equinox, the sun always moves between the two Tropics and, for this reason, it is impossible for other parts of the earth to be heated;[62] and [he believed that] the zones and regions of latitude[63] remain eternally in the same arrangement. Why did he not say: because of the circular motion[64] of other planets? Because it had already been determined that all the planets move only through the extent of the band of the Zodiac, which is called the narrow, beaten[65] path of the wanderers; and some of them pass through [only] some small part of it. Why did he not say: because of the circular motion of the *primum mobile?* Because he did not know of any other motion than the diurnal, and there was, in his time, some suspicion of a motion of retardation, similar to that of the planets. Why did he not say: because of the circular motion of the heavens? Because he did not know what it was or could be. Why did he not say: because of the circular motion of the earth? Because he believed, almost *a priori*, that the earth was immobile. Why then did he say [*propter solem et circumlationem*]? Because the truth, which makes itself heard through natural effects, forced him to do so. It remains, then, that the cause[66] is the sun and motion. I say the sun, because it is the only thing which diffuses and communicates vital force.[67] I then say motion, because if either the sun did not move to the other bodies or the other bodies to it, how could it receive what it does not possess or give what it has?[68] It is therefore necessary that there be motion, and that of the kind that is not incomplete; but, just as it causes the renewal of certain parts, it must bring renewal to those parts which, being of the same condition and nature, have the same passive power[69] to which, if nature is not unjust, the active power must correspond.

But we can find much less reason why the sun and the whole society[70] of stars should turn around this globe than that it, on the contrary, should turn with respect to[71] the universe, making its annual circle around the sun and variously turning all its sides away from and inclining them toward the sun, as to the living element of fire, in certain ordered successions. There is not a single reason why, without a sure purpose and urgent occasion, the innumerable stars (which are so many worlds, some bigger than this one) should have such a violent relation to this particular one. There is no reason which makes us prefer to say that the pole [of the celestial sphere] trepidates, the axis of the [universal] world nutates,[72] the pivots of the universe totter and, as if it were possible, that larger and more magnificent globes toss, turn, twist, piece themselves together[73] and, spiting nature, dismember themselves in such a way that the earth thus perilously comes to attain the center as that body which alone is heavy and cold, as the savants of optics and geometry can prove.[74] Such proofs notwithstanding, it is not possible to prove that the earth is different from any other body which shines in the firmament, either in its substance or matter or in its position. For if this body can be embraced[75] by the air in which it is fixed, the others can likewise be embraced by the air[76] which surrounds them; if they can cleave the air by themselves, by virtue of their own souls and natures, circling some center, so no less can this one.

SMI. I pray you, give great importance to this point because, as for me, I hold it as a most certain thing that the earth moves of necessity, [and I reject the possibility that] the stars are fixed and pinned onto the tapestry of the sky.[77]

But for those who have not understood it, it is better to announce this argument as a main subject[78] rather than to touch on it in a digression. But, if you would please me, proceed immediately to specify to me the motions to which this globe is subject.

TEO. Most willingly, because this digression would have occasioned too much delay in clinching, as I wished, the necessity and the fact that all the parts of the earth must participate successively in all aspects and relations to the sun, making themselves subject to all kinds of complexions and appearances.[79]

Now then,[80] to this end it is fitting and necessary that the motion of the earth be such as to produce certain changes: [so that] where the sea is, there was a continent, and *vice versa;* where there is heat, there was cold, and *vice versa;* where it is habitable and more temperate, it was less habitable and temperate, and *vice versa;* in conclusion, every part comes to have every view of the sun which every other part has, so that every part eventually participates in every life, every generation, every felicity.

First, then, in the space of twenty-four equal hours the earth moves around its own center, exposing its back as much as possible to the sun. This it does for the sake of its

own life and those lives contained in it, and gives, as it
were, respiration and inspiration with daily heat and cold,
light and darkness. Secondly, its own center circles the
shining body of the sun in about three hundred sixty-five
and a quarter days, for the regeneration of the things that
live and dissolve on its back; so from the four points of the
ecliptic[81] arise the genesis of the generation, adolescence,
maturity and decline of its inhabitants.[82] Thirdly, for the
renewal of centuries it partakes of another motion by
which the relationship that this upper hemisphere of the
earth has to the universe, passes to the lower hemisphere,
and the latter becomes the upper hemisphere.[83] Fourthly,
for the mutation of configurations[84] and complexions of
the earth it is necessary[85] that there be another motion by
which the orientation[86] that the near vertex[87] of the earth
has toward a point near the arctic pole exchanges with the
tendency of the opposite vertex toward the opposite point
of the antarctic pole.

The first motion is measured starting from the equi-
noctial point of the earth, up to its return to more or less the
same point. The second motion is measured from an
imaginary point on the ecliptic (which is the path of the
earth around the sun), up to its return to more or less the
same point. The third motion is measured by the orientation of a hemispheric line[88] of the earth (considered as a
horizon) with respect to the universe, up to the return of the
same line, or one proportional to it, to the same orientation. The fourth motion is measured by the progress of a
polar point of the earth, in relation to the projection[89] of
some meridian passing through the other pole, until the
time when it presents more or less the same aspect as
before.[90]

Now we must consider that, even though we say that
the earth has four motions, all of them nevertheless com-
bine into one compound motion. Consider that of these
four motions, the first derives from that motion which
makes it seem that everything moves over the poles of the

world, as they say, during one natural day. The second derives from that which makes it seem that the sun in one year goes around the entire Zodiac, passing every day, according to Ptolemy in the third part of the *Almagest*,[91] through fifty-nine minutes, eight seconds, seventeen thirds, thirteen fourths, twelve fifths, and thirty-one sixths; according to the *Alphonsine Tables*,[92] through fifty-nine minutes, eight seconds, eleven thirds, thirty-seven fourths, nineteen fifths, thirteen sixths, fifty-six sevenths; according to Copernicus, through fifty-nine minutes, eight seconds, eleven thirds.[93] The third motion derives from that which makes it seem that the eighth sphere[94] moves over the poles of the Zodiac in the direction opposite to the diurnal motion, as we see from the order of the signs, but so slowly that in two hundred years it shifts no more than one degree and twenty-eight minutes, so that it takes forty-nine thousand years[95] to complete the circle. The principle of this motion is attributed to a ninth sphere. The fourth motion is derived from the trepidation back and forth which the eighth sphere is said to perform over two equal circles imagined in the concavity of the ninth sphere, above the ascendants of Aries and Libra in the Zodiac;[96] it is derived from that motion which is seen to be necessary because the ecliptic of the eighth sphere is not always so disposed as to intersect the equinoxes at the same points. Sometimes the intersection is in the head of Aries, sometimes outside it to one side of the ecliptic or the other; that is the reason why the greatest declinations of the Zodiac are not always the same and the equinoxes and the solstices therefore continually change, as in fact has been observed for a long time.[97] Do consider that, even if we say that the motions are four, they nevertheless contribute to a compound motion. Secondly, consider that, even though we call them circular, none of them is really circular.[98] Thirdly, consider that, even though many have toiled to discover the true law of these motions, their efforts have been as useless as the efforts of those who have yet to try, since none of the motions are entirely regular and capable of geometric description.[99] There are thus four motions, and there must not be more nor less (I mean to say diversities of local mutation in the earth) of which one irregular one necessarily renders the others irregular, as I would like to describe with the motion of a ball tossed in the air. [Figure 9.][100]

First of all, the center of the ball goes from A to B.[101] Secondly, while the center moves from high to low or from low to high, the ball turns around its own center, moving the point I to the position of the point K and the point K to the position of the point I. Thirdly, while gradually turning, it advances along its way, [increasing its] turning speed or else losing and diminishing it (as happens to the ball which, while rising upward from where it at first moved faster, it then moves more slowly; and *vice versa* in returning downward, and in medium proportions at middle distances whether it is ascending or descending). In the course of this, the orientation which characterizes the half of the circumference which is marked by 1, 2, 3, 4 will come to characterize the other half marked by 5, 6, 7, 8.[102] Fourthly, this turning is not proper,[103] that is, it is not like that of a wheel which turns with the circular impetus which arises from the moment of its weight.[104] Instead, it proceeds obliquely, since it is [the turning of] a globe which can easily turn in any direction; thus, the point I and the point K do not always pass through the same straight line, so that inevitably, sooner or later, whether it moves interruptedly or continuously, it must accomplish a motion by which the point O comes to be where the point V was and *vice versa*.[105] [Any] one of these motions which is not regular suffices to assure that none of the others will be regular; if one is not known, all the others will become unknown. Nevertheless, there is a certain order, in which [the motions] approximate or deviate from regularity more or less; of all these irregular motions, the most regular, that one which is closest to being ideally regular, is that of the center. Next is the more rapid diametric motion [of the

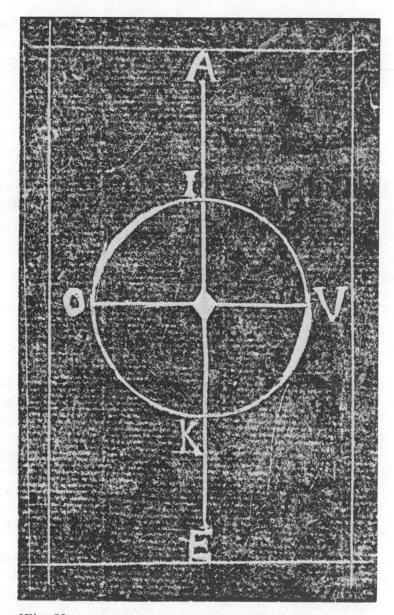

[Fig. 9]

By permission of the Houghton Library, Harvard University

223

ball] around [its] center. The third is that which, together with the irregularity of the second (which consists of an access of speed and slowness), changes the whole orientation of the hemisphere bit by bit. The last one, which is most irregular and uncertain, is that which interchanges the sides; namely, sometimes [some part,] instead of going forward, goes backward and, with the greatest inconstancy, [the motion] eventually comes to exchange the situation of opposite points.[106] Similarly with the earth: first of all, it has the motion of its center, which is annual and the most regular of all and, more than the others, similar to itself. Second, and less regular, is the diurnal motion. Third is the motion we call hemispheric. Fourth, and most irregular, is the polar or colural motion.[107]

SMI. I would like to know with what order and rule the Nolan will have us understand these motions.

PRU. *Ecquis erit modus? Novis usque semper indigebimus theoriis?*[108]

TEO. Don't worry, Prudenzio! Nothing good in the old ones will be wasted. To you, Smith, I will send the Nolan's dialogue, entitled *Purgatorio de l'inferno,* where you will see the fruit of redemption.[109] And you, Frulla, keep our discourses secret so that they cannot reach the ears of those we have bitten again,[110] [and] so that they will not become angered at us and come to give us new occasions for treating them even worse and thus giving them still greater punishment. You, Master Prudenzio, make an end, and let it be only a moral summary of our tetralogue,[111] since the speculative occasion, taken from the Ash Wednesday Supper, is already over.

PRU. I conjure thee, O Nolan, by the hope thou hast in the most high and infinite Unity which animateth thee and which thou adorest, by the eminent numens who protect thee and whom thou honorest, for thy divine genius which defendeth thee and in which thou trustest, beware of vile, ignoble, barbarous and unworthy conversations. In this way thou wilt not come by chance to such rage and such reclusiveness as would perhaps make thee like a satiric Momus[112] among the gods or like a misanthropic Timon[113] among men. Remain thou long close to the most eminent and generous heart of Monsieur de Mauvissière (under whose protection thou hast begun to publish such solemn philosophy), so that mayhap there will come to be most sufficient means, through which the stars and the puissant celestial deities will guide thee to such a place that thou wilt be able to look at such bestiality from afar.

And ye others, O noble personages, are conjured by the sceptre of the refulgent Jove, by the renowned civilization of the descendants of Priam,[114] by the magnanimity of the Quirinal[115] senate and people, and by the banquet of nectar which the gods are celebrating over boiling Ethiopia: If by chance another time should come when the Nolan, in order to do you service or pleasure or favor, comes to spend the evening in your houses, arrange matters so that he is protected from similar encounters. And, when he must return to his house under a dark sky, if ye care not to have him accompanied by fifty or a hundred torches, which, even though he had to march at midday, would not be lacking if he should come to die in a Roman Catholic land,[116] have him accompanied, at least, with one torch. Or, if this seems too much to you, lend him a lantern with a tallow candle inside so that we will have rich material for speaking of his welcome in your houses, which is not possible now.

Adiuro vos,[117] O Doctors Nundinio and Torquato, by the diet of the anthropophagi, by the skin of the cynic Anaxarchus, by the enormous serpents of Laocoön and by the festering sore of St. Roche,[118] to remember, even if you be in the profound abyss[119] and at the day of Last Judgment, that rustic and boorish pedagogue who taught you manners, and that other arch-ass and ignoramus who taught you how to dispute, so that they can pay you back the misspent outlay and the interest on the time and brains they made you lose.

Adiuro vos, O London boatmen, who with your oars ply the waves of the haughty Thames, by the honor of Evenus and Tiberinus[120] for whom the two famous rivers are named, and by the celebrated and spacious tomb of Palinurus,[121] guide us to port for our money.

And ye others, O *Trasoni*,[122] wild and bestial representatives of the rude masses, are conjured by the caresses the Strimoneae gave to Orpheus,[123] by the last service the horses did to Diomedes and to Semele's brother[124] and by the petrifying power of Cepheus' shield;[125] that, when ye see and meet foreigners and travelers, if ye will not abstain from your grim and furious looks, at least abstain from your renowned knocks.

I conjure you again, all together, some by Minerva's shield and lance, some by the multitudinous progeny of the Trojan horse, some by the venerable beard of Aesculapius,[126] some by the trident of Neptune, some by the kisses the mares gave to Glaucus,[127] that some other time you make your achievements[128] known to me with better conversations, or else be silent.

THE END OF THE ASH WEDNESDAY SUPPER

Notes to the Fifth Dialogue

1. It., *moto mondano.*
2. It., *in mezzo l'aria.* In the Fourth Dialogue (p. 180) Bruno explicitly identifies his own term "air" with Moses' use of the word "firmament." This *aria* is presumably distinct from the commonplace air and the upper, pure

Aristotelian air which serves to render the earth perfectly spherical. (On the latter, see the Third Dialogue, pp. 158-61.)

3. It., *la maggior e minor.*

4. I.e., line of sight.

5. This is another example of Bruno's confused thinking on the subject of distances, angular separations, radial distances and tangential distances. See the Third Dialogue, pp. 139 ff.

6. It., *accidenti;* i.e., accidents in the Scholastic sense.

7. It., *virtù.* This word means "force" and "power" as well as "virtue."

8. You have hit it on the nose.

9. Parmenides was an ancient Greek philosopher, a native of Elea, who, with Zeno, was at the head of the Eleatic school (*ca.* 475 B.C.). He was the first Greek philosopher who based his picture of the universe upon logical reasoning and defended it by rational arguments. From his primitive logic developed the Platonic dialectic, Aristotelian logic and the whole Western tradition of philosophical reasoning; Plato named a dialogue after him. Melissus was a philosopher of Samos.

10. It., *selva.*

11. *Ethera* was a word commonly used by the ancients (meaning "pure air" or "ether") to distinguish the pure sky—that is, the heavens—from the dross air of the sublunary world. Cf. n. 26, Pref. Epist.

12. Bruno's use here of the word "mirror" (It., *specchio*) adds weight to the view that he was not a pantheist, at least at the time when he wrote the *Supper.* One may extend the word "mirror" to signify an image, or even an "ambassador" or "nuncio," as Bruno suggests in this passage. But a mirror image is in any case distinct from the thing itself—here the infinite Deity.

13. Ital., *corridori*, runners. We have translated the word literally in the previous sentence, but it would seem awkward to do so here.

14. It., *machine.*

15. It., *virtù.*

16. It., *sensibile.*

17. I.e., the black mineral.

18. It., *nel ferro è come un senso.*

19. Cf. W. Gilbert, *De magnete* (published in 1600 but probably written almost entirely before 1580). Gilbert makes a fundamental distinction (as Bruno does not) between electrostatic forces and magnetic forces. Beginning with solid arguments from experiment, he attributes the former to a material cause and the latter to a formal cause. His view is distinct from, though not incompatible with, Bruno's: ". . . there is that concord (without which the universe would go to pieces), that analogy, namely, of the perfect and homogeneous parts of the spheres of the universe to the whole, and a mutual concurrency of the principal forces in them, tending to soundness, continuity, position, direction, and to unity. . . . [N]or was it downright madness, in the judgment of Scaliger, for him to grant the lodestone a soul; for the lodestone is incited, directed, and orbitally moved by this force, . . . and it seems to be very like a soul." (Book II, Ch. III. S. P. Thompson *et al.*, transls., New York, 1958, pp. 67-68.)

However "modern" Gilbert's work on the magnet is, we can still detect (as in the above passage) the vestiges of the influence of Plotinus and Marsilio

Ficino. Bruno, however, is deeply indebted to both Plotinus and Ficino vis-à-vis the motive power of soul, without breaking new ground and advancing beyond such Neoplatonic platitudes as did Gilbert.

20. It., *più vigoroso.*

21. It., *mobile.*

22. It., *reggine.*

23. Here again we see an example of the ambiguous attitude of Bruno toward the role of mathematics in natural science. (See nn. 67 & 68, Dial 3.) Earlier, Bruno has not hesitated to adduce geometrical proofs (correct or otherwise) of physical phenomena. He is, however, uncertain as to how far one can identify the mathematical demonstration with the physical reality (cf. Teofilo's remark immediately following). Indeed, Bruno believed in Hermetic *mathesis*, not mathematics, and he wrote a treatise, dedicated to the Emperor Rudolf II, against mathematicians: *Articuli adversus mathematicos.* For a discussion of Bruno's *mathesis* and emblems, see Yates, *GB&HT,* pp. 313-315 & passim.

Bruno's view of the distinction between mathematics and physics, together with his general confusion concerning both, has again led him into error concerning fact. Bruno has argued that it is the length of the day which governs the climate, and not the elevation of the sun. In fact, both are significant; that the elevation of the sun can be the dominant effect (and not a mere "accident") is clear in the case of the tropics, where it can be quite hot despite the fact that the length of the day never varies much from twelve hours, and in the case of the arctic regions, where it does not get very hot in spite of the fact that the summer sun is always above the horizon. Bruno here criticizes contemporaries who apparently understood this point quite well. He probably raises the matter in his zeal to demonstrate the vital importance in his system of the mutual interchange of virtue among neighboring stars; this is essential to the sense in which he views them as living beings.

24. It., *potenza.*

25. It., *non repugnante.*

26. It., *necessario;* necessary in a sense implying just sufficient.

27. These are exceedingly difficult questions.

28. It doesn't look so to me. (It is not clear whether Smith's last remark is addressed to Prudenzio or to Teofilo.)

29. This is also the standard Aristotelian view.

30. It., *proprie continente.*

31. Cf. Copernicus, *De revolutionibus* I, 8.

32. It., *caggiona atti di violenza.*

33. These are Aristotelian terms.

34. It., *un certo empito.*

35. That is, within the crystalline sphere which carries the moon. Fire, being the lightest of the terrestrial elements in the Aristotelian view, tends upward as far as possible, and comes to rest at the sphere of the moon. Bruno is denying this, since he must dispense with the crystalline spheres in his infinite universe.

36. Probably Bruno means that all things tend to their natural centers as far as space allows. This, however, negates the notion of levity, the centrifugal tendency of fire and air in the Aristotelian system. That Bruno intends just this

is implied in what follows; Bruno is substituting a mutual vital tendency of all things for the absolute tendencies of Aristotle.

37. It., *vivi continenti.*

38. I.e., the Aristotelians.

39. Steam . . . vapor: It., *vapore; esalazione.*

40. It., *exalazione.*

41. Later, in *De immenso* (in *Opera* I, i, 218) Bruno maintained the rotatory motion of the sun around its own axis: *"omnis astra circuire, etiam fixa, inter quae Sol est unus."* Solar rotation was first observed by Galileo in 1610, and announced in his *Lettere intorno alle macchie solari.* Bruno appears to have been the first to suggest solar rotation, though obviously not on a scientific basis.

42. It., *faccia.*

43. *Timaeus* 41 A-B. "Dissolve" is used in the sense of "die."

44. Bruno is excluding God from the necessity of continual alteration, and perhaps the soul and such other nonmaterial entities as angels, as well.

45. See the Introduction, pp. 30-1.

46. It is this teleological view of motion which Galileo had to reject with the greatest vigor in order to found the modern science of kinematics.

47. *Meteorologica* I, 14, 1-10; an almost literal translation.

48. It., *giro.* See also, below, p. 217 and nn. 58, 60, and 61.

49. It., *complessioni e virtù diverse.*

50. Ancient city of northern Egypt, east of Alexandria, on the Nile Delta.

51. Memphis is a city of middle Egypt, long the residence of the Egyptian pharaohs; Argos was the capital of Argolis, in the Peloponnesus; Mycenae was a city in Argolis, of which Agamemnon was king.

52. These examples are also taken from Aristotle, *Meteorologica* I, 14, 12-15.

53. *Meteorologica* I, 14, 16.

54. A. Cappelli, *Cronologia, cronografia e calendario perpetuo* (Milan, 1960), p. 133, indicates that St. Felix of Nola was martyred around A.D. 265.

55. It., *passi;* actually a measure of about 2½ feet.

56. Some editions have *Libra;* Libya seems to make more sense.

57. It., *abiti.*

58. See nn. 47 and 48, above, and n. 60, below. Aristotle says, "the sun and its course."

59. It., *raggione.*

60. On account of the sun and revolution (i.e., in the sense of "cycle" or "course," if Bruno is keeping to the meaning of Aristotle in *Meteorologica* I, 14, 4; however, Bruno is quoting from an ancient Latin translation of Aristotle's work, which was printed in 1507 [and thus Aristotle's meaning may have been somewhat changed in translation]. Cf. *Libros Metheorum Aristotelis Stagirite peripateticorum principis, cum commentariis fidelissimi expositoris Caietani de Thienis, noviter impressos ac mendis erroribusque purgatos* [Venice, 1507], f. 20r).

61. On account of the circular motion of the sun.

62. Presumably Bruno here means, "to be heated in a manner different from the present one."

63. It., *clima.* The English equivalent, "clime," is given in OED in the following relevant contexts: "1553: A clime is a porcion of the worlde betweene South and North, wherein is variacion in length of the days, the space of halfe an houre. 1594: Every clime consisteth of two Parallels."

64. It., *circulazione.* Cf. the use of *giro* in this sense, p. 215 and n. 48, above.

65. It., *trito.* Florio gives English equivalents connoting both "narrow" and "well-worn." Since both seem appropriate here, we have given both.

66. I.e., of the renewal of the earth.

67. It., *virtù vitale.*

68. We have already seen Bruno argue that motion is essential to interaction and change.

69. It., *potenza.*

70. It., *università.*

71. It., *a l'aspetto dell'.*

72. It., *nutar.* This word, implying "nods," should not be interpreted as suggesting that Bruno knew of what we today call the nutation. This minute motion was discovered by Bradley in the early eighteenth century, using sophisticated telescopic equipment.

73. It., *rappezzarsi;* to patch oneself up.

74. This is the standard Copernican argument that denying the motion of the earth necessitates attributing a much larger motion to the entire universe. The argument assumes a prominent, but not central, role in Galileo's *Dialogue on the Two Great World Systems.* The neatness with which the Copernican system fits into Bruno's larger cosmology is especially clear here. The last phrase in this long sentence is, of course, intended ironically.

75. It., *vagheggiare;* to contemplate with pleasure, to gaze fondly upon.

76. Here again, *aria* is used in the sense of firmament. See n. 2, above.

77. It., *che sii possibile quella intavolatura ed inchiodatura di lampe.*

78. I.e., for a separate dialogue.

79. It., *abiti.*

80. In the following passage Bruno describes the motion of the earth according to the Copernican system, not as it is found in *De revolutionibus,* but according to his own interpretation and imagination. Bruno not having a correct understanding of geometry, and not knowing well its language, his explanation is confused and obscure. Unlike Copernicus, Bruno does not adduce each of the second two motions to account for a single set of observed phenomena. Indeed, this is explicitly contrary to his aim, since he argues that in the final analysis heavenly motions cannot be dissected into circles (even though he insists there are exactly four elementary motions).

81. I.e., the two equinoxes and the two solstices.

82. It., *cose* (can mean "possessions").

83. Bruno has in mind the precession of the equinoxes. He implies that this process results in an inversion of the earth's axis; actually it results in a steady cyclical change in the relation between the seasons and the position of the earth in its orbit as evidenced,,for example, by the position of the sun in the zodiac.

The third motion is distinct from Copernicus' third motion, which he postulated to account for the fact that over the course of a year the orientation of the earth's axis remains nearly fixed with respect to the fixed stars; Copernicus thought that, in the absence of a specific motion, it would remain fixed with respect to the sun. The small difference in period between Copernicus' second and third motions accounts for the precession of the equinoxes; Bruno does not seem to have grasped this point.

84. It., *volti.*

85. It., *necessariamente gli conviene.*

86. It., *abitudine.*

87. It., *vertice.* Bruno makes a distinction between the pole (vertex) of the earth and the celestial pole. In the Ptolemaic system, the former is imaginary and the latter real; in the Copernican system these roles are reversed. From his terminology, it is not clear that Bruno is consistent in the distinction.

In other cases where he uses common terms not appropriate to his system, Bruno carefully states that he is speaking "in the common fashion."

88. I.e., a specific radius lying in the equatorial plane of the earth.

89. It., *dritto.*

90. See the Introduction, pp. 31-2, for a discussion of Bruno's four motions.

91. Cf. Ptolemaeus, *Syntaxis mathematica* III, i (Heiberg ed.), pp. 191 ff.

92. Bruno merely has *Alfonso,* for the king who sponsored the *Tables.* The *Alphonsine Tables,* compiled and calculated in order to update the observations needed to calculate planetary positions (a need arising from observational errors in earlier work, and from the imperfection of the Ptolemaic system) were the work of a group of astronomers gathered around King Alfonso X (el Sabio, 1221-1284) in Toledo, *ca.* 1270.

93. These long-obsolete units are further divisions of angles in sixtieths; i.e., 1 minute = 60 seconds; 1 second = 60 thirds, etc. The limit of observational accuracy before Galileo was about 30 seconds at best; the further refinements given here are futile arithmetic exercises.

94. I.e., the sphere containing the fixed stars.

95. The precession period was open to question in the sixteenth century. The value given in the Alphonsine Tables is 49,000 years. Ptolemy's value of approximately 24,000 years, adopted by Copernicus, is much closer to the correct value of about 26,000 years. However, the belief in a variable rate of precession due to the effects of trepidation made a firm statement as to the period impossible. See N. M. Swerdlow, "The Derivation and First Draft of Copernicus' Planetary Theory: A Translation of the *Commentariolus* with Commentary," in *Proceedings of the American Philosophical Society,* 117/6 (1973), pp. 423-512.

96. See n. 109, below.

97. This is a garbled account of the so-called trepidation, an irregular wobbling and/or variation in the inclination of the earth's axis (in Copernican terms). The theory of trepidation was abandoned when better observations became available in the seventeenth century. It is distinct from the real but very minute nutation, which was first observed by Bradley in the eighteenth century. There were several theories of trepidation current in the sixteenth century. Some were based on simple observational errors, and others on misinterpretation

(sometimes at several removes) of the original observations. The theories were often confused together and garbled; Copernicus was himself misled by an ambiguity of Regiomontanus, itself based on a theory of al-Battâni, which was probably founded on a misinterpretation of pre-Ptolemaic data. See Swerdlow, "Derivation and First Draft of Copernicus' Planetary Theory," p. 446. It is no surprise that Bruno is vague on this point. See n. 72, above.

98. There is no basis for taking this as an anticipation of Kepler's views. Note the following sentence.

99. Cf. p. 152.

100. In what follows, the reader will note that the lettering in the figure is not the same as that used by Bruno in the text; this has occurred before, in other figures.

101. B presumably corresponds to E in the figure.

102. Presumably 1, 2, 3, 4 refer to points on the upper hemisphere and 5, 6, 7, 8 to points on the lower.

103. It., *retta*.

104. It., *che corre con l'impeto d'un circolo, in cui consista il momento della gravità*. This is a very difficult passage to interpret and to translate. So far as we can tell, Bruno is thinking of a wheel which spins on its axis as it rolls down an incline, and whose axis is therefore constrained to be perpendicular to the direction of motion of the wheel. In any case, Bruno's subsequent meaning is clear: A sphere can turn about any axis, regardless of its orientation relative to the direction of translational motion.

105. This motion, which Bruno considers analogous to precession and trepidation of the equinoxes, will not in general result in interchange of the positions of points O and V, but rather in a description by the axis OV of a cone. Bruno is strongly impelled by his philosophic notions, however, to discover motions which result in the interchange of every point with every other, including the poles O and V.

106. It., *viene al fine a cangiar la sedia d'un punto opposito con la sedia d'un altro*.

107. The colure is a great circle drawn through the poles and either the equinoxes or the solstices. Its motion is due to the precession. Bruno sees in it a mechanism for interchanging the poles. See n. 105, above.

108. When will it ever be ended? Will we continually need new theories?

109. *The Purgatory of Hell*, a dialogue written by Bruno not later than 1583, is now lost; therefore it is impossible to know for certain what the "fruit of redemption" is. V. Spampanato, *Vita di G. B.* (Messina, 1921), p. 375, opines that this dialogue must have dealt with a subject matter similar to that in the *Spaccio della bestia trionfante*, as well as having answered Smith's last question. See n. 112 below, for an indication of the content of the *Spaccio*. Spampanato's suggestion would seem to be valid. The essentially non-physical nature of Bruno's "physical" arguments in this Dialogue is indicated by his thoroughly Platonic-Hermetic discussion of the causes of motion, as well as by his frequent references to the Zodiac and its various signs. These references may be Brunian signposts leading us toward the reform of the heavens (and of the signs of the Zodiac) found in the *Spaccio*. Thus, while on the surface it appears incongruous that Bruno follows his discussion of the earth's motions with the promise of

another work on "the fruit of redemption," this apparent incongruity is resolved when we see, once again, that he is using the Copernican system, together with his additions to it, as a hieroglyphic key to the "magical" vitality of the Hermetic understanding of the Eucharist; when we see, once again, that Bruno's purpose in the *Supper* is not physical, but religious and social—that is, Hermetically reformatory and irenic.

110. Cf. nn. 14 & 29, Pref. Epist.

111. This is a final mocking rejoinder to Prudenzio's grammatical quibbles in the First Dialogue (pp. 83-4, above) as well as to his generally pedantic nature.

112. Momus is a speaker in Bruno's *Lo Spaccio della bestia trionfante (The Expulsion of the Triumphant Beast)*. Momus had been expelled from the council of the gods to the star at the tip of Callisto's tail because he had spoken against the gods and had argued too severely against their errors. He was finally admitted back into their company and was made an extraordinary herald, able to reprehend vices without regard to the title or dignity of anyone. Along with the divine Sophia and Isis, Momus speaks in the *Spaccio* at an assembly of the gods which is concerned with reforming themselves and the celestial images. From this there would follow a general reform of mankind, along with a return of Egyptian (i.e., Hermetic) religion and ethics.

The effectiveness of this approach to reform of the world is based on the idea that the cleansing of the celestial images reforms the lower world *via* the celestial influences upon the latter. See Yates, *GB&HT*, *sub. nom.* "Bruno, Spaccio. . . . "

113. A famous misanthrope of Athens.

114. I.e., the Romans. Because of Bruno's supposed mission on behalf of the French king to England (see Introduction), Bruno could also be referring to the French; there was a legend, popular in the Middle Ages and Renaissance, that the French royal line had been founded by the Trojan refugee, Francus.

115. I.e., Roman.

116. Since he had been traveling throughout Catholic lands in northern Europe without trouble, Bruno probably has Italy specifically in mind here. He must have had some misgivings about returning to Italy. See the Introduction, pp. 16, 21.

117. I adjure you.

118. Anaxarchus of Abdera (fl. 340-337 B.C.), on being beaten by the tyrant Nicrocreontus, kept saying, "Beat, beat the flesh of Anaxarchus, since you cannot beat Anaxarchus." (Diogenes Laertius, *Lives* IX, 58-59.) Laocoön, the son of Priam and Hecuba and priest of the Thymbrean Apollo, was killed at the altar by two serpents, along with his two sons, (Vergil, *Aeneid* II, 201 ff.). St. Roche is a French saint famed for his miraculous healing of the victims of the plague in the fourteenth century. He caught the plague and healed himself; even today he is invoked against physical disease in France and Italy.

119. I.e., Hell.

120. The deities of the river Evenus in Aetolia, and of the Tiber.

121. Aeneas' pilot, who fell into the sea near Latium, where there is now a promontory named after him. Cf. Vergil, *Aeneid* VI, 379-381.

122. Pluralized form of Trason, a violent and uncouth character in a Roman comedy.

123. The Maenades, infuriated at being rejected by Orpheus, tore him to pieces on the banks of the Strymon, a river on the Macedonian-Thracian border. Cf. Ovid. *Metamorphoses* XI. 1 ff.

124. Diomedes and Polydorus, Semele's brother, were torn to pieces by horses. Cf. Seneca, *Troades*, vv. 1118-1119; ibid., *Hercules furens*, vv. 1176-1177.

125. This is a puzzling allusion. It was Perseus, the suitor and later the husband of Cepheus' daughter, who turned his enemies to stone with the head of Medusa the Gorgon, whom he had slain.

126. Son of Apollo and the nymph Coronis, deified after his death as the god of healing. Cf. Ovid, *Metamorphoses* XV, 621-744. Aesculapius is identified with Asclepius and thus with the *Asclepius*, which is part of the *Corpus Hermeticum* (cf. Yates, *GB&HT*, pp. 35-40 & passim).

127. Glaucus was torn to pieces by his own horses, out of revenge by Venus. Cf. Vergil, *Georgics* III, 266-268.

128. It., *fatti*.

SELECTED BIBLIOGRAPHY

Editions of *La Cena de le ceneri:*

Bruno, G., *La Cena de le ceneri,* a cura di G. Aquilecchia (Torino, 1955).
———, *Dialoghi italiani,* con note da G. Gentile, terza edizione a cura di G. Aquilecchia (Firenze, 1972).
———, *Opere italiani,* ed. G. Gentile (Bari, 1925-7).
(There are numerous earlier editions as well.)

Works on Bruno:

Salvestrini, V., *Bibliografia di Giordano Bruno ed degli scritti ad esso attinenti.* Pisa, 1926. (2nd posthumous ed.: L. Firpo, ed. [Firenze, 1958]). A general bibliography of works published before 1958; exhaustive with respect to works in Italian.
Berti, D., *Vita di Giordano Bruno* (Firenze, 1867).
Boulting, W., *Giordano Bruno, His Life, Thought, and Martyrdom* (London, s.d.).
Clemens, F. I., *Jordano Bruno und Nicolaus von Cusa* (Bonn, 1947).
Corsano, A., *Il pensiero di Giordano Bruno nel suo svolgimento storico.* Firenze, 1940. (2nd ed.: 1948).
Firpo, L., *Il processo di Giordano Bruno* (Napoli, 1944).
Fraccari, D., "L'Impostazione antimatematica del problema della natura nella *Cena de le ceneri* di Giordano Bruno," *Rivista critica di storia della filosofia,* fasc. III, anno V (giul.-sett. 1950), pp. 179-193.
Gentile, G., *Giordano Bruno e il pensiero del Rinascimento.* Firenze, 1920. (2nd ed.: 1925).
Giusso, L., *Scienza e filosofia in Giordano Bruno* (Napoli, 1955).
Klein, R., "L'Imagination comme vêtement de l'âme chez Marsile Ficin et chez Giordano Bruno," *Revue de Métaphysique et Morale* (no. 1, 1956), pp. 18-39.

Kristeller, P. O., *Eight Philosophers of the Italian Renaissance* (Stanford, Cal., 1964).

Lerner, L. S. & Gosselin, E. A., "Was Giordano Bruno A Scientist?: A Scientist's View," *American Journal of Physics*, 41/1 (1973), pp. 24-38.

———, "Giordano Bruno," *Scientific American*, 228/4 (1973), pp. 86-94.

McNulty, R., "Bruno at Oxford," *Renaissance News*, XIII (1960).

Mercati, A., *Il sommario del processo di Giordano Bruno* (Città del Vaticano, 1942).

Michel, P.-H., *The Cosmology of Giordano Bruno* (Ithaca, N.Y., 1973).

Nelson, J., *Renaissance Theory of Love: The Context of Giordano Bruno's "Eroici furori"* (New York, 1958).

Olschki, L., *Giordano Bruno* (Bari, 1927).

Santillana, G. de, "De Bruno à Leibniz," in *La Science au XVIè* (Paris, 1960).

Singer, D. W., *Giordano Bruno, His Life and Thought* (New York, 1950).

Spampanato, V., *Vita di Giordano Bruno, con documenti editi e inediti* (Messina, 1921), 2 vols.

Tocco, F., "Le fonti più recenti della filosofia di Giordano Bruno," *Rendiconti all' Accademia dei Lincei* (Roma, 1892).

Védrine, H., *La Conception de la nature chez Giordano Bruno* (Paris, 1967).

Westman, R. S., *Magical Reform and Astronomical Reform: The Yates Thesis Reconsidered* (Los Angeles, 1976) (in press).

Yates, F. A., "Giordano Bruno's Conflict with Oxford," *Journal of the Warburg and Courtauld Institutes*, II (1938-9), pp. 227 ff.

———, "The Religious Policy of Giordano Bruno," *JW&CI*, III (1939-40), pp. 181-207.

———, "The Emblematic Conceit in Giordano Bruno's *Gli Eroici Furori* and in the Elizabethan Sonnet Sequences," *JW&CI*, VI (1943), pp. 101 ff.

———, *Giordano Bruno and the Hermetic Tradition* (Chicago, 1964).

———, *The Art of Memory* (London, 1966).

Other works:

Cassirer, E., *The Individual and the Cosmos in Renaissance Philosophy*. M. Domandi, transl. (Philadelphia, 1972).

Cassirer, E., Kristeller, P. O., & Randall, J. H., Jr., eds., *The Renaissance Philosophy of Man* (Chicago, 1956).

Festugière, A.-J., *La Révélation d'Hermès Trismégiste* (Paris, 1950-4), 4 vols.

Ficino, M., *De vita coelitus comparanda* (Basel, 1576).

Florio, J., "A Worlde of Wordes" (1958), *Anglistica & Americana*, CIV (New York & Hildesheim, 1972).

French, P., *John Dee: The World of an Elizabethan Magus* (London, 1972).

Garin, E., *L'Umanismo italiano*. Bari, 1952. (2nd ed.: 1958).

_____, *La Cultura filosofica del Rinascimento italiano* (Firenze, 1961).

_____, *Scienza e vita civile nel Rinascimento* (Bari, 1965).

Gosselin, E. A. & Lerner, L. S., "Galileo and the Long Shadow of Bruno," *Archives internationales d'histoire des sciences*, 25/97 (1975), pp. 223-46.

Johnson, F. R. & Larkey, S. V., "Thomas Digges, the Copernican System and the Idea of Infinity of the Universe in 1576," *Huntington Library Bulletin*, 5-6 (1934), pp. 69-117.

Johnson, F. R., *Astronomical Thought in Renaissance England* (Baltimore, 1937).

Klibansky, R., *The Continuity of the Platonic Tradition during the Middle Ages* (London, 1939).

Koyré, A., *From the Closed World to the Infinite Universe*. R. Tarr, transl. (Baltimore, 1957).

_____, *Etudes galiléennes* (Paris, 1966).

_____, *La Révolution astronomique: Copernic, Kepler, Borelli* (Paris, 1961).

Kristeller, P. O. & Randall, J. H., Jr., "The Study of the Philosophies of the Renaissance," *Journal of the History of Ideas*, 2 (1941), pp. 499 ff.

Kristeller, P. O., *The Philosophy of Marsilio Ficino* (Gloucester, Mass., 1964).

_____, *Studies in Renaissance Thought and Letters* (Roma, 1956/1969).

Lovejoy, A. O., *The Great Chain of Being* (Cambridge, Mass., 1936).

Martin, A. L. *Henry III and the Jesuit Politicians* (Geneva, 1973).

Nock, A. D. & Festugière, A.-J., *Corpus Hermeticum* (Paris, 1945, 1954, 1972). Vol. I, ed. by A. D. Nock, transl. by A.-J. Festugière; Vol. II, ed. by A. D. Nock, transl. by A.-J. Festugière; Vol. III, ed. & transl. by A.-J. Festugière; Vol. IV, ed. & transl. by A. D. Nock & A.-J. Festugière. (In French.)

Plattard, J., "Le Système de Copernic dans la littérature française du XVIe siècle," *Revue du XVIe*, 1 (1913), pp. 220 ff.

Renaudet, A., *Préréforme et humanisme à Paris pendant les premieres guerres d'Italie (1494-1517)* (Paris, 1916/1953).

Rice, E. F., Jr., *The Renaissance Idea of Wisdom* (Cambridge, Mass., 1958).

Schmidt, P. M., *La Poésie scientifique en France au XVIè siecle* (Paris, 1938).

Testi umanistici sul'ermetismo. Testi di L. Lazzarelli, F. Giorgio Veneto, C. A. di Nettescheim. Ed. by E. Garin, M. Brini, C. Vasoli, P. Zambelli. (Roma, 1955).

Walker, D. P., *Spiritual and Demonic Magic from Ficino to Campanella* (London, 1958).

———, *The Ancient Theology: Studies in Christian Platonism from the Fifteenth to the Eighteenth Century* (Ithaca, N.Y., 1972).

Yates, F. A., *John Florio* (Cambridge, Eng., 1934).

———, *The French Academies of the Sixteenth Century* (London, 1947).

———, *The Theatre of the World* (Chicago, 1969).

———, *Astraea: The Imperial Theme in the Sixteenth Century* (London, 1975).